The Computer Major's Guide to the Real World

By Alan Simon

BARRON'S

First edition published 1999 by Barron's Educational Series, Inc.
© Text copyright 1999 by Alan Simon
Design and illustrations © copyright 1999 by Barron's Educational
Series, Inc.

All inquiries should be addressed to:
Barron's Educational Series, Inc.
250 Wireless Boulevard
Hauppauge, New York 11788
http://www.barronseduc.com

International Standard Book No.: 0-7641-0840-9

Library of Congress Catalog Card No.: 98-74563

Printed in THE UNITED STATES OF AMERICA

9 8 7 6 5 4 3 2 1

TABLE OF CONTENTS

CHAPTER 1
FINDING THE *RIGHT* FIRST JOB

INTRODUCTION

If you're still in school while you're reading this book, then most likely what's uppermost in your mind is finding your first job after graduation. No, make that finding the *right* job after graduation. There are countless opportunities awaiting you out there in the real world; how do you know which ones are right for you? And then, from that "short list," which one should you accept if it's offered to you?

In this first chapter we'll discuss the ins and outs, ups and downs, and nitty gritty of everything—and I mean *everything*—you need to know so that you're not sitting behind some computer screen three months into your first job wondering, "How could I have been so stupid as to come here to work?"

We'll discuss the following topics:

- **SELF-ASSESSMENT**—why your job search starts with a thorough understanding of your background and capabilities, strengths and weaknesses, and personal aspirations.
- **WHERE YOU CAN AND SHOULD INTERVIEW**—of the hundreds of thousands of companies out there, which could be right for you.
- **RÉSUMÉS AND COVER LETTERS**—how you can best present your capabilities to make yourself stand out from the others with whom you'll be competing.
- **INTERVIEWS**—what you should say and ask . . . and not say and ask during interviews.
- **SITE VISITS**—what happens when you're invited to visit a company's location out of town.
- **COMPENSATION**—a brief discussion, since salary, benefits, and other aspects of your compensation are covered in Chapter 2.
- **MAKING YOUR CHOICE**—so how do you decide which offer to accept?

TAKE A LOOK INSIDE:
THE ART OF JOB-RELATED SELF-ASSESSMENT

No, you haven't picked up the wrong book by mistake; this isn't one of the zillions of self-help books on the market. But bear with me, okay?

Before you start thinking about companies, jobs, geographical locations, and everything else you need to decide about that all-important first job, you *first* need to take a look inside and gain as thorough an understanding as you can of your own capabilities and aspirations.

Why? That's an easy question to answer. There is no such thing as a "computer job." Or to be more precise, there are actually hundreds of very different types of computer jobs. For example, developing business application software such as inventory or payroll programs is very different from developing systems software such as operating systems or compilers. Assuming you want to be a hands-on software developer, which of these many paths is likely to be the most comfortable—and rewarding—one for you?

So let's start by taking an inventory of the following items.

YOUR EDUCATIONAL PROGRAM

Are you a business computer major; that is, in a program in a college of business administration entitled computer information systems (CIS)—or are you studying management information systems (MIS)? Or are you a computer science major (CS), perhaps enrolled in part of an engineering school program? If you're a business computer major, chances are you've been taking courses such as systems analysis and design, database management systems, and a variety of business-oriented programming classes. You've also been taking electives in finance, accounting, marketing, and management.

In contrast, a computer science major usually takes courses in operating systems, compiler construction, advanced algorithms, and similar topics. Some CS programs have courses on computer hardware in addition to systems and other software.

Why is this important? If you're a business-oriented MIS or CIS major, your best chances for early career success will usually be in a position with characteristics similar to your academic program. This might involve creating business applications software, rather than working as part of a large systems programming team at a vendor such as Microsoft developing a new compiler or operating system. Similarly, a computer science major might relish the chance to, say, work as part of the Windows NT development team at Microsoft, but would find developing business applications to be "somewhat less challenging" (okay, boring).

Basically, you want to understand which of the many aspects of the computing world your education has given you some background in. Next, assuming you've been doing well in those areas and like them, you must understand what jobs out in the real world are a "natural progression" for you . . . and which ones aren't.

THERE ARE NO SET RULES that state business computing majors can only be successful in business-oriented computing jobs or that CS graduates can only find happiness working on systems software at a vendor. A case in point: me!

As both an undergraduate and graduate student, I majored in business computing: computer information systems at Arizona State University as an undergraduate, and immediately afterwards studied management information systems as a graduate student at the University of Arizona. A business-oriented computing career was where I'd end up, right?

Not exactly, courtesy of the United States Air Force, where I spent my first four years after graduate school as a computer systems officer. The Air Force decided to assign me to a systems and communications programming job although my background was business-oriented and I'd never taken any courses in systems programming. Fortunately, I received a tremendous amount of training during my first year in the Air Force and actually enjoyed the career broadening I received before I left the military and rejoined the business side of the computing profession.

So you may very well find yourself taking a slightly-out-of-the-ordinary career path as you make the transition from college to the ranks of technology professionals out there, as I did. The trick, as we'll discuss later in this chapter, is to make sure that the company where you decide to work is willing to commit to the training you'll need to round out your academic background to help you be successful in the early months of your professional life.

AN HONEST ANSWER TO THE QUESTION, "DO I LIKE WHAT I'M DOING?"

There's no shame in admitting to yourself after two or three years of "classroom computing" you don't have the passion for computer technology—at least as a professional calling—that you thought you did. Or maybe you need to think hard about which aspects of the field you enjoy—or don't. Surfing the Internet and checking out cool web sites is one possibility, or maybe designing and creating web HTML (hypertext markup language, the language of the Internet) pages would bring out the artistic side you never knew you had. But debugging C or Visual Basic programs is tedious, frustrating, and—let's be honest—not a whole lot of fun. Or perhaps you find that programming is a struggle for you and consistently have trouble with programming assignments.

Wait . . . don't panic if you're thinking, "Oh, no, that's me! Did I waste my education? What do I do now?" No, you didn't, and what you do is keep a clear mind. Many, many, *many* types of jobs may not be "computer jobs" in the traditional sense (that is, dealing with aspects of software development). Instead, they build on the foundation and knowledge you gain as a computer major and permit you to participate in the information technology boom in some other manner. Example: got a knack for sales? Well, did you know that many people in the computer industry do exceptionally well (financially) selling computer hardware, software, or both? Those people aren't programmers or analysts and may know next to nothing about the technical workings of the products they're selling. Yet most will admit that they picked up a tidbit or two from their college computer courses, maybe just enough to spark their interest in selling computer products. A computer major with a talent for sales might really do well.

So before you hesitatingly and uneasily trudge off to a series of interviews for hands-on computer positions, make certain that you *want* to start your career in that direction. If you don't, lots of "sort of" computer jobs are out there waiting for you, and your efforts will likely be better expended in one of those directions.

YOUR LIFESTYLE PREFERENCES

Do you want to stay in (or return to) your hometown? Do you want to travel . . . and how much? Are you looking for a nine-to-five job, or do you thrive on (or at least are willing to put up with) 70 or 80 hour work weeks? Chapter 4 discusses the tradeoffs you may—or may not— want to make in the personal and work sides of your life. The time to figure out your preferences is *before* you even start interviewing.

YOUR APPETITE AND TOLERANCE FOR RISK

Some technology career paths are (relatively) safe . . . established companies, proven technologies, low-risk job changes and progressions. Other paths are filled with risk—but also with the potential for high rewards. In the latter, you might go to work for a startup company for a lower salary than you'd receive elsewhere but, in exchange, getting a bucketful of stock options. A sudden layoff could be around the corner if the company doesn't succeed, but then again you might end up with a large sum of money if the company goes public and your options increase dramatically in value. (And in tough times, large companies have layoffs, too.) Your personal appetite for risk may vary radically from that of someone else graduating with you, earning the same degree from the same school, in the same year. You need to have a good idea of how comfortable you would be with riskier job opportunities so that you can tailor your interview schedule and candidate employers accordingly.

YOUR CANDIDATE COMPANY PORTFOLIO

After you've done your homework and taken a long, honest look at your capabilities, short-comings, and interests, your next task is to figure out where you will be interviewing. There is no magic number of interviews. You might interview at five different companies throughout (and perhaps immediately after) your last year in college, or maybe ten, or possibly fifteen or even twenty. But remember those hundreds of thousands of potential employers out there. How do you (1) develop your "short list" and (2) prioritize the companies on that list?

ON-CAMPUS INTERVIEWS

First and foremost—and easiest (I'll explain in a moment)—are the companies who choose to interview on your campus. By "easiest" I mean simply this: A company that decides to interview at your college is *explicitly stating* that they would like to hire some number—perhaps one or two, perhaps dozens—of newly minted computer graduates from your school. Simply put, they wouldn't be wasting their time conducting interviews if they weren't serious about hiring for positions that they could successfully fill with you and your peers.

Chances are that you're well aware of the on-campus interviewing process at your particular school. On most campuses, notices of which companies will be interviewing—and when—start appearing early in the fall term to give seniors and those in their last year of graduate school plenty of time to begin preparing for interviews and the entire job recruiting process. Most schools' career centers provide guidance and assistance with all aspects of the interviewing process, from preparing résumés to scheduling interviews to providing company background. Check with your career center—and also your school's department—*early* to find out what is offered at your particular school.

Here's the trick: Do your homework! For example:

- Check out the companies' web sites on the Internet.
- Find out *specifically what job type(s)* the company is interviewing for to make sure that they match with your particular career objectives and background, as identified during your self-assessment.
- Find out how many job openings of each type the company is trying to fill and whether they'll all be filled from your school or if the company is conducting on-campus interviews at other schools (either nearby or elsewhere in the country).
- If possible, find out the particulars of the jobs that interest you: the possible location(s) and how much travel might be involved.
- Look for hints of potential problems—sudden and brusque cancellation of a scheduled interview—that could be early indicators that the company might be a difficult place to work.

- If possible, try to contact one or more recent graduates from your school who went to work at a company in positions similar to the one you're seeking and find out how they're doing. Your department may keep track of who is working where, and in this day of near-universal e-mail it's usually fairly easy to contact someone.

REFERRALS

Perhaps your older sister works at Microsoft or Oracle or AT&T or maybe some small Internet consulting firm . . . wherever. Does she like her job? Does she like the company? Does she think the company has a bright future?

CAREER TIPS

FREQUENTLY CHECK YOUR COL-LEGE'S BULLETIN BOARD or intranet site or wherever on-campus interviews are listed. Newcomers to the on-campus interviewing process could show up at any time, and you don't want to miss out on THE JOB just because you checked the on-campus interview list once, early in your last year, and then didn't look again for months.

Whatever the size of the company, it's likely to have dozens, if not hundreds, of jobs posted internally that your sister can check out. Most of them may not be suitable for a newcomer to the computer field (though if, say, you're finishing graduate school and you had several years of experience before you went back to school, you could very well have the qualifications for some of those positions). Or maybe the company *is* conducting on-campus interviews . . . just not at your school. Your sister could put you in contact with the hiring organization and open a door that you might not know about through your on-campus channels.

THE INTERNET

Many fast-growth companies devote part of the "hiring" portion of their respective web sites to entry-level positions for new college graduates. You could poke around companies that you've heard of or use one of the many Internet search engines to find pages for (for example) "college+ computer+job" or "entry+computer+job" or other combinations.

CAREER TIPS

"SISTER" (IN THE ABOVE EXAMPLE) could be brother or brothers or sisters or friends or father or mother or mother's friend or anyone. You get the idea. Use your network of connections to open as many doors as possible.

CLASSIFIED LISTINGS

Chances are that you won't find a whole lot of job listings from the Sunday classifieds in your local paper that are directed towards new hires. But some companies do list these, particularly in major metropolitan areas. Fast-growing consulting firms, for example, occasionally advertise in papers such as *The Philadelphia Inquirer* and *The New York Times* that they have special programs to train newcomers to the computer field for particularly hot areas. So you could find a few leads this way.

RÉSUMÉS, COVER LETTERS, AND OTHER MATERIAL

Here's your first tip: Forget all the traditional advice about the type of paper on which you print your résumé being an all-important weapon in your job search. In these days of faxing and e-mail, the chances of your résumé being seen in its "native" form decrease daily.

"Fax or e-mail me his (or her) résumé" is what I tell recruiters or internal human resources (HR) people when I'm considering hiring someone, and I study the *content* of the résumé. The paper is meaningless because it's being printed on whatever paper is in *my* fax machine or printer, and it would be silly for me to determine someone's suitability for a position based on such triviality.

What *does* still matter, though, is that your résumé:

- is free of spelling and grammatical errors;
- is "visually pleasing" (that is, has proper and consistent spacing);
- clearly describes your unique qualifications and attributes . . . but does *not* exaggerate them;
- isn't too short or too long, but just right in length;
- is designed to trigger the reader's interest and make him or her *want* to talk with you in person.

Books abound on how to prepare résumés—and cover letters—and a number of them are dedicated to the particular needs of college students' job searches. A list of some of them appears at the end of the chapter, and Appendix A includes a sample cover letter and résumé.

One last word in this area . . . I referred to "other material" in the section heading. Sometimes, an interviewer may want to see examples of your work: programs you've written, documentation you've prepared, or perhaps reports and recommendations from your systems analysis instructor. A couple of comments about this:

THIS CAUTION DOES NOT APPLY TO GROUP WORK—a program created by a team of which you were a member, or a systems analysis report that was produced by you and several teammates. The real computing world is one in which teamwork is *highly* valued and, is, in fact, necessary in most situations. Demonstrating your ability to be a productive part of a programming or analysis team can reflect positively on you during the interview process. *However,* you should not rely solely on group-work examples because sometimes it's difficult to pinpoint exactly what portions of the work were yours. And even when you can clearly point to several code modules or several parts of a report as your contribution, an interviewer may still want to see if you can complete work solely on your own. So have examples of both types of work available, if possible.

- Your school work *does* matter, after all! It's not enough to just get a passing grade and move on; interviewers could look at your classroom computer-related work as a predictor of your on-the-job performance. High-quality code with appropriate comments and internal documentation—even for relatively simple programs—reflects positively on you. Conversely, poor-quality code that exhibits lots of bad programming practices—*even though it's only school work*—could easily eliminate you from further consideration for a position. Likewise, reports that are spell-checked and grammatically correct, and of course well organized, are another asset in your job search.

- Use your own work! Aside from the obvious ethical lapse (that's putting it kindly!) if you represent someone else's work as your own as part of your interviewing process, consider the embarrassment should the person whose work you "borrowed" use the same exact program or report as representative of his or her work to the same company. That would not be a good thing . . .

THE INTERVIEW

Entire books have been written about the art of interviewing, and I recommend that as you have the time and energy, you page through some of them. What I'm going to do in this section is more specific: present you with the highlights of interviewing for your first job in the computer profession. Basically, the material in this section covers your Critical Success Factors (CSFs): CSFs are business-speak for some relatively small number of items (out of a much larger, longer list) that if they go right, predict that you'll most likely be successful in what you attempt to do. Your interviewing CSFs include the following items.

BEING A GOOD LISTENER . . .
AND HAVING THE INTERVIEWER RECOGNIZE THAT

The interviewer says, "So tell me about yourself." And you do . . . for 45 minutes straight, and the interview is only one hour long. Wrong!

- Your answers to questions should be brief and to the point.
- Try as hard as you can *not* to interrupt the interviewer when he or she is speaking. Keep the "uh-huhs" to a minimum. Wait until he or she finishes the entire question before beginning your answer . . . otherwise you might find yourself answering a question that you thought was going to be asked but in reality was slightly different than you anticipated.
- Try to absorb everything the interviewer tells you...it's never good to ask a question and the answer begins something like "Well, as I told you earlier,..."

GIVING CONSISTENT ANSWERS

Some interviewing sessions will be conducted with multiple interviewers. That is, you'll spend half an hour or an hour with one person, then move on to speak with another, then another. Make sure that your answers to the same question asked by more than one interviewer are consistent. For example, don't tell one interviewer that you're really looking forward to traveling as part of your job and then tell another that you're ambivalent about travel. Likewise, you aren't helping yourself if you tell one interviewer that you really want to be a hands-on developer and then tell a second person that you would rather be hired into a non-coding position.

ASKING "THE RIGHT AMOUNT" OF QUESTIONS

Even though the interviewer controls the tempo of the interview, you should strive to have a balanced interview . . . about the same number of questions asked by you as the interviewer. Asking questions shows that you're not just a passive participant in the interviewing process, and that your "active" behavior will carry over into the real world, where everyone—even programmers—*must* ask questions and engage other people in dialog as part of daily activity.

ASKING THE RIGHT QUESTIONS

You should ask questions that are relevant to the company and the job(s) for which you're interviewing. It's okay to ask semipersonal questions such as, "What is the thing you like most about working here?" However, be careful: Asking the question, "What are the things you like least about working here?" is likely to be an instant turn-off.

COMING ACROSS AS FLEXIBLE

For your first job, it's highly unlikely that you're in a position to be making many demands: a particular position based in a particular office with a very, very high salary and lots and lots of stock options. Instead, you want to give the impression that the company should—*must*—hire you into some position, somewhere, because you're the type of person they want working there, one who can be a team player and fill more than one role. Even in "nerdy" companies you need to have more skills in your bag of tricks than just being a whiz-bang programmer.

COMING ACROSS AS STABLE

The facts of life in the business world, particularly in computer technology, are these: The days of lifelong employment in one firm are all but gone. An example: me! In twenty years in the computer industry, the longest I've been with any one company is just over four years. (In contrast, my brother has been with one company for ten years, and he started there directly out of graduate school and has only worked with two companies in his career. But he's a rarity.)

Nevertheless, most hiring managers desire to keep their employees for as long a time as possible because it's expensive and time-consuming to replace departing employees. Therefore, you want to inspire confidence in the people with whom you're interviewing that you'll be a stable employee, that is, one who isn't going to resign half way through a project.

How do you get this impression across? Well, for starters, you don't come out and say, "Hey! Guess what? I'm a stable person!" But you can point out:

- the organization that you joined as a freshman and remained a member of throughout your college career.
- the summer job that you started before your sophomore year and returned to each summer.
- the ten-hour-per-week computer lab assistant work-study job that you've had for the past two years.

DEMONSTRATING YOUR PORTFOLIO OF TECHNICAL SKILLS

Even though you're interviewing for an entry-level job, the more you can demonstrate that you're a top-notch C programmer or that you've written ten different functioning applications in Visual Basic, the better off you'll be when compared to your competition.

COMING ACROSS AS A FAST LEARNER

Okay, technical skills aside, there is a *big* difference between school programs and the type of software you'll be developing in the real world. To be blunt: You're in for some real surprises when you start developing software in business settings. Therefore, you need to convince the interviewers that you're a quick study when it comes to the facts of the real-world computing life. Many, many things aren't covered in school programs (or only a few, anyway) such as software version control, tape library management, deployment of software to hundreds of PCs, and so on. But you'll be learning these techniques, and your job success will often depend as much on these skills as your programming abilities.

COMING ACROSS AS ENERGETIC

For most of you, it won't be a nine-to-five world out there. You want the interviewers to see you as the type of person who can be energetic at 8:00 or 9:00 P.M.—four or five days a week for several months, if necessary—when project success depends on team productivity . . . and civility towards one another.

COMING ACROSS AS A REAL PERSON

When I'm interviewing people—entry level and experienced—I put a lot of emphasis on whether the candidate comes across as a real person, someone with interests outside of work (whatever they may be), someone who has had setbacks in his or her career and has overcome them . . . basically, someone whom isn't just a one-dimensional (I hate to use this term, but I will) geek. You want to give the impression that you can grow in your role with the company; you can talk with business people and translate their requirements into technical criteria; and, when the time comes, you can oversee the work of others (see Chapter 6).

THE SITE VISIT

You may find yourself interviewing for a position with a firm located in a distant city. For example, assume that you're in your senior year at Arizona State University (my alma mater in Tempe, Arizona), majoring in computer information systems. You sign up for an on-campus interview with a software firm in Boston, and the interview goes so well—you do a great job and the interviewer is very impressed with you—that you're asked to fly to Boston for an all-day Friday interview extravaganza, followed by an invitation to a Friday dinner and reception and then a Saturday picnic gathering for all of the interviewees from all the different schools (75 people in all). They'd like to consider you for a position as an entry-level business systems developer, and they want to spend some time learning more about you, not only professionally but personally.

Beware! Even though all of the topics discussed in the previous section apply to the series of interviews through which you'll be going (for example, consistent answers), you need to be aware of some other considerations during the site visit:

BE CERTAIN OF ALL TRAVEL LOGISTICS

I know, I know, this sounds like some fairly basic common sense, but it's not so much your own ability to get from point A to point B that should concern you. Keep in mind that large companies handle travel plans for dozens, perhaps hundreds, of people every day. Further, many companies have a travel agency handle their reservations and arrangements rather than someone directly on their staff.

The point is this: It's all too easy for you to think that you have a flight on a particular day from Phoenix to Boston, but you need to confirm your reservations—call the airline to double check and then call again just before your flight. Do the same for your hotel reservation, the rental car (if applicable), and anything else on your travel path.

In the business world, travel arrangements get messed up all too often if you don't stay on top of all the logistics. It may sound petty, but your ability to make sure that travel problems don't affect your performance is part of your job (albeit a small one). So you want to make sure that you aren't blindsided by travel problems for your site visit, which would affect your interviews.

BE PUNCTUAL TO ALL EVENTS

Even if you were up late the evening before (more on that in a moment!), make sure that you show up on time to everything that is scheduled for you . . . not only the interviews but also dinners and social events.

HAVE ENOUGH CASH ON HAND, AND (IF POSSIBLE) MORE THAN ONE CREDIT CARD

Here's a tip: Just in case there are no automatic teller machines (ATMs) nearby (or the one closest to the hotel you're staying in is broken), you should have enough cash with you to cover any expenses you might anticipate. You should also have one or two checks with you, plus (if possible) more than one credit card. On several occasions I've been checking into a hotel when the credit card I tried to use was refused for some unexplained reason (no, I wasn't over my credit limit . . . at least not those times!). Having another credit card on hand has been, shall we say, very important on those occasions.

Now this may all seem rather superficial, particularly if the company is supposed to be paying for all of your expenses, but (here's another personal anecdote) I've also checked into hotels that were supposed to be prepaid, but they weren't. It's always best to discretely ask later about being reimbursed for any expenses you had to take care of (but shouldn't have had to) rather than presenting a lot of up-front problems that distract from the reason you're in Boston in the first place: your job interview!

WATCH YOUR DRINKING!

Now you probably didn't think you'd be getting a lecture about alcohol moderation in a book about computer careers, did you? Well, this isn't exactly a lecture, but more of a warning about what is considered proper behavior during events that are part business, part social. Maybe you heard that the employees at this particular company you're visiting "do some serious partying." And wouldn't you know it, at both the Friday dinner and reception and the Saturday picnic, things seem pretty lively among the employees who have been invited to the events. Lots of revelry, boisterousness, and generally, very much like the party you were at last weekend.

But make no mistake—you're *not* at that college party. After you're hired and have become one of the group, then you can feel comfortable interacting with your co-workers in a carefree manner. But for now, you need to look at this Friday dinner and the Saturday picnic as extensions of your interview because you are being evaluated. A drink or two throughout the dinner and after might be fine, and so too might a beer or two at the Saturday picnic. But don't get "plastered" (or even unsteady) because that could easily hamper your chances of receiving a job offer.

BE YOURSELF . . . SORT OF

There's no point in putting on a facade that is very different from the real you. If you tend to be the class clown type, don't necessarily hide that. In the real world, we value people who are multidimensional, who can alleviate the tension of tight deadlines by participating in a late-night, in-office dart war (that is, shooting rubber-tipped or foam-tipped darts from toy weapons . . . yes, this kind of thing really does go on out there!). At the same time, though, be a bit on guard

WARNING

THIS ADVICE APPLIES even if you know one or two people who are already employed there (say, friends from your school who graduated a year earlier). Remember that your friends are most likely relatively low-ranking employees—barely above entry level—and not the people who decide whether or not to hire you. Don't treat this reunion as an occasion to relive your wildest college partying times.

throughout the entire site visit, especially when meeting with or speaking with senior-ranking company officials. For example, the site visit isn't the time to test whether or not a hiring manager's political views are in synch with yours. Tread carefully around any conversations that cause your warning antennae to tingle.

BE (PHRASING THIS DELICATELY) PROFESSIONAL IN YOUR PERSONAL INTERACTIONS

Ahem! Remember the advice about being careful not to drink too much, that you're there to interview, not to party? Well, the same general advice applies to, shall we say, budding romantic encounters. This isn't moral advice, but rather practical. In the real world, people do form relationships with co-workers, clients, or others they meet through their business dealings. *However,* a general uneasiness still prevails among many in the business world when personal and professional matters intermingle.

Suppose the student from the University of Chicago (another candidate) with whom you become involved during that weekend isn't offered a position there, but you are. Would you still accept the job? Perhaps the employee with whom you become involved is an underachiever and is terminated between the time you accept a job offer there and when you report to work after graduation. Will that color your view of the company and get your career off to a bad start?

People are people, and things do happen. But if at all possible, if only during the site visit, separate personal and professional desires. For what it's worth, it will also be good practice for when you get out there in the real world.

FIND OUT THE INSIDE STORY

What you're told about the company during an interview session on your campus is one thing; what actually occurs there on a daily basis could be something else indeed. Watch for hints that those first descriptions were too rosy:

- three of your six interviewers cancel their sessions because they didn't get back in time from out-of-town work because a project is in serious trouble.
- you hear sarcastic remarks by an employee (interviewer or anyone else) such as, "So, did they tell you that you'll only be traveling 20 percent of the time? That's what they tell all of us . . . right!" Or, perhaps, "Well, here comes the newest batch of suckers . . . I mean job candidates."

WHAT YOU NEED TO LEARN

Your primary objective throughout the entire job search process—from your earliest research to what may seem like an endless stream of interviews and possible site visits—is to convince at least one company to offer you a position. However, the chances are very good that you'll receive more than one job offer. In fact, in good times such as the last half of the 1990s, it isn't uncommon for energetic, talented computer graduates to have five, six, maybe even ten job offers. The same was true during most of the 1980s, and even in slower economic times (the early 1980s and early 1990s, for example), most graduates with computer degrees still received a couple of job offers (though possibly with lower starting salaries than in better times).

WARNING

DON'T JUST ASSUME you'll take the job with the highest starting salary! Although money is certainly important, you could conceivably find yourself much more excited about an opportunity that pays a few thousand dollars less than your highest offer but just *feels* like the right job to take. That's why the items discussed below are so important.

So, that primary objective aside, what *you* need to get from your interviews and the rest of your job search process is enough information so *you* can decide where *you* want to work. Aside from the obvious—compensation (discussed in the next section and then in more detail in Chapter 2)—you need to know many, many things to make the best possible employment decision.

So you need to do your best to learn the following:

WHAT IS THE EXACT JOB DESCRIPTION FOR THE POSITION YOU'LL BE HIRED FOR?

Perhaps you've been interviewing for several different types of jobs with one employer. Which position are you being offered? Exactly what tasks will your job involve and what are the details of those tasks? For example, "software developer" is, to put it mildly, a catch-all term. You need to know:

- what application (for example, an inventory management system);
- whether you'll be working on a project that's just starting up or joining an on-going project team;
- what programming language(s) or development environment(s) you'll work in;
- what your specific tasks will be. Coding new modules? Doing testing and quality assurance (QA) on modules written by more experienced and senior developers? Modifying existing code to meet new requirements?

You must also be absolutely certain about the job location. For example, you may have interviewed at company headquarters in Boston, but the job positions they're offering are actually in Iowa. (Not that I'm saying that's a bad thing! I live on a farm and, personally, would rather work in Iowa than Boston.)

WHAT TRAINING WILL YOU RECEIVE AND WHEN?

Will you be expected to hit the ground running from your first day, with no formal training? You should hope not, since you're most likely interviewing for an entry-level position, but you do need to know if that's the case. Find out whether you'll be expected to learn everything you need to know solely from on-the-job training (that is, working with and being mentored by more experienced employees) or if you'll be sent to formal classroom-style training in a programming language or database management system or whatever tools you'll be expected to use as part of your job.

WHAT IS YOUR IMMEDIATE MANAGER—AND HIS OR HER MANAGER—LIKE TO WORK FOR?

Maybe you've met the person who will be your manager as part of the interviewing process, or maybe you haven't. Even if you have, the person could act significantly different during an interview session than on the job under pressure. Try to find out as much as you can about what it's *really* like to work for this person. (Suggestion: instead of partying, use social settings during a site visit for this kind of dialog and research.)

WARNING

ALTHOUGH ON-THE-JOB TRAIN-ING is valuable in learning the real world aspects of a programming language or development environment, all too often the people from whom you're supposed to pick up these pieces of knowledge are extremely busy and pressured in their own tasks and deadlines and don't have the time or patience to give your training as much attention as they should. Or, even if they do have the time, they might be (to be kind) "training challenged"—that is, they might be great technologists but can't effectively teach others about the rudimentary aspects of new job skills. You need to discover these things because at some point—usually sooner than later—you'll be expected to pull your own weight. When that time comes, you don't want to be in a situation where you haven't been taught the additional skills and you're facing deadlines, with no help on the horizon. Get these things cleared up *before* you begin a job, not after!

WHAT ARE YOUR CLOSEST CO-WORKERS LIKE?

As with your manager-to-be, you would like to have an idea what your co-workers are like, particularly those with whom you'll be working most closely. With luck, they're all a good bunch of people who are talented, personable, and make the workday . . . well, less worklike. But luck doesn't always prevail . . . you could find yourself as the only "normal" person working with a group of antagonistic, bitter, sarcastic . . . you get the idea.

WHAT ARE THE COMPANY'S FINANCIAL DETAILS?

You need to find out the inner financial workings of smaller companies such as a startup consulting firm or a new company trying to develop Internet software. Is the company's financing provided solely by its founders, or is there investment funding from an outside firm behind this company (such as a larger company or a venture capital firm)? The answers will give you an idea of how stable the company is likely to be, particularly if a downturn occurs. They are also factors to consider when you evaluate any company stock options you receive as part of your compensation package (see Chapter 2). For larger, established companies such as IBM, Fidelity Investments, Coca-Cola, Microsoft, and any other household name, you still want to find out something about how the company has been doing financially (discussed next). Nearly all these companies are public firms, meaning that their stock is traded on a stock exchange. (Occasionally, you find a large privately held firm, such as one of the large "Big 5" consulting companies. These very large firms, however, are different than a startup in terms of any worries about the company's survival or source of funding.)

IS THE COMPANY ON AN UPSWING OR DOWNTURN?

Have times been good at the company lately? Are profits up? Is employee stability good (low turnover), which means that people not only like to work there but see a bright future. Or is the company going through tough times, with lower earnings, poor employee retention, and an uncertain future? Ideally, you want to find yourself working at a company on the upswing, particularly as an entry-level employee. Should layoffs come, guess who's likely to be early in line for severance?

WHAT IS THE COMPANY'S HISTORY OF LAYOFFS?

WARNING

EVEN IF THERE IS A NO-LAYOFF POLICY (written or unwritten), it may not last forever, as with one of my former employers . . . Digital Equipment Corporation (now part of Compaq).

What is the company's recent (in the past five to ten years) history of layoffs?

Try to find out *why* layoffs occurred when they did, and under what circumstances. Was it because a large project was concluded and the entire project team was terminated because there wasn't follow-on work? Did layoffs occur even as profits were rising—but not fast enough? These answers will give you a good sense of the culture of the company you're considering going to work for.

HOW ARE YOU EXPECTED TO SPEND YOUR FIRST THREE YEARS AT THE COMPANY?

Suppose you're hired to work on a one-year development project. Will you then be expected to spend the next two years as part of the applications maintenance team, doing modifications to and correcting errors in the code you and your teammates developed? Or will you then transition to a new development project because other employees do the maintenance on all existing applications? Are you likely to remain working in the same company location? The same business organization? The more you learn about these items, the more you can make intelligent choices about where to live—an apartment or a house? what part of town? how long of a lease? —or whether or not you should buy a new car.

CAREER TIPS

JUST BECAUSE A COMPANY may have a shady, less than desirable history regarding layoffs doesn't mean that spending a year or two there at the beginning of your career is necessarily a bad idea. Perhaps the pay is so outstanding and the technology with which you'll be working so exciting that it's worth the risk of a bit of job instability because you'll be much more marketable after your stint there. We'll discuss this a bit further in Chapter 15.

THE AMOUNT—AND TYPE—OF TRAVEL YOU CAN EXPECT

Maybe you like travel, or perhaps you don't. Even if you are looking forward to business travel, you want to find out whether yours will involve long periods out of town (several months or longer, for example), or a series of shorter but more regular trips (such as a few days every couple of weeks). Will you be allowed to return home on weekends when you're out of town for extended travel (commonly called "fly backs"), or will you have to remain in the city in which you're working? Can you keep your frequent flyer miles (as contrasted with the company getting them)?

HOW MUCH ORGANIZATIONAL CHANGE HAS OCCURRED IN THE PAST YEAR?

How often has the company reorganized? You want to find this out because many of the other things you learn as part of your research (travel, your manager, even the specifics of your job) could be nullified in the twinkling of an eye as the result of a reorganization. Organizational change is a reality, even a necessity, in the business world; good companies evolve and change to adapt with their environment, new opportunities, and challenges. So I'm certainly not cautioning you to stay clear of companies that are undergoing, or have recently undergone, organizational change. Rather, you do want to get an idea (if possible) of whether the change has had a positive effect or, conversely, could be detrimental to you.

WHAT IS THE LEVEL OF PROJECT STABILITY?

Suppose that in the past year, your potential employer has initiated 15 different projects. How many of them were completed successfully? How many of them are still on-going and are likely to be successful? How many have been canceled because of problems that couldn't be overcome? How many projects were canceled for "other reasons" such as the effects of organizational change as discussed above? The greater the overall project stability in the organization has been, the more likely your job (and possibly burgeoning career) is going to be stable and less prone to disruption.

WHAT'S THE STATE OF EMPLOYEE MORALE?

You don't want to simply ask interviewers and others the blunt question, "How's morale around here?" Mostly, you'll hear, "just fine," whether or not morale is good. But you can put together a composite of employee morale by asking as many people as possible, at as many levels (senior management, middle management, and developers and analysts like you would be) such questions as, "What's the best thing, the thing you like most, about working here?" and "What is the thing about working here that you would most like to change?"

WHAT IS THE COMPANY'S EXPENSE REIMBURSEMENT POLICY?

Of course you'll be reimbursed for expenses such as out-of-town travel! Ah, but you need to find out *exactly* how you'll be reimbursed. Will you get a company credit card? If so, are the charges billed directly to the company or do you have to pay the bill first then have the funds reimbursed to you? How often are you reimbursed? Are airplane tickets paid for by the company or do you pay for them and then get reimbursed?

This may seem like an off-the-wall item, but it can make a big difference in your finances. Most companies where I've worked either require you to use your own credit cards for travel expenses or issue a "company credit card" that is really yours—you make the payments—and then you submit travel vouchers for approval. This means that (1) you need sufficiently high credit limits on your personal card(s) to cover these expenses, and (2) you need to consider what would happen if your reimbursement is delayed, such as when your manager is on vacation and isn't there to sign your travel voucher. Could you cover these expenses out of your own pocket temporarily? All it takes is one or two expensive, short-notice airline tickets that you have to put on your credit card and before you know it, you're over your credit limit or, at best, paying off only part of the expenses and having to pay interest on the amounts you can't cover because you haven't been reimbursed.

WHAT'S THE COMPANY VACATION POLICY?

How many days of vacation do you get a year? How many holidays? How many "floating holi-days" (basically, additional vacation days)? Are there any restrictions on when you can take vacation, such as not when other members of your project team are on vacation because of the project schedule?

WHAT IS THE PERFORMANCE REVIEW POLICY?

How often is your performance reviewed? If it's once a year, is it on the anniversary of your hiring date, or is it a consistent date within the company? When will you be eligible for your first performance review? If you're promoted, do you automatically get a salary increase? These—and many other important questions—are discussed in more detail in Chapter 2.

IS THIS THE RIGHT ORGANIZATION WITHIN THIS COMPANY TO WORK IN?

In any large company (and many medium-sized ones), there are organizations that are the place to be and others that are, shall we say, less beneficial to your career. If possible, you want to be in one of the better organizations; your career will profit in the long run.

COMPENSATION

Because there's so much to say about compensation, I've split the subject out into an entire chapter (the next one, Chapter 2). So check out the discussion about salaries, bonuses, stock options, and all the rest there.

DECISIONS, DECISIONS

So the big moment is here! You have to decide among the three or five or more job offers and the decision isn't easy. One moment, you think that the position as a developer with the software development company in San Francisco, working on their new personal finance program, is the job of your dreams. The next moment, you think you should go with the consumer products company in New York in their information technology (IT) department because it will give you a chance to learn the hot area of data warehousing.

This decision—a critical, all-important one that will affect most aspects of your life for years to come—is obviously one you don't want to (make that *can't*) make lightly. But don't fear: help is on the way, directly below.

The following chart gives you a consolidated way to measure different attributes of each of your opportunities, weighted for importance *to you* (more on that in a moment), and develop a weighted score for each.

It's important to note that you aren't obligated to select the opportunity with the highest score, of course. The primary purpose of this chart is to give you a way to collect and organize all of your thoughts and help you sort through the hundreds of details about all of the jobs that you've been absorbing for months.

THE JOB ATTRIBUTE CHART

The table below shows the type of chart you can create to help you compare your job opportunities. You can tailor the specific job factors, the weighting factors (more on those in the next section), and the range of scores (0 to 10 in the table below; 10 is the highest and 0 the lowest). That is, you could take the category of "job responsibilities" and divide it into several subcategories: day-to-day tasks; equipment you'll work on (your own laptop or workstation, for example); and one or two others, each with its own weighting factor and score.

JOB ATTRIBUTE CHART

JOB FACTOR	WEIGHTS	JOB 1		JOB 2		JOB 3	
	(1–5)	SCORE	TOTAL	SCORE	TOTAL	SCORE	TOTAL
Job responsibilities	4	8	32	4	16	8	32
Near-term compensation	4	7	28	5	20	10	40
Long-term compensation	3	7	21	5	15	10	30
Living location	2	6	12	9	18	2	4
Work lifestyle	5	5	25	9	45	8	40
Managers and co-workers	3	6	18	8	24	4	12
Opportunity to learn	3	6	18	2	6	10	30
Career growth potential	2	6	12	2	4	10	20
Intangibles	3	8	24	9	27	2	6
Total Score			**190**		**175**		**214**

The idea is to create a total score for each of your job opportunities (and though the table above shows three, you're not limited to that number; you can create as many columns as necessary). This will give you an idea which one or two of them stand out as the best when you take all the various factors together.

You are under no obligation to automatically select the job offer that receives the highest score; what you want to do is solidify your thinking that (in the above example) your first preference is Job 3, your second choice is Job 1, and Job 2 trails the other two. Further, note the wide difference in scores between Jobs 3 and 2. That difference is greater than the difference between Job 3 and Job 1. So you may, after your first pass, decide to eliminate Job 2 from consideration and concentrate on the other two.

WEIGHTING FACTORS

The reason to include weighting factors is not to utilize something, however rudimentary, from that statistics or quantitative analysis class taken your sophomore year. Rather, what you want is some way to give the job factors that are most important to you more significance in the scoring process than those that matter less. In our example, we've used a system where 5 is the highest value and 1 is the lowest. Again, you could tailor the weighting in your own chart any way you like, such as using a scale from 1 to 10. I'd recommend not becoming overly complex, though.

You'll note that "living location" has a weighting factor of 2, whereas "job responsibilities" is weighted as a 4. This means that in *your* particular decision-making process, the tasks and responsibilities you'll have in your first job are more important to you than where you'll live. Then, if you look at the "raw scores" you've given for Job 1, you'll see that "job responsibilities" has a value of 8, giving a weighted total value of 32. Similarly, "living location" has a value of 6 but since the weighting (the significance) isn't as great as the job responsibilities, the weighted value is 12.

ABOUT EACH ITEM

The job factors in the chart are largely self-explanatory, but a brief description of each is included below.

Job and Responsibilities

What will you be doing? What development systems and programming languages will you use? What will your role be on a development project team?

Take all of this into consideration and give it a score that represents whether you'll be doing really cool stuff or—conversely—routine, ho-hum tasks that will make the workday seem very, very long.

Near-Term Compensation

We'll discuss all aspects of compensation in Chapter 2. For now, the value for near-term compensation will be the salary and *expected* first-year bonus (that is, not the maximum you *could* receive as a bonus but rather what you're likely to receive). You can rate the offers against each other: your highest salary offer might be a value of 10 if, say, it's for lots more money that you had expected to receive, or perhaps it's a 7 or 8 if it's your best offer but mostly in line with the offers that your friends are receiving. You can then rate the other offers' near-term compensation accordingly: An offer that is significantly lower, for example, might receive a 2 or 3.

Long-Term Compensation

Do you get stock options as part of your offer, or are you going to work for an established company that doesn't give new employees stock? If you do get stock, what does the long-term outlook seem to be? If you're working for a start-up, it could be significant (or it could be nothing; you never know!). Alternatively, if you go to work at a fairly stodgy, slow-growing large company, there could be some long-term potential but not as much as at the start-up.

Living Location

Living location is certainly a personal part of the score. For example, someone who graduates from the University of North Dakota and wants to remain near home after graduation would likely give a job offer from a North Dakota software company a 9 or 10 score, while someone who grew up in Arizona and went to school there and despises the cold and the snow, might give that same offer a 1.

You should also take into consideration factors such as cost of living and related matters. You might love New York City, for example, but on an entry-level salary the cost of living might be so prohibitive that you would have to share a place to live if you want to live in the city (or live in New Jersey or somewhere else outside the city). If you don't want to have a roommate, and you don't like long commutes, then factor those items into your scoring.

Work Lifestyle

Here are two extremes by which you can score what life will be like during your hours at work. On the most positive side, the type of job you would likely give a value of 10 would have:

- **FLEXIBLE HOURS**—all that matters is getting your work done, and if you want to sleep late and work late, that's okay according to company policy.

- **FLEXIBLE WORK LOCATION**—working at home, or taking your laptop with you to a park and spending the day there, is not only tolerated but actually encouraged!

- **PLENTY OF EQUIPMENT**—you have your own PC with a complete set of software for everything you need to do; you don't have to wait in line to use one of a handful of PCs in your office.

- **TEAM SPIRIT**—you will receive a tremendous amount of hands-on assistance from the day you arrive, and your work is monitored (though not in an overbearing way) to make sure you progress on course.

- **A REWARD-ORIENTED CULTURE**—if you do a good job, you get rewarded . . . not only at performance review time but throughout the year—perhaps the company pays for tickets for a play or dinner or sends a project team that is doing well on a weekend ski trip.

- **TRAVEL**—your travel is just right for your particular needs. A three- or four-day trip once a month, to really great places, with a chance to go early and stay late and do some sightseeing and have some fun!

In contrast, I would give a job with the following characteristics a very low score:

- **"PUNCH-CLOCK MENTALITY"**—you are expected to show up no later than 7:30 A.M. every morning and leave no earlier than 5:00 P.M. every afternoon; there is no such thing as comp time even if you worked all weekend or pulled an all-nighter. Attendance factors more into your annual review than your job performance. Lunch is 45 minutes—no more, or you have to make up the time at the end of the day. By the way, you are expected to work a minimum of 45 hours every week regardless of workload.

- **"FACE TIME MENTALITY"**—you had better be at your desk during work hours! If you're not sitting at that desk, you're obviously not working.

- **LACK OF EQUIPMENT**—you're part of a new project team and you're assigned to a prototype team. However, no one on the team will be receiving PCs until . . . well, sometime next month, because due to budget shortfalls, the company has a hold on all expenditures. Therefore, even though the clock is running on your tasks and deliverables, you have no way to do your work.

- **A MISTRUSTFUL ATMOSPHERE**—maybe people aren't sabotaging each other's code, but they certainly aren't helping each other! You are pitted in competition against the others with whom you're working. Some amount of competition is certainly healthy and tends to bring out the best in rising stars at a company, but here it's a "if he wins, you lose" culture when it comes to projects, job tasks, and other attributes of your day-to-day work life.

- **A PENALTY-ORIENTED CULTURE**—not only aren't there the little pleasant surprises along the way, but you're "whacked" immediately—and publicly—for mistakes. And believe me, as an entry-level person you'll be making plenty of mistakes as part of your job; you *have to,* or you don't learn.

- **A BAD TRAVEL SITUATION**—you receive an e-mail at 3:00 one Friday afternoon telling you that you had better be on a plane at 7:30 that evening to fly from Philadelphia to Los Angeles. A project out in L.A. is in trouble and you've just been assigned to the project team, beginning Saturday morning. How long will you be in L.A.? Well, don't plan on coming back to the East Coast any time in the next few months because you'll be working seven days, and 80 or 90 hours each week. Your weekend trip to the Jersey shore with the nonrefundable condo deposit? Too bad. That's the way it goes.

So how do you come to know these kind of things? Refer to the discussion earlier in this chapter about the things you want to find out during your interviews and, if applicable, site visits. By asking such questions as, "What do you like best about working here?" and "What would you most like to change?" you can, over time, piece together a pretty good idea of whether work life will be a 10, a 1, or somewhere in between, should you accept that job offer.

Managers and Co-Workers

Though your manager and your co-workers factor into what work life will be, I recommend scoring the "people aspect" of each opportunity separately. You might, for example, score work life high based on such factors as flexible time and location and manageable travel. Yet the person for whom you will be directly working (you've been told by others who work for him) explodes into streams of profanity as he screams at project team members when deadlines are missed. Or perhaps the manager seems like a good person for whom to work, but two of your prospective co-workers give you a bad feeling, and you've overheard remarks about their incompetence and how everyone else on the team has to pick up their workloads in addition to their own.

Opportunity to Learn

Everything you've found during your research about training—classroom and on-the-job—factors into the score you give each job offer for providing you with the opportunity to learn. Will you be broadening your technical skills, learning about the Internet and doing HTTP and HTML development, something you've always wanted to learn? Will you be working as part of an organization that has several top-notch data warehousing architects, giving you the opportunity to learn a great deal about that rapidly growing technology area?

Potential for Career Growth

What is your sense of what your career would be like at some future point—say, seven years out—should you remain with that employer? Will you have a chance to grow from being a software developer to a lead project architect and then a project manager? Will you have the chance to switch to related career fields—say, selling computer consulting services—should you tire of the hands-on work? Does the company promote people from within to newly created management positions, or do they almost always hire from the outside?

Intangibles/Sixth Sense

I would strongly recommend trying to get in tune with your sixth sense about each of your job opportunities. Aside from your scores for all of the factors, does an opportunity *feel* as if it will be a good one? For what it's worth, every time I've gone against my sixth sense I've been sorry and wound up in, shall we say, less than desirable work situations.

Although the "intangibles" category has a weighting factor of 3 in the chart on p. 19, you'll see that I've increased it to a factor of 5 in a revised version of the chart on p. 26. Whatever weighting factor you decide to use for your own particular decision-making process, don't ignore your sixth sense when it comes to making your choice.

STUDYING THE EMPLOYEE AGREEMENT

Most companies require you to sign an employee agreement—basically, a contract—as a condition of your employment. Usually you sign it on your first day of work, or perhaps you'll receive a copy before your starting date that you're to review, sign, and bring with you.

> **WARNING**
>
> **DON'T WAIT UNTIL YOUR FIRST DAY** of employment, or even until after you accept the offer! You should study the employee agreement of each company that gives you a job offer as part of your evaluation process. Why? Read on, and you'll have a pretty good idea of some of the traps that could be waiting for you should you not do so.

The Basics of the Employee Agreement

The employee agreement usually covers some rudimentary conditions of your employment:

- explicitly stating that you're working for the company as an employee;
- that your employment is "at will"—that means you aren't obligated to remain employed there for some finite period of time nor is the company required to maintain your state of employment for six months or a year or two years or some other duration. Rather, you can resign whenever you want, usually with two weeks notice (as specified in the agreement), or the company can terminate your employment for any reason, also with some stated amount of notice and pay during that period.
- that you certify there is nothing in your background that could inhibit your ability to perform your job, such as an obligation from a previous employer that prohibits you from working there (more on that later);
- that software and documentation you create as part of your job tasks are the property of the employer or a customer of that company, as determined by the particulars of any company-customer agreements;
- that you're required to keep confidential internal information about the company and, if applicable, its customers.

The above items should all be acceptable to you, though you want to make sure that you're comfortable with the language and there are no ambiguities or uncertainties as to any of the terms. *If you have any doubts, get someone such as an attorney to review the agreement and give you his or her interpretation of the wording!*

Some companies also insert clauses in the agreement dealing with what is commonly called a *noncompete agreement,* and this is where problems can easily arise. This isn't to say that an employee agreement with a noncompete clause is automatically a bad one. Some noncompete clauses are fairly bland and straightforward, stating that (for example) should you go to work for a competitor you can't divulge any of the company's trade secrets to your new employer (this is basically a confidentiality agreement). Another commonly found—and usually acceptable—noncompete clause comes into play when you go to work for a consulting firm and you're prohibited from resigning and going to work for a customer of that firm for which you did consulting work. This type of clause usually covers a finite period, starting with the date of your resignation and then goes for six months or a year (some stretch the period to two years, and this is getting a bit ridiculous . . . but not as ridiculous as some of the examples we'll discuss in a moment). A variation on this consulting noncompete clause may have it applying only to clients for whom you worked in the past year rather than any client for whom you worked at any time during your employment there.

Watch Out For . . .

However . . . let's look at some other noncompete clauses that are, in my opinion, far too restrictive, most of which usually apply to computer consulting firms. For example:

- You are prohibited from going to work for *any* client of an employer for the next two years, even if you personally never worked on a project for that particular client company.
- Adding to the above clause, you are also prohibited from going to work for any *prospective* client—any company that the consulting firm made a sales pitch to in the past two years, even if they did no work there—for a period of two years.
- You are prohibited from going to work for any of the consulting company's competitors for a period of two years, with "competitor" being defined as any consulting or software company that does business in any state in which the employer has a client.

CAREER TIPS

NEVER **ALLOW A COMPANY to "force" you into signing a new, more restrictive employee agreement after you are already working there! The** legalities of doing so probably vary from state to state but aside from whether or not it's legal, you have just received an early warning indicator that (1) there are problems afoot at that company, or (2) things have changed significantly since the time you began working there, and you can expect further unpleasantness soon.

These are *real* noncompete clauses! I've seen each of these at prospective employers or, in one situation, an employer that attempted to tighten its current employee agreement and require its employees to sign the new, more restrictive version. In one situation, I was doing contract consulting work for a firm and was considering joining them as a full-time employee. However, after reviewing the highly restrictive employee agreement that I was handed, I declined the offer and remained a consultant for the next project (my last one with them).

Sometimes you can ask a company to amend or delete certain clauses in the employment agreement in accordance with your circumstances. However, most companies decline to do so, and you may very well find yourself in a decision-making mode as to whether you *really* want to—or should—go to work there if the agreement is too restrictive or problematic.

Looking Ahead:
The Executive Employment Contract

Later in your career as you're being considered for executive-level positions, you may be considering an opportunity for which there is an executive employee contract. Like the basic employment agreement, this is a legally binding arrangement that spells out the details of your tenure of employment. However, an executive employee contract is often for a specific duration, say two or three years, and may include executive-level aspects such as buyout clauses if the company is bought by another firm (the so-called "golden parachute"), a severance amount (and associated conditions) should your employment be terminated, and similar details. Don't expect to see such items in a basic employment agreement for an entry-level software developer, but know that at some point in your career, probably after you've been working at least ten years, you may encounter this type of arrangement. In those circumstances, *definitely* get professional legal assistance while you're negotiating such an agreement.

 CAREER TIPS

AFTER STUDYING A COPY of each company's employee agreement, your sixth sense about the company will be accurately tuned to the rating you should give in that category. A particularly restrictive employee agreement that seems unfairly inhibiting is usually an accurate indication that things might not be that pleasant at that employer after you get settled in, especially if business starts slipping. Conversely, an employee agreement that covers the basics yet doesn't attempt to restrict your career should you choose to leave usually tells you that you won't have too much of a hassle during your time there.

MAKING A SECOND PASS AT YOUR SCORING CHART

So you've gone through the first iteration of your scoring chart. You turn down one job, but then they counteroffer, increasing the salary by $5,000. Another company tells you that the project they discussed with you has been canceled, but they still want you to work there . . . and they describe another project that doesn't sound nearly as exciting as the original one.

Or you start to reconsider some of the weighting factors you first assigned. You decide location may be less important than you had thought. Or, because of a personal situation (such as a family illness) it becomes a more important, maybe even the most important, factor.

You should continually refine your chart as your job search proceeds and you learn more (or information changes) about each opportunity. Compare the following chart to the previous one and you'll see how your decision-making process might change after giving a second thought to different aspects of each job, plus your personal preferences and what's important to you (as represented by the weighting factors).

JOB ATTRIBUTE CHART

JOB FACTOR	WEIGHT	JOB 1		JOB 2		JOB 3	
	(1–5)	SCORE	TOTAL	SCORE	TOTAL	SCORE	TOTAL
Job responsibilities	4	8	32	4	16	8	32
Near-term compensation	4	7	28	5	20	10	40
Long-term compensation	3	7	21	5	15	10	30
Living location	4	6	24	9	36	2	8
Work lifestyle	5	5	25	9	45	8	40
Managers and co-workers	5	6	30	8	40	4	20
Opportunity to learn	3	6	18	2	6	10	30
Career growth potential	2	6	12	2	4	10	20
Intangibles	5	8	40	9	45	2	10
Total Score			230		227		230

SUMMARY

Don't feel too overwhelmed by the large amount of material covered in this chapter. If, perhaps, you thought finding your first computer job was simply a matter of going through a few on-campus interviews and then accepting the offer with the highest starting salary . . . well, you could do it that way, but you have a much greater chance of being happier and satisfied in your first job if you put a little more effort into the entire search. By doing your homework, asking the right questions, and applying a bit of discipline to your decision-making process (courtesy of some variation of the chart introduced in this chapter), you'll be much less likely to be thinking, "Oh no! What did I get myself into?" after you've entered the computer profession.

INTRODUCTION

For many readers, we've gotten to the best part of this book. Money! Uppermost in the minds of most college graduates (or soon-to-be graduates) is how much they'll be paid to ply their trade in the computer profession. And believe me, this interest, concern, or whatever you want to call it (obsession?) in how you'll be compensated will continue throughout your career.

While there is much, much more to your first job and the next one and the one after that than how much you're paid, there is no escaping the importance of compensation to your job satisfaction. More important than immediate gain, though, is that your compensation is an enabler of much of what you'll be able to do with the rest of your life. From your first days of life in the real world, how well you live, how much you're able to give to charity, and other aspects of your life will be largely driven by your compensation.

With that preamble behind us, we need to thoroughly discuss the many different aspects of compensation so you have an idea of how salary, bonus, stock options, and all the other pieces of your earnings fit together. This information will help you evaluate different initial postgraduation job offers and then, later in your career, consider opportunities to change employers and pursue new jobs.

We'll discuss:

- your salary, which will almost always be the most significant aspect of your compensation for your first job after graduation
- different models for how your salary might be increased (some better for you than others)
- everything you wanted to know about bonuses
- company stock and stock options
- overtime pay and comp time, should they be part of one or more of your job offers
- vacations and holidays
- benefits (or lack thereof, as you might be surprised to find out!)

SALARY

In almost all offers, the most significant piece of your compensation will be your *base salary*. This is the number that you've heard bandied about by your friends and last year's graduates, and that you've studied in your research on the Internet and in magazines. For example, "I got an offer of $35,000 from Company X" or "The average starting salary for computer science graduates for Phoenix-area companies is expected to increase this year by 5 percent to $33,000." These numbers—$35,000 and $33,000—are the *base* portion of your *total annual compensation*.

It's *critical* to recognize that the following equation applies for most job offers:

$$\text{salary} \neq \text{total annual compensation}$$

Total compensation includes not only your hiring salary, but your annual bonus (should you be eligible for one and should it be paid), a signing bonus (if applicable), plus any overtime pay and "guaranteed" additional earnings (such as automatic increases from company stock purchase plans, which we'll discuss later).

For purposes of this section, though, we're going to concentrate on the salary portion of your compensation. By the end of this chapter, you can put this information together with all the rest to get a pretty good idea of the true total value of your job offers.

HIRING SALARY

 WARNING IF YOU HAVEN'T DONE your homework in all of these areas and factors listed above, then you *must* do so before you even begin discussing salary with any companies.

Negotiating your hiring salary is very much like buying a car. You have an idea of the salary ranges you can expect, given such factors as your major, the school you attended, the city or cities in which you're considering working (salaries and compensation often vary geographically, as we'll discuss), the general state of the economy, the demand for computer graduates and how it has varied from the previous year (upward or downward trend), and so on.

Naturally, you would like to receive as high a salary as possible. But at the same time, an employer who makes you an offer would rather pay you a salary of $32,000 than $35,000. There will be some negotiating, some give and take. You may lower your expectations a little bit, and the company may come up slightly in their offer. The company could throw in a few extras in lieu of additional salary, perhaps a few more vacation days each year or maybe a signing bonus.

 CAREER TIPS IF YOU'RE A GRADUATE STUDENT with several years of work experience behind you before you entered graduate school, or (as is increasingly common) you did a significant amount of computer-related part-time or even full-time work during your college days, then that experience may very well factor into your salary expectations and possibly make you a candidate for higher-level positions. For example, if you have the equivalent of two years of C++ programming experience on "real applications" that you gained from a summer job after your sophomore year and continued for most of your junior and senior years, you can likely seek higher-paying positions with correspondingly greater responsibility than your classmates who lack that experience. See Chapter 1 and the discussion about self-assessment to help guide you in figuring out where you fit into the job search hierarchy.

As with buying a car, where you may be considering a couple of different models at different dealers, you're most likely looking at several opportunities. Likewise, a company might have a larger supply of "customers" (that is, prospective employees) than they have open job slots.

So let's start talking about the initial offer and then move to a discussion of negotiations and other factors.

The Initial Offer

Whenever possible, you want the company to make the initial offer instead of making it yourself, saying during an interview "I'd like to get a starting salary of $35,000." As someone just entering the computer field, you can do this more easily than more experienced technology professionals. Why? Because most companies are much less flexible about their budgets for new computer employees. For example, a company may be looking at hiring 15 entry-level people, each of whom will be paid somewhere between $30,000 and $34,000, with no variation permitted according to the company's budget.

More experienced professionals, however, are often looking at higher-level positions with more variability in what a company will pay, and therefore companies usually try to get a job seeker to make the first move about salary expectations so they can work within a range around those expectations. Companies do this even if they could (if necessary) go much higher in starting salary to hire someone they really want.

WARNING

SOMETIMES THE PERSON making you a verbal offer might ask you the following very loaded question: "What do you think about the offer?" *Never* get into a discussion on the phone and say something like "It's great!" or "I have an offer from Company Y that is $3,000 higher," or anything like that. Be elusive. Say something like "I'm excited to receive an offer." Don't get steered into negotiating on the spot since you're not likely to be prepared to do your best.

So the likely scenario is this: You'll receive a call or a letter from a human resources manager or some other person at a company that is making you an offer (or maybe you'll get a call first followed by a letter), and you'll be told that the company is offering you a position to be a C developer, Visual Basic developer, or general software developer (or whatever the position is), with a starting salary of, say, $33,000. You'll be given some period of time to accept or reject the offer.

For more experienced computer professionals seeking higher-level positions, the period of time will typically be relatively short: one week, perhaps two. However, for the entry-level positions offered to you while you're still in school, you're often given more time, perhaps even several months if you're offered a position in, say, November of your senior year, and graduation isn't until May.

Alternatively, you may interview with a company in October or November but since they're interviewing at many different campuses, you may not receive a job offer, should one be forthcoming, for several months, perhaps only shortly before graduation. It's important to find out the timing of job offers in the context of the interviewing process when you're going through interviews. This gives you a good idea of whether or not you might have to wait months to receive an offer from the company of your dreams, should you interview with them very early in your last year of school.

Signing Bonus

Some companies offer a signing bonus as part of your compensation package. This is particularly true when the demand for computer professionals outstrips the supply of qualified candidates, such as in the mid- and late 1980s and the mid- and late 1990s. Before you start getting too excited, though, keep in mind that even companies that do pay signing bonuses to new entry-level employees in addition to those who join

NOTE

A FEW ORGANIZATIONS, particularly governmental or nonprofit ones, may have no flexibility at all in what they can offer you as your starting salary. There is one and one salary only for an entry-level developer and it's nonnegotiable, no matter how uniquely qualified you might be, or how competitive the job market is, or any other factors. So keep that in mind as part of your evaluation criteria when the time comes to negotiate a revised offer (should you wish to work there).

them at a higher level usually pay a few thousand dollars and not much more. So when you read articles in the business or technology press about "the return of the $100,000 signing bonus," don't expect to see such an offer coming your way.

Many companies hold back signing bonuses from initial offers, then during job offer negotiations will add one to the total offer, sometimes along with an increase in the offered base salary, sometimes as an alternative to the increase.

Any way you look at it, a signing bonus is desirable. But there are certain things you need to learn about any signing bonus that you're offered, including:

WARNING

IN SOME LARGER COMPANIES, your signing bonus might "fall through the cracks" because the human resources (HR) department might not communicate that information to the payroll department, for example. Be persistent! If you're owed a signing bonus by a certain date and you haven't received it, then talk to anyone and everyone to make sure you're paid what you're owed!

- **WHEN IT'S PAID**—Will you receive it the day you start work? In your first paycheck? Or will it be paid after some type of checking-you-out-as-a-full-time-employee period, which could be as long as three or six months? Obviously, the sooner the better.

- **ANY PAYBACK PERIOD**—Signing bonuses often have as a condition a period of time, usually one year, in which the bonus (or a portion thereof) must be paid back if you resign. For example, over a one-year period a prorated portion of your $5,000 signing bonus must be returned. If you resign six months into your employment to go somewhere else, you would owe $2,500.

Negotiating

So you receive the offer letter. And another, and another, and before you know it, you're ready to start making the decision about where you're going to work. As part of the evaluation process (see Chapter 1), you also want to be negotiating the financial aspects of the offers with each company.

CAREER TIPS

DON'T BE AFRAID to negotiate smartly, worrying that if you ask for more money the company will withdraw the offer. That does occasionally happen, but if they really want you to come work there, one of two things will happen. First, they will raise their offer, maybe not to the point that you're totally satisfied (in which case you can continue to negotiate). Or, alternatively, they could tell you, "Sorry, we can't go any higher, but we really want you to come work for us." Perhaps the company representative is being truthful—they really can't raise the offer—or perhaps not. But the point is, don't be afraid to ask.

A general rule of thumb is that a company *expects* you to ask for more money, so they'll rarely put their best offer forward on their first try (remember the car buying analogy). Therefore, it's a good tactic to call the HR person (or whomever is your point of contact) to discuss the offer at each company that you're considering seriously.

Try to make them make the first counteroffer. This means that instead of saying something like, "The offer is for a starting salary of $33,000; I'm looking for $36,000," you should try, "Can we see about raising the starting salary, as I'd very much like to come and work here." Very often the company representative will ask you "Well, what are you thinking about?" and try to engage you into stating your expectations. It's okay if you want to say, for example "I'm looking for $38,000" when in your mind you'd be happy with $36,000. Again, remember the car buying analogy.

A couple of cautions pertain to salary negotiations. Specifically, while bluffing is acceptable, you don't want to be caught outright in a lie.

- **ACCEPTABLE**—Saying "I'm looking at several other offers." If you're asked about the other salaries you're being offered, it's okay to say, "The highest one is $39,000" when in reality it's $37,000. The key: staying within a reasonable distance from your own highest offer, and possibly knowing that one of your friends actually did get an offer of $39,000 from another company (assuming, of course, your friend isn't exaggerating!).

- **RISKY**—Saying "My highest offer is from Company X for $38,000, and I'm going to take that offer unless I receive a higher starting salary from anyone else." This is risky for two reasons. First, the above statement makes you come across as fairly mercenary and almost exclusively money-oriented. The company then might perceive you as the type of person who

WARNING

IF A COMPANY SHOULD ever contact you after you accept a job offer, but before you begin work, and tell you that they need to lower your starting salary for some reason such as "we had a bad quarter and our budgets were cut" or (this one's worse) "we made a mistake in our offer letter, and we are capped at $30,000 each for new employees, not the $33,000 we offered you," then *run!* This isn't negotiating, this is a sign that something is seriously wrong at the company . . . financial problems, a culture where they don't value employees and are very likely to do things like that throughout your time there, or whatever. Once you accept a job offer then *those* are the terms of your employment, not some revised and lowered salary. How would you like it if you signed a contract to buy a car for a certain price and then, when you went to pick up the car, the dealer said, "Oh, I'm sorry, I can't sell the car to you for that price anymore but I can let you have it if you'll pay an extra $500."

would accept an offer and then, just before you were to begin working there, call them up and say, "Sorry, I'm taking another job elsewhere." The other reason is that if your offer from Company X is $36,000, not $38,000, it's possible that the person to whom you're speaking *knows* that. How? Companies survey other companies to see what they offer for various positions at various levels, and it could be widely known that Company X's top offer for this year for entry-level computer science graduates is $36,000. Possibly, too, you may not have an offer from Company X. If your other offers evaporate you could have used a fictional job offer to drive off the real ones, leaving you in a not-so-desirable position.

Factors to Consider

As you're negotiating salary with your short list of prospective employers, keep in mind the following things.

1. GEOGRAPHICAL LOCATIONS—A starting salary of $35,000 to work for a company in the San Francisco area is not equivalent to an offer of the same amount to work in Pittsburgh. Why? Cost of living differences. An apartment in San Francisco or elsewhere in the Bay Area could cost you upward of $1,500 a month, whereas in Pittsburgh you could live fairly comfortably for about $500 a month in rent. Perhaps you need to pay several hundred dollars a month for parking at an apartment in San Francisco (or New York or another high-cost-of-living city), whereas parking doesn't cost anything extra in cities with lower costs of living.

It's *likely*—but not certain—that a company in a higher cost of living area will adjust its salaries accordingly, so the average starting salary in San Francisco might be $45,000 this year whereas in Pittsburgh or Phoenix or Cleveland, most computer science and MIS graduates are receiving salaries of perhaps $5,000 less. You need to factor cost of living into your negotiations and evaluation, and figure out how much money you'll have left after covering essentials.

2. YOUR WEIGHTING FACTORS—See Chapter 1 for the discussion of how to weight the importance of salary and compensation as part of the overall picture when you're considering job offers. If salary is of relatively low importance, you should still negotiate but you may not want (or feel comfortable) pushing very hard as part of your negotiations for higher starting salaries on the offers.

3. THE JOB LEVEL YOU'RE BEING OFFERED AND YOUR EXPERIENCE—If you have real world experience behind you, then you should be competing for higher-level jobs. Therefore, don't sell yourself short when seeking opportunities and their corresponding starting salaries. More important, you can use this experience as part of your negotiating strategy, for example, saying, "I took part in two successful development projects that used Visual Basic when I was in college, and I was in charge of testing and quality assurance."

INCREASES AND PERFORMANCE REVIEWS

As you're focusing on securing job offers and trying to decide among them, you should also find out as much as you can about companies' systems of salary increases and performance reviews. Basically, this information is as much a part of your compensation as your starting salary, signing bonus, and the rest.

Companies' policies vary widely. Here are some of the things you must find out about and some of the things to watch for.

When Performance Reviews Are Done

Some companies review your performance on the anniversary of your hiring date. Others review all employees performances at a single time each year, regardless of hiring date. In the latter situation, you could find yourself very much at a disadvantage if, for example, everyone is reviewed in September of each year and you begin working at the company in July or August. Chances are you won't have many real accomplishments on record during your first month or two on the job, particularly if you spend most of that time being trained. As a result, you could go through the first review cycle without receiving a salary increase. The next time you'd be eligible for review is the following September, meaning that you'd have gone through 13 or 14 months from your hiring date to your first chance for a salary increase instead of 12.

Some companies have two regular review cycles each year for different groups of employees (one in the spring and one in the fall, for example). In these situations, you want to find out when you'll first be eligible for review: the next one or the one six months later.

Other Occasions for a Performance Review

Some companies permit their managers to do performance reviews at times other than during the official review cycles. This way, if you're doing a stellar job you could be promoted and receive a salary increase before you otherwise would.

What the Company's Ranking System Is Like

Some companies call them "grades," others use the term "corporate title," and others might use "level." Whatever the phrase, each company usually has some type of hierarchy ranging from the company's chief executive officer (CEO) or equivalent to, at the lower end, entry-level administrative and support staff members. You need to understand not only at what level you'll be coming in but also things like how long it takes to move from one level to another, what the criteria are for promotion, and the additional compensation aspects at each level. That way, you can better gauge what level you're likely to reach in successive years.

If Salary Increases Are Granted if You're Not Promoted

Suppose you go through a review cycle and for whatever reason you're not considered quite ready for the next level. Do you still get an annual salary increase? If so, what is the likely percentage or amount?

If Salary Increases Are Higher if You're Promoted

You also want to know if you will receive a higher increase if you're promoted than if you're not when your review cycle comes around. Perhaps surprisingly, companies often will give you the same 6 percent or 8 percent regardless of how you're rated and whether or not you're promoted. (This can be a warning sign that later in your career there your salary would likely stagnate because excellent performance isn't correspondingly rewarded.)

If Promotions Are Automatically Accompanied by Salary Increases

Another spin on the promotion-salary increase relationship is finding out whether or not a promotion means that you will always receive a salary increase. Basically, this is the real-world version of the sitcom-standard "Well, we can't pay you any more money but we can give you a title" joke you sometimes see in workplace settings. Trust me, though, it's not very funny in the work world when it occurs and you find out that your excellent work isn't going to bring you commensurate financial reward.

The Likely Range of Increases

Most companies produce an annual or semiannual range of salary increases as determined by their budgeting process. Some rigidly hold their managers to those ranges, while others permit their managers to go above (sometimes *way* above!) the top end of that range to either reward the best-performing employees or to make up for past shortfalls. For example, I once "inherited" a group of data warehousing professionals (when I joined a consulting firm as an executive) that was relatively underpaid compared to their peers in other technical specialties within the company, let alone the marketplace for data warehousing consultants. In the first review cycle, I gave some of the more underpaid employees generous increases that, in some cases, were double the high end of the recommended range. The next review cycle I increased the salaries of two of my regional managers by 25 percent—*way* above the high end of the salary increase range—to bring them in line with new hires with equivalent levels of responsibility.

The reason you need an idea of this type of information (and you'll most likely get it through unofficial channels, such as one-on-one conversations during a site visit with your future peers) is because as time goes on, and overall market salaries outstrip the pace of official increases within most organizations, you want to see if your salary will catch up with the marketplace. One of the most aggravating things you'll come across in your career is to have a new employee at the same level as you, maybe even a level or two lower, be hired for significantly more money than you're making . . . and company policy prevents your salary from being adjusted accordingly.

BONUSES

Bonuses are an extremely variable portion of your overall cash compensation. In some companies, they don't exist (or barely do) for lower ranking employees, while in others, entry-level employees could receive 15 percent, 20 percent, or even more of their base salary when they've done a good job and the company is doing well.

Your offer letter will most likely state whether or not you're eligible for a bonus, and give *some*—but definitely not all—of the details. Listed below are the things you want to find out from your conversations about each of your offers.

WHAT IS THE TARGET AMOUNT?

This is the easiest item to learn and is almost always contained in your offer letter. The letter will either specifically state an amount or percentage of your base salary. It's important to understand, though, that this amount is the target and the amount you actually receive could be higher, lower . . . or even nonexistent. Read further for more details.

IS THE AMOUNT PRORATED?

Most companies prorate bonus payments depending on when you're hired. If you're offered a starting salary of $38,000 with a 10 percent target bonus (and therefore a $3,800 target bonus amount), and if you start work on July 1, you will likely be eligible for 50 percent of that amount your first year, or $1,900. Or if you start on October 1, your eligibility would be 25 percent, or $950.

ARE YOU EVEN ELIGIBLE IN YOUR FIRST YEAR?

CAREER TIPS

MAKE SURE YOU FIND OUT if there's a cutoff date for bonus eligibility when you set your start date!

Some companies set a cutoff date after which any employees' start dates make them ineligible for participation in the bonus program that calendar year. For example, if the company sets a September 1 cutoff date and you begin work on September 3 that year, you aren't eligible for any payment at all even though you will have worked almost one-third of the year.

WHAT ARE THE CRITERIA?

You need to know two things about the company to figure out how much of your target bonus you are likely to receive. The first is the company's *funding policy*. Many companies set aside a certain portion of their earnings to fund the bonus pool. As long as the target earnings are met (usually each quarter), the bonus pool is fully funded. The second is your company's *eligibility criteria.* Specifically, assuming the bonus pool is fully funded, how does the company determine the exact amount that you and your colleagues (and others at your company) will receive? For example, your criteria as an entry-level employee might include whether your project is successful (or on schedule, if it's still in progress) or whether you pass certain training classes. They might also involve some intangibles such as whether you perform administrative tasks. For example, in a consulting company, this might mean filling out your time sheet each week to indicate the amount of time you've spent on various aspects of your project plus other tasks. Ideally, most or all of the criteria for your bonus eligibility will be objectively measured, but eligibility often has a subjective aspect, meaning that factors such as whether or not you get along with your supervisor or manager factors into his or her recommendation for the amount you should get.

IS THERE AN UPSIDE?

The funding policies and eligibility criteria described above usually result in a decrease in the bonus you actually receive relative to your target. Put another way (and to be a bit cynical), the chances are pretty good that you'll get less of an actual bonus than you were originally told. However, some bonus programs offer some or all of a company's employees an "upside potential," or the chance to get more than the target amount if things go very, very well. Perhaps the upside will apply if the company's earnings vastly exceed expectations (sort of a profit-sharing program), or perhaps the company has individualized criteria, such as, if you are a project manager, successfully delivering your project weeks early and significantly under budget.

DOES THE TARGET AMOUNT INCREASE IF YOU RECEIVE A SALARY INCREASE?

If you receive a salary increase during the year, your target amount should be adjusted higher, even if the percentage stays the same. For example, if your salary on January 1 is $30,000 and you receive an increase to $35,000 on July 1, and your target bonus percentage changes from 10 percent to 15 percent, then your target amount should be calculated as follows:

$$(\$30,000 \times 10\% \times .5) + (\$35,000 \times 15\% \times .5)$$

WHAT ARE THE IMPORTANT DATES WITH REGARD TO PAYMENT?

Every bonus program has certain important dates as part of its rules. The phrase "Christmas bonus" (or "holiday bonus") is the most common, signifying a bonus given some time during the December holiday season. However, many companies pay bonuses early the following year, usually in February or March. They time these bonuses thus because funding and eligibility criteria related to company performance (revenue, earnings, specifically identified decreases in certain types of expenses, etc.) aren't usually known until the year's final financial analysis is completed. It's important to know this so that you don't, for example, plan a January ski trip based on the bonus amount you expect to receive at Christmas and then learn that it's not paid until some time in March.

Likewise, many companies who pay bonuses early the following year set an "earn date" equal to that payment date. That means if you leave the company for a new employer in, say, January and the bonus payment date is in February, you do *not* receive any portion of the bonus, even though you were there during all of the previous year. Other companies *supposedly* (though I've never actually seen one that does this) set an earn date of December 31, meaning that you will receive the bonus payment in March for which you're eligible (subject to funding and eligibility criteria) even if you resign some time in January or February.

Other variations include:

- **EARLY PARTIAL PAYMENTS**—if everything is on track through the third quarter, the company might do an early partial payment some time in December of, say, 75 percent of the target bonus amount, with the balance coming on the official pay date early the next year.

- **QUARTERLY OR SEMIANNUAL PAYMENTS**—if eligibility criteria are set by quarter, a company may pay bonuses on a quarterly or semiannual basis. The advantage of this is that your cash flow increases throughout the year (that is, you don't have to wait until the end of the year for the additional cash income).

- **"EXTRA BONUSES"**—this usually applies to more senior managers and those with sales responsibilities: significant accomplishments with a financial impact result in some employees receiving additional bonus amounts in addition to their annual target amounts, usually on a sporadic basis.

WARNING

WATCH OUT FOR the "total compensation" pitch in which the company tells you that your total compensation will be, say, $44,000. Before you start jumping up and down with excitement, thinking that's $7,000 more than the amount you expected to receive as a starting salary, look further into the details . . . where you may find that you're actually being offered a salary of $33,000 with a target bonus amount of $11,000. Then you look further and find out that the company's bonus payment record has been somewhat sporadic the past few years, and employees usually receive less than half of their target amounts. So more likely, you're looking at first-year compensation of around $38,000, which is less than one of your other offers of $39,000 with a 10 percent bonus that is very likely to be paid. (Not only that, but in the first offer your cash flow throughout the year is based on the $33,000 . . . you might not receive that additional $5,500 until sometime early the following year, meaning that you could be scraping by for a while until you receive that amount, should it even be paid.) Make sure you don't get confused by offers based on a total compensation amount that, when you look deeper, is an amount that would more accurately be termed "total *potential* compensation."

WHAT IS THE METHOD OF PAYMENT?

Are bonuses paid in cash? This may seem like a silly question, but it isn't—some companies pay part or all of employees' bonuses in stock or stock options in lieu of cash. If your target bonus amount is $20,000, there is a big difference between receiving $20,000 in cash compared with $10,000 in cash and $10,000 in options to buy stock at a fixed price. The stock price would have to double for the options portion of the bonus to make up for the $10,000 "lost cash" as compared with an all-cash bonus.

WHAT IS THE COMPANY'S BONUS PAYMENT HISTORY FOR THE PAST THREE YEARS?

Has the company fully funded its bonus pool for the past three years? If not, what percentage did it fund? How much did the average entry-level developer (assuming that's the position you're being offered) receive each of those years?

STOCK

More and more entry-level employees find themselves with an *equity component* to their compensation packages. That is, they have a chance to share in gains of the stock of the company where they work.

You're likely to encounter two different kinds of equity components: (1) plans where you can buy company stock at a discount, and (2) stock options. Both are discussed in the sections below.

COMPANY STOCK PLANS

We'll start with the simplest form of equity participation, the opportunity for you to buy shares of your new employer's stock. You could do this on your own if the company is a publicly traded one (that is, its stock is listed on the New York Stock Exchange, the NASDAQ over-the-counter market, or some other stock exchange) by calling up a stock broker and buying some number of shares at the prevailing market price.

But company stock plans let you buy the stock at a *discount* to the market price. I've worked for two different employers that had nearly identical company stock purchase plans that were set up as described below. Other companies' plans may vary somewhat from these setups, so you need to get the details from any prospective employer with a similar plan.

First, you can elect to set aside some percentage of your salary, from 1 percent to 10 percent, to put into the stock purchase plan. That amount is withheld from each of your paychecks. Assume that you have a salary of $36,000, and you're paid twice each month, meaning that the gross amount of each paycheck is $1,500. Therefore, if you fully participate in the stock plan, $150 is withheld from each paycheck, along with tax and other deductions.

Next, the company sets up two six-month periods each, with a starting and ending date. For this example, let's use May 1 and November 1 as the boundaries of each period. Assume you start working for the company in July; that means that you are eligible to participate in the program starting with the first paycheck after November 1, and by the following May 1 you've set aside $1,800 ($150 × 12 semimonthly paychecks). We're assuming no pay increases during that time to keep this example simple.

Now it gets a little bit more complicated. The company needs to set a purchase price for your $1,800 worth of company stock . . . basically, the price per share that will determine how many shares you can buy. It's often calculated as follows:

- The company takes the *lower* of two different stock prices: the closing market price on the first trading day of the period (November 1 or, if that day falls on a weekend, the following Monday) and the last trading day of the period (May 1 or, if that day falls on a weekend, the previous Friday). Assume that the company's stock price was $30 on November 1 and $35 on May 1, the company will select the $30 figure.

- Next, the company discounts that selected amount ($30 per share) by a designated percentage . . . 15 percent in the examples from these two companies. This sets the actual purchase price per share at $25.50 ($30 × .15).

- You can now determine the actual number of company shares that you'll purchase. Since $1,800 has been set aside, and the price per share is $25.50, you will be given 70.588 shares of stock for your money ($1,800/$25.50). Sometimes you are given fractional amounts (the .588 in this example); other times the actual number of shares is rounded down (to 70 in this example) and the remaining small amount of money is carried over into the next purchase period.

And that's basically it! Well, not exactly; the all-important question that you need to ask yourself—and also answer—is "What do I do with this stock?"

You could hold on to the stock as part of your personal savings and investments as you would hold on to any other stocks or mutual funds. If the company's outlook seems bright, you can hope the stock goes up and you can sell it for more money in the future. You have been given the opportunity to buy stock at a fairly good discount from the going market price. Because the company's stock purchase plan used the lower price from the beginning of the six-month period ($30) instead of the prevailing market price ($35), and *then* discounts that lower amount, you've essentially bought a $35 stock for $25.50!

Which leads us to your other choice: sell the stock immediately and pocket the profit! You need to be aware of any restrictions on selling the stock or "logistical problems" (we'll discuss both of those in a moment) but assume that you could turn around and on May 2 immediately sell your shares. Assuming that you've received a rounded amount—70 shares—you could sell all of your stock for $2,450. Since the actual cost of those shares to you was $1,785 (not $1,800; remember that $15 was carried over into the next period of the plan because of the rounding of the number of shares), you have gained $665.

Even if the stock had gone down during the period, you can still sell at a profit. Assume that the price on November 1 was $35 and the stock dropped to $30 by May 1. The amount of shares you will be given in exchange for your money doesn't change, since the company uses the lower of those two figures (still $30) as the figure from which the discount is taken. However, should you want to sell your shares immediately, you would receive $2,100 for them (70 shares × $30 per share), and your gain would be $315 ($2,100 − $1,785).

You need to find out the following about your company's stock purchase plan—and consider other factors—before you decide how much to contribute (or whether to contribute at all!):

1. **YOUR PERSONAL FINANCIAL SITUATION**—Using the above example, how is your personal situation affected by not having the money you're setting aside available to you immediately? Or, put another way: if you take away $300 each month from your available cash on hand, does that cause a problem in meeting your expenses? You may look at the above example and figure, "Oh well, I'll just rough it for a while because of the automatic profit I'll get six months later." But read on . . . that "automatic profit" could evaporate if the company's policies don't permit you to sell the stock immediately should you want to do that.

So make sure that you can afford to not have that money available to you. Basically, pretend that it's gone forever when you figure out how much you want to contribute. Maybe you don't want to go with the 10 percent maximum amount in the first period you're eligible to contribute; instead you might put in 3 percent or 5 percent of your salary.

2. **ANY COMPANY CONTRIBUTION LIMITS**—During the early stages of your career, you most likely won't be affected by any company-specified limits on the amount you can contribute. But some companies put limits on the total amount you can contribute in any given

period. When you're at the higher range of the salary spectrum you may not be able to contribute the full maximum amount (say 10 percent) of your salary. But this won't affect you for a while, and many companies don't have limits on the contribution amounts.

3. **THE DETAILS ABOUT HOW OFTEN—AND WHEN—YOU CAN CHANGE YOUR CONTRIBUTION, CANCEL YOUR CONTRIBUTIONS, OR REENROLL**—Most companies have a policy that requires you to enroll in a particular contribution period a few weeks before the period starts. No enrollment, no participation until the next period comes around. Also, you cannot change your contribution amount during a period, or disenroll (stop contributing) until the end of the period. Just make sure you understand all of the guidelines.

4. **SELLING RESTRICTIONS**—All in all, company stock purchase plans are a good benefit, and you can add a little bit—or a lot—to your annual income. *But*—and this is a "big but" (no puns intended)—you can only be assured of the "guaranteed return" if you can automatically sell your shares immediately and pocket the gain, rather than hold onto the stock as part of your investments.

If the company has a program set up to handle your stock electronically, and the day (or the day after) each transaction date you can make a phone call and sell your shares should you wish to do so, then there is really no risk in participating. But do make sure that setting the money aside for six months, unavailable to you, won't cause any financial strain.

But . . . some companies still handle stock purchased through company programs the old-fashioned way, with paper stock certificates. Further, it may be weeks, even months, before you receive your certificates. And given the volatility of the stock market, it's easy to see how you might have a built-in automatic gain of thousands of dollars the day your purchase price is set (say the stock price has skyrocketed during that six-month period) but by the time you receive your certificates two months later, the stock has plummeted because of bad earnings or overall stock market weakness. Thus, not only has your gain evaporated, but the market share price is now *below* your discounted (or so it was then) purchase price, and you've *lost* money.

So be careful! Make sure that a good thing doesn't turn bad simply because a company's policies are set up in such a way that you can't be as flexible as you could be in the stock market in general. After all, it's your money and *you* have to protect it!

5. **TAX LAWS**—Tax laws for stock sales change frequently. Currently, if you hold a stock for longer periods of time before you sell it then you will pay less tax on any gain than if you sell it immediately (when it would be taxed as ordinary income). For what it's worth, my recommendation is to think of tax laws about long-term capital gains *after* you consider whether or not you want to (or can afford to) hold on to stock purchased through your company's plan. Put another way, don't hang onto the stock just because you can pay lower taxes if you sell it a year later . . . there may not be any gain on which to pay taxes at that point and you could have lost money by holding onto a bad stock.

Company-sponsored stock purchase plans in privately held companies—those who have yet to "go public" —are *very* different than those of publicly traded companies, as described above. I don't want to overgeneralize, but you are usually better off with a stock option program (discussed in the next section) than a stock purchase plan if you go to work for a privately held company.

The details will vary from one company to the next, but here's what you might expect. The company sets a purchase price based on some type of calculation, such as a multiple of its book value, its revenue, or some other measure. You then purchase some or all of the number of shares you've been authorized to buy and hand over the cash to the company . . . perhaps all at once or maybe through payroll withdrawals similar to those of publicly traded programs.

But what happens then? If the company eventually goes public, or if it's purchased by another firm, you can then sell your shares for the going price. Until then, though, you are almost always *severely* restricted on what you can do with the stock. You can't easily sell it because it's not publicly traded, and besides, there are usually restrictions that prohibit you from selling stock to anyone outside the company on your own. Sometimes you're allowed to make your own deal and sell shares to other employees of the company, or back to the company, but at a set (usually low) price, such as your original purchase price or the current book value of the company.

Should you leave the company's employ you are usually obligated to sell the stock back to the company, again at a low price that will usually be the same as your purchase price. So basically, you will wind up having given the company an interest-free loan if you aren't able to cash in down the road if the company goes public or is sold, and your money was locked away—you couldn't get at it—for (possibly) years.

All in all, stock options (discussed next) are a better deal for you in a privately held company, mostly because you don't have to put out any money until (or if) you have the opportunity to cash in on gains if the company goes public or is sold.

EMPLOYEE STOCK OPTIONS

Even though I mentioned stock options in the context of working in a privately held company, you can receive stock options working for a private *or* public company. The discussion below applies to both situations except when I specifically note a distinction.

The Basics

A stock option is exactly what the phrase implies: an option for you to purchase stock. While you can play the options market in most publicly traded stocks, we're specifically discussing stock options you receive from your employer as part of your compensation package . . . options to purchase some number of shares of your employer's stock.

There are two primary differences between a stock option plan and a company-sponsored stock purchase plan (described above).

First, you don't have to set aside any money, either a lump sum or through payroll withholding. Therefore, your personal cash flow isn't affected by your eligibility for a stock option program, no matter how many shares are part of your own option plan.

Second, the price for your options is set on the date they are granted to you and that price—called the *strike price*—doesn't change. This means that, for example, if you are granted the option to purchase 1,000 shares at $10 and five years later, after the company goes public, the stock is valued at $70, you can still pay $10,000 for those 1,000 shares and then immediately sell them for $70,000, or a $60,000 pre-tax profit.

Actually, the details are a bit more complicated so let's look at each aspect of a stock option program.

The strike price. The strike price is usually set at "fair market value" because otherwise, there are tax implications should you be granted a strike price below the market value. If you're working for a publicly traded company, fair market value is the closing stock market price on the day of your options grant. If you're working at a privately held company, there is usually a formula similar to that set for employee stock purchase programs at a private firm. (This is described in the previous section: based on a multiple of book value, or earnings or revenue, or some other measure).

Your actual grant date. Often the date you're actually granted the stock options—and thus the strike price you receive—is *not* your starting date, but some company-specified date. Sometimes, it's once each quarter, such as when the company's board meets. Or it could be less frequent, such as at the company's next *annual* board meeting. The reason the grant date is important is that you may join a fast-growing company, and the day you start work the stock price is, say, $30. But after the company reports great earnings (and the stock market is hot!), the price has risen 50 percent to $45 by the time your grant date rolls around. Therefore, your strike price is $45, not $30, meaning that if you have, say, 1,000 options you will have to pay $45,000, not $30,000, for those shares. So when (or if) you exercise those options, you will receive $15,000 *less* in your profit than if you had been able to receive $30 as your grant price.

The vesting period. The concept of an options vesting period is a complex one, but I'll give you a simple example. But please, please make sure you check the policies of your employer (or prospective employer if you're still considering offers) so you thoroughly understand the details. Say you're granted 1,000 options with a four-year vesting period. This could mean that each month, 1/48 of your 1,000 options—or 20.833 shares—are vested, meaning that should you want to you could execute those options and sell the stock. (More on executing options coming up later.) So at the six-month point, you have 6/48 of your options vested; at the twelve-month point, you have 12/48, or 1/4 of your options vested; and so on.

Alternatively, four-year vesting could work this way. At the one-year anniversary of your grant date, 25 percent of the options, or 250 shares, are immediately vested. Then a year later, another 25 percent become vested. At the three-year period, another 25 percent, or 75 percent in total, of the options can be executed. Finally, at the four-year point, all of your options are fully vested. This means that, for example, at the point between the year one and year two anniversary dates you can still execute only 25 percent of the options; you don't have access to the next "batch" (another 25 percent) until the next anniversary date. You might see a combination of the above two plans: 25 percent executable on your first-year anniversary of the grant date, followed by equivalent (1/48) monthly vesting of the remaining shares.

The reason that it's important to understand the particulars of each company's vesting period is that even if the stock shoots very, very high and your options are worth tens or hundreds of thousands of dollars in profits, by the time you have an opportunity to exercise those options the value could be worth much, much less . . . or perhaps nothing at all if the stock price has dropped below your strike price.

Expiration dates. Stock options usually have an expiration date, such as eight or ten years after the grant date. This means that you have to exercise your options by that date or they expire. See the next item for the discussion of what is meant by "exercising the options."

Exercising the options. Well, basically when you exercise an option (or a package thereof) you pay a sum of money, representing the number of shares you're exercising (some or all) multiplied by the strike price per share, and in exchange you receive that many shares of stock that you can then sell (and receive your profit) or, if you wish, hold as part of your investments.

Cashless transactions. What's that? You don't happen to have an extra couple of hundred thousand dollars in cash laying around when it comes time to exercise your options? Don't worry; most option plans are administered through a brokerage that has a "cashless transaction policy" whereby they keep track of how many options you have and, when you call them to exercise some number of options, they calculate the gain you are due and mail you a check for that amount. Basically, you don't have to borrow the money to buy the options and then turn around and sell the stock and then pay off the loan . . . it's all done for you.

Additional grants. Most companies with stock option plans provide you with the opportunity to receive additional grants of stock throughout your career there. Upon promotion; annually, after you reach a certain management level within the company; or periodically, after you've done a spectacular job on a project or some other work.

Special conditions. Sometimes a company may *reprice* options if the stock price drops significantly below its highest strike price (usually the strike price from the most recent batch of options grants . . . remember that every time the company makes a grant of stock options the price will likely be different than on the previous occasion). Why would they do this? Stock options are not only a compensation tool of an employer but also a retention mechanism. If a company fears that a significant portion of their employees will leave because their options are now worthless (that is, the market price is below their strike price) the company may choose to reprice their options—basically, lower the strike price by reissuing options with new terms and conditions.

Another special circumstance applies to people at certain levels within the company, such as all vice presidents within a consulting firm, and restricts them from exercising options during certain periods of the year. For example, all executives to whom the blackout period applies may be restricted from all trading in the company's stock, including exercising options, during the time just before quarterly earnings are announced until a week later. The idea is to prevent insider trading. Make note of any restrictions on trading, but most likely they won't apply to you as a new employee.

Private company considerations. If you're working for a privately held company that has yet to go public, and you have stock options about to expire, then you have a choice to make. You can either exercise your options and pay for those shares of stock or you can let your options expire, meaning that they're gone forever. Seems like an easy choice, right? Well, if you exercise your options you *cannot* sell your stock on the open market because the stock isn't publicly traded . . . the company hasn't gone public yet. Therefore, when you go to work for a privately held company you need to ask what their strategy is regarding when (or if) they plan to go public, offer the company for sale to another firm (which will give you an outlet for selling your shares), or some other change. If for some reason the plan is to remain privately held, then be careful! If you'll be permitted to share in company profits along with other employees, then you'll be receiving equity-related income in that manner rather than through the sale of your company shares. Otherwise, if it doesn't look as if you'll receive some form of income as a result of your partial ownership of the company (as represented by your stock), then the stock option plan is basically worthless.

Should You Make a Tradeoff Between Salary and Equity?

You may find yourself facing a situation in which you're considering an offer with a smaller company—perhaps a startup firm that isn't yet publicly traded—and you receive an offer that is somewhat—perhaps significantly lower—than the going market rate for someone of your experience. For example, you may receive an offer for an entry-level position with a starting salary of $25,000 when most of your other offers are upwards of $35,000.

But in exchange for this lower salary, you receive a large number of stock options as part of your compensation package—say tens of thousands of options. The idea is that you make a tradeoff now, by accepting a lower salary, and if the company is very successful you will make lots and lots of money down the road when the company goes public and the stock price is much higher than your strike price.

The same tradeoff philosophy is sometimes found in more established companies, including those that are already publicly traded. Salaries are a bit on the low side compared with the company's competitors but you receive a large number of options as part of your compensation package.

This may sound like a familiar scenario to anyone who has read about (or perhaps known) recent college graduates who went to work for startups focusing on Internet technologies in the mid- and late 1990s and made millions of dollars from their stock options. Sounds pretty attractive, right? Who in his or her right mind would pass up such an opportunity?

Well, consider that great wealth by way of stock options is a very cyclical occurrence. The same thing happened in the early 1980s when personal computers were first introduced and that industry took off. Then again in the mid- and late 1980s when networking took hold. But in between, particularly around the 1990 recession and during other stock market downturns, the chance to make vast stock options profits all but evaporated.

Then consider what happens when a company fails, or doesn't do so well and just plods along. Even though you've made the salary-options tradeoff and taken less money than you could have otherwise made, you can't make up that difference and your chance to make money from that stock is gone, perhaps forever.

So the best scenario you can hope for is an acceptable salary, about what you would receive

NOTE FOR WHAT IT'S WORTH, rather than accept a ridiculously low, almost trivial salary in exchange for a bucketful of stock options, consider that in most of those cases your share of the total equity of the company will be rather small, probably less than 1 percent. The vast majority of the gains, if any, will go to the venture capitalists and the company's founders and the board members. So if you really want to work very, very hard for very little salary in hopes of big gains down the road, you should consider striking out on your own where *you* will be one of the principals who will receive the lion's share of the rewards.

from any of your offers, but you also have a not-so-insignificant number of stock options as part of the package that give you some upside. Maybe the number of options, and corresponding upside, isn't as great as in other situations but then again, neither is the risk if the stock portion of your compensation doesn't work out.

OVERTIME PAY AND COMP TIME

Some companies do offer overtime pay as part of your compensation package. You'll usually find this at consulting companies that bill you out by the hour to the firm's clients. The company may have a policy authorizing overtime pay for all hours you work past some number, such as 45 or 50 per week. Understand, though, that the company isn't doing this out of the goodness of their collective corporate hearts. Rather, it's a retention tool to make working 60 or 70 hours a week (as you may find yourself doing) palatable and to keep you from going to work somewhere where you'll work fewer hours.

Alternatively, the company may have a comp time policy. For example, the company's "standard" work schedule may be no more than 180 hours per month. The policy may state that if you work extralong hours for several weeks and things are fairly routine and non-hectic the last week of the month, you can take off some hours to keep you at the 180 maximum for that month. Or if you're on a project that requires you to keep working past the 180 maximum, you can get credit for some (usually not all) of those hours once things settle down a bit and take some time off. If you can't do so then you might receive overtime pay instead.

Find out about these policies, should they exist, because they can factor into your overall compensation and help you decide where to work.

VACATIONS AND HOLIDAYS

Typically, you will receive two weeks of vacation each year as an entry-level employee. Additionally, some number of holidays (usually between six and eleven) are also days off from work.

With regard to holidays, almost all companies give you the following days off:
- New Year's Day
- Memorial Day
- Fourth of July
- Labor Day
- Thanksgiving Day
- Christmas Day

If New Year's Day and Christmas Day fall on a weekend, you are usually also given off a Friday or Monday.

Now comes the complicated part. Some, but not all, companies also give you time off for the following holidays:

- Presidents Day
- Columbus Day
- Veterans Day

Other companies set holiday days such as the day after Thanksgiving, or (should Christmas and New Year's Day come on a Thursday) the day after Christmas and/or the day after New Year's. Still other companies have "shutdowns" during the week between Christmas and New Year's.

Then there are what are known as "floating holidays," or some number of days that you can use on, say, Veteran's Day and Columbus Day should you choose to do so, or you can use them on other days. Basically, floating holidays are like additional vacation days, so if you have four floating holidays and two weeks of vacation, it's like having just under three weeks of vacation.

So far, this seems pretty straightforward. But you need to be aware of each company's policies on your vacation because your compensation can be affected—positively *or* negatively—in various ways:

- **WHETHER THE COMPANY HAS A CARRY-OVER POLICY OR A USE-OR-LOSE POLICY**—Suppose you can't, or choose not to, use all of your vacation within the calendar year you receive it. Some companies let you carry your unused days over to the next year, while others have a use-or-lose policy . . . if you don't use your vacation days, you lose them. If they have a *buyback policy* then at least you can get paid for days you don't use. If not, and you can't take your vacation because of obligations at work, you're basically out of luck.

- **HOW MUCH VACATION YOU GET YOUR FIRST YEAR**—Some companies give you a prorated amount of your authorized vacation days in your first year (that is, if you start working on July 1 and entry-level employees have two weeks of vacation a year, you'll get one week). Others have policies where if you start past some date—usually October 1—you have to wait until the following year to receive *any* vacation at all.

- **RESTRICTIONS ON WHEN YOU CAN TAKE VACATION**—Some companies prohibit certain employees from taking vacation during certain periods. For example, a software company that releases new software in December of each year might black out the entire period from September 1 until the end of the year for its project and support teams so they can be available for the last-minute software development activities and to support the initial releases of its software.

BENEFITS

Benefits are another part of your compensation package. In this section, I'll focus primarily on things to watch out for when you're looking at smaller firms. This way, you'll know the questions to ask so that you're not unpleasantly surprised.

CAREER TIPS A COMPANY'S VACATION POLICY can tell you a lot about what it will be like to work there. The more generous—and less restrictive—a company's policy is, the more likely you'll enjoy working there. Conversely, a company with lots of restrictions on when you can take vacation; that is very stingy in the amount of vacation days it gives you; and has a use-or-lose policy without a corresponding buyback policy, is probably going to be the type of employer from which you'll want to find an escape fairly soon.

CAREER TIPS **AS A GENERAL GUIDELINE to help your evaluation, the less you personally have to pay for your benefits through payroll deductions, and the better and more thorough the coverage is, the better off you'll be . . . and, as with vacation policy and many of the other topics we've discussed, the more likely you are to be happy working at that employer.**

There is much, much more to the subject of employee benefits than we have the space to discuss, so after reading through the basics in this section (and these are only the basics), you should do some research on your own about the details of health insurance, life insurance, and other aspects of employee benefits.

HEALTH BENEFITS

Almost all companies will give you medical insurance coverage (but see the discussion of when you might *not* have such coverage). Many also have dental insurance, and some have vision assistance as a separate program.

The details of health plans vary widely from one company to the next. Some companies have one and only one plan available, and that's all you get, good or bad. Other companies have different plans for different geographies or business units, and where you live and work will decide what health plan you receive. Still other companies give you a choice of plans: one is a health maintenance organization (HMO), another a preferred provider organization (PPO) plan, and another a more traditional health insurance plan. Consult the details of each plan when you have a choice—or, for that matter, even if you don't have a choice—so you know what's covered and what isn't. When in doubt, ask.

An important question to ask is whether your health insurance coverage is automatic, and if it takes effect on the first day of your employment. I was once rudely surprised when I joined a company and several weeks into my employment I needed to go the doctor and discovered that I did *not* have health insurance coverage. In fact, the insurance wouldn't be effective until sometime later in my employment. (Needless to say, this indicated that this wasn't a very good place to work!) So find out if you have *first-day automatic health coverage*. If so, then you're all set. If not, my recommendation is to think twice about going to work for that company.

Look at the various costs associated with health insurance as part of evaluating an offer. Some companies pay most or all of your insurance premiums, others require you to pay a substantial amount out of each paycheck for your coverage. Insurance for you as an individual is always lower than if you're also insuring your family, so make sure you have the right amount as part of your calculations.

If you leave an employer after working there for a while, you are eligible under the federal COBRA law to remain covered by your employee health insurance for up to 18 months should you need to do so. You will now have to pay the *complete* premium, which includes the subsidized portion that had been withdrawn from your paycheck. But at least you will have coverage if you have any time before you start a new job with new health coverage.

LIFE INSURANCE

Life insurance isn't probably on the uppermost of your mind if you're in your early twenties and just graduating from college, but if you have a family—or soon will—you should start at least looking at insurance coverage. Most companies give you a modest amount of company-paid life insurance, often some multiple—usually two or three times—your annual salary (though often with some cap at the upper end). This is *term insurance,* meaning that there is no cash value to the policy.

You may have the opportunity to purchase additional life insurance through the company but check their rates compared with other insurance you can get directly from insurance companies; you don't want to overpay.

DISABILITY INSURANCE

You may have disability insurance as part of your benefits. Some companies pay for your disability insurance; others require payments from you along with your health benefits.

Short-term disability insurance covers you if you need to be absent from work for health reasons for a short period of time. If you're affected by a debilitating health problem and can't work, then long-term disability insurance becomes effective. Usually, long-term disability insurance covers a portion of your salary (such as 75 percent).

RETIREMENT AND INVESTMENT PLANS

Fewer and fewer companies these days have traditional pension plans: the type where after working there 20 or 30 years you receive an annual payment of some amount of money based on your years of service and how much you earned during your career.

Most companies are switching to 401(k) plans in which you invest some percentage of your salary into the company's plan, and that money is then invested in stocks, mutual funds, bonds, or some other vehicle. Every company can set up its own 401(k) with a variety of investment choices, so you need to see what your options are.

Some companies match your contributions, meaning that if you invest $5,000 during the year into your 401(k) plan, the company also puts in $5,000. Other companies have partial matching policies, such as 50 cents for each dollar you put in, or 100 percent matching but only up to $2,000. When the company has a matching plan, it may restrict your access to the matching portion, perhaps requiring it to be in your account for three years; if you leave the company's employment before that period is up you can only take your own contributions and earnings with you, not those of the company.

MEDICAL ACCOUNT PLAN

Some companies give you the opportunity to set aside a certain amount of pre-tax money into a medical account plan that you can use for medical expenses that aren't covered by your health insurance. The catch is that if you don't use that money, you lose it. So be careful when you figure out how much—or if—you want to participate in such a plan.

EDUCATIONAL BENEFITS

Most firms give you the chance to take classes and receive full or partial reimbursement. However, companies' plans vary widely. Some are very generous: full reimbursement, even at expensive schools, for example. Other plans require you to attend a relatively low-priced school; cap the amount of benefits you can receive each year; or require you receive an A or B for full reimbursement, otherwise you only receive partial reimbursement.

Other companies may require you to repay any educational benefit if you resign your employment within some period of time (usually one or two years) after receiving a payment. So be sure you clearly understand the policies of each company's educational reimbursement so you can evaluate whether or not that's a benefit you will be able to use should you choose to work there.

Looking ahead, some larger organizations have programs where you can go to school on a full-time basis for a master's or doctorate degree, and still receive your salary while you're in school. The tradeoff is that you then incur an employment commitment (three years, for example) during which you must pay large sums of money back to the company if you resign. (Such programs are common should you go to work as a computer development officer in the U.S. military, so check with the details of your particular service's programs.)

THE "CAFETERIA PLAN"

Suppose you are married and your spouse has a very good health plan through his or her employer, including coverage for you. To you, health insurance may be a benefit that you can't really use. But you want to complete your master's degree, and the company's somewhat meager educational benefits aren't enough to cover your expenses.

What will be of interest to you is a company that has adopted the "cafeteria plan" approach to benefits. That is, you have the opportunity to pick and choose from a list of benefits, eliminate those you don't need, and possibly increase the amounts allocated to other categories. The amounts you receive with which to work will usually vary according to your level within the company.

RELOCATION ASSISTANCE

If you'll be moving to a new city, you'll want an employer to cover relocation expenses for you. Chances are that as an entry-level employee you won't have an entire household of furniture and personal belongings for you and your family (though later in your career that will certainly be possible). But if you're going to be moving more than you can, say, stuff into the hatch area and backseat of your car, then you want to make sure that you're not stuck with an expensive bill to cover a professional moving company's services.

OTHER BENEFITS AND PERKS

Company cars . . . mileage reimbursement for using your own car on business . . . keeping your frequent flyer miles . . . first-class upgrades on airlines . . . reimbursement for health club payments or being able to work out in the company's exercise room . . . low-interest loans to buy a computer for yourself . . .

Every company has a comprehensive list of what you can and can't receive payments for and other related aspects of your compensation. Typically, the higher your rank within a company, the more generous the plans are. Therefore, you need to get a good idea of all the different aspects of what might be available to see the positive—or negative—impact on your income. For example, if you need to use your own car for regional travel (say, to drive from Philadelphia to New Jersey every day for a consulting project, a round trip of around 100 miles) and you are *not* reimbursed, that out-of-pocket money for gas and wear and tear on your vehicle can quickly add up. Other companies might have policies where you are reimbursed for business travel only if the amount of your drive is greater than your regular commute. So if you live 50 miles from your office but usually work at home, and then suddenly have to drive 40 miles each way, every day, to a client site because of a new project, then you have to absorb those transportation costs.

SUMMARY

Well, we've covered a lot of material in this chapter. Chances are that first on your mind is the base salary you'll receive from the company whose offer you'll accept. However, as we've discussed, there are many, many other items you need to be aware of with regards to compensation and considering various offers.

It's strongly recommended that you consult additional references about benefits and related matters, and *thoroughly* study all company-provided material about their particular benefits programs and other matters such as stock option details, overtime pay policies, and everything else we've discussed in this chapter.

 YOU MIGHT FIND YOURSELF considering a position where you have *no* benefits. For example, you might be looking at what is in effect a consulting contract working with a firm, assisting them on a client project. Because of the particulars of tax law you're considered an employee, and you have taxes withheld from your regular payments (which aren't really a salary because the amount may vary according to the number of hours you work and other factors). But in these contracting-like situations, it is rare for a company to cover health benefits, life insurance, or any of the other items discussed above. Similarly, you won't receive pay for holidays or vacation. You don't work, you don't get paid.

So why would you consider going to work in such a situation? One simple answer: more money! Because of the tenuous, unpredictable nature of such arrangements you will usually receive more (sometimes much more) per hour of actual work than you would if you were a salaried employee. So considering such an opportunity is certainly advisable should a good one present itself to you, with one caveat: make absolutely sure that your pay—whether hourly or daily—is *significantly* more than you would receive should you accept another offer elsewhere as a salaried employee. You will probably have to purchase health insurance on your own (perhaps using COBRA—discussed earlier—from a previous employer), and you could find yourself without any income (basically unemployed) for several weeks or months (or even longer, in slower economic times) after a contractual arrangement ends and before another begins. Therefore, you not only want to be receiving more money per hour of work but you also want to be tucking some of that money away in case you need it to live on.

CHAPTER 3

GETTING READY TO START WORK

INTRODUCTION

In this chapter we'll discuss a variety of "preparatory" items. We'll talk first about the things you need to do before you begin your new job and then, next, topics of concern to you during your first days with your new employer, and a few do's and don'ts . . . sort of your code of conduct.

The first part of this chapter is just good old common sense advice and is presented primarily to make sure that in the excitement of getting ready for the real world workforce you don't get sidetracked, overlook important items, and get your career off to a rocky start. Afterwards, we shift our discussion to items particular to the first days of your career as a computer professional.

BEFORE YOU START WORK: PERSONAL MATTERS

You want to have *everything* in order on Day One of your new job. By "everything," I mean exactly that: everything in your personal life and everything that can be considered a prerequisite to starting your job. This section presents a checklist that you can use, with commentary and advice about each item.

YOUR EDUCATION

Make sure that everything to do with your degree is in order and completed. If you have any, uh, "troubles" your last semester after you've accepted a job offer—such as having to withdraw from a course or receiving a failing grade—make sure that you do something to cover that missing class. Make it up in summer school, or take an alternative course to make up those credits. But be sure that by the time you start your new job, you have everything settled.

 WARNING WHATEVER YOU DO, *don't* just forget about (read: ignore) your missing credits. Or, worse, state on your résumé that you have completed your degree when in fact you haven't. Eventually, possibly years later, you'll get caught shading the truth and you could very easily be dismissed from a job that you've already begun.

Alternatively, contact your new employer *immediately,* as soon as you realize you have a problem, and explain the difficulty. Then, if necessary, make arrangements to delay your start date until you have a chance to complete your degree, or perhaps take a make-up course after you start work.

RELOCATION PLANNING

If you'll be moving to another city to start your new job, you either (1) need to have your living arrangements settled before you arrive, or (2) make sure that your new employer will take care of temporary living logistics—and expenses—for you.

If the company doesn't have a temporary living expense policy, then they should pay for a house-hunting (or apartment-hunting) trip for you. Make sure that you go to the city that will be your new home at least a month or two before you're going to begin work, and that by the time you leave you have a lease set on an apartment or house. If you're going to be buying a condo or house, have all the details settled, including a move-in date.

Some companies permit you to start working without having to worry about these details and until you find a place to live, they will put you up at their expense in a furnished apartment or a suite-style hotel. This second alternative is often preferable, and if your new employer has a temporary living policy, I recommend taking advantage of it. That's because unless you really know the new city very well (because you lived there in the past, for example), you often don't know all the ins and outs that can make living there pleasant . . . or, conversely, very unpleasant.

For example, most major cities and metropolitan areas have absolutely horrendous rush-hour commutes. It's not uncommon to spend an hour (or more) in bumper-to-bumper, slow-moving traffic to move ten miles or less. Since you'll likely be spending long hours at work, you may not want to add two hours each day—ten hours each week!—sitting in traffic.

So if you spend the first few weeks, maybe even a month or two, in company-paid temporary living quarters, you'll not only save money by not paying rent or a mortgage, you'll also get a chance to really learn the city and figure out where living might be easiest for you. You might choose to live further away from work (but going *against* the prevailing rush-hour traffic) than you would have before you saw those long, long lines of cars. Or maybe you find a place of worship that you really like and you decide to live on that side of town. Or perhaps you and several of your new co-workers decide to all get together to rent a large house instead of each living in an apartment.

The point is that rather than rush into a particular set of living arrangements and then regret your decisions (which will possibly weigh on your mind and affect your attention to your work), you're better off camping out for a while at company expense and taking your time finding a place to live.

MOVING ARRANGEMENTS

If you'll only be moving a few belongings to a new city, your moving arrangements are very simple: load your car, fill it with gas, and take off! But if you'll be moving more personal belongings and furniture, as you will later in your career, and particularly if you have a family at that time, then you'll be dealing with moving vans, restrictions on what you can and can't move, and all the rest of those fun details.

Start making those arrangements early, at least a couple of months before your scheduled arrival. Perhaps you need to have your belongings kept in storage while you're staying in temporary housing (see the previous section). Make sure that the moving company not only has you on their schedule but also has the types of services that they'll be providing to you on their list, such as storage, dual location moves (for example, picking up your belongings from your family's home and your fiancé's from that person's home, if the company is paying for both of your belongings to be moved), whether you will pre-pack your belongings or if the movers will do the packing, and any other special services.

Make sure that you have a list from the moving company of what they will and won't move according to their policies. For example, perhaps a moving company won't move flammable items, so you need to pack those items yourself and drive them in a car, or buy new ones when you arrive at your new city.

Some companies have a policy where they will let you do a "self-move" and pay you part or all of the difference between that and a professional moving service. For example, if you (1) pack your own goods, (2) rent a moving truck from a company such as U-Haul or Hertz Penske, and (3) drive the truck yourself to your new home, then they will not only reimburse you for your expenses but also give you a little extra cash. *However,* having been part of several self-moves, they are not a lot of fun! If you're going a fair distance (such as part or all the way across the country), you might run into endless road construction, bad weather (especially in the winter!), or other hazards along the way. My own personal suggestion is to think twice about any self-move. If you do opt for that approach, have a friend or family member go with you to share the driving, help increase your safety on the road, and generally pass the time.

YOUR PERSONAL TRANSPORTATION

If you're driving to your new location, then make sure your car is road-worthy and have any repairs made well before you start your trip. If you have decided to buy a new car and can do so before you start your job (from savings, for example, or as a graduation present) then have that vehicle in your hands with enough time to find any unanticipated problems and get them fixed.

If you're flying then make sure you have all your arrangements set—and double-checked—including how you will get from the arrival airport to wherever you're staying (a hotel, temporary living quarters, or your new apartment).

SPECIAL MOVING CIRCUMSTANCES

It's possible that you will be starting work for an organization in which living arrangements—temporary *or* permanent—don't apply to you, at least not right away. For example, a few companies have a military-style "boot camp" (okay, maybe more of an orientation program, since you won't be going on ten-mile runs and doing dozens of push-ups!) for their new employees. These programs take place on a campuslike setting, and you and your new colleagues will live in dormitories for several months while you go through long, long hours of training.

If you accept an offer with such an intensive orientation program, then you need to find out if you'll need to make your post-training living arrangements before you start the training program or if you can do so during the program.

FINANCIAL "ASSISTANCE"

Some companies give you advance pay with interest-free repayment periods once you begin work. This way you can have a little extra money for car down-payments, apartment security deposits, or any other start-up expenses.

If possible, make arrangements for advance pay before you start work (contact the company's human resources department) and have a good idea of when you'll receive any payments.

The same is true for signing bonus payments (see Chapter 2). Likewise, solidify any arrangements for any other money you're expecting (such as a last paycheck from your current employer).

"RIGHT TO WORK" MATERIAL

Anyone who has started a job in recent years knows that employers now require you to produce certain documentation that "proves" your right to hold that job. If you're a U.S. citizen, you need to produce a passport (if you have one) or a mixture of a driver's license, social security card, birth certificate, military papers, voter registration, or other material.

If you're not a U.S. citizen, then you have requirements that depend on your immigration or work permit status.

In either situation, you *must* make certain that you know what material you need to bring with you when you start the job so your employment (or at least your pay!) isn't delayed.

GETTING AN EARLY START ON YOUR JOB SKILLS

I *strongly* recommend that you pursue a course of self-study from the moment you accept a job offer until you begin work. By self-study, I mean the following:

1. **GET AN ACCURATE LIST OF TECHNOLOGIES AND PRODUCTS YOU'LL BE USING**—As part of evaluating your job offers, you've (I hope) done a significant amount of research and asked many questions, so you should have no doubt as to what you'll be doing after you start work. If you'll be doing hands-on programming, you should know what language (for example, Visual BASIC, C, C++, Java); on what operating system platform (for example, Windows NT or UNIX); and with what supporting technologies (for example, a Visual BASIC front-end to a Microsoft SQL Server database in a client/server environment).

2. **GET ACCESS TO SOFTWARE**—If you'll be a Visual BASIC (VB) programmer, go out and buy a copy! (Assuming you have a PC; if not, then you should seriously think about buying one unless you want to wait and take advantage of an employer's low-interest loan program, if they have one—see Chapter 2). And start playing around! I mean exactly that: playing. Write some fun programs so you'll get into the inner workings of what VB does, and you'll see first hand what works well and what limitations you may run across. Create a program to keep track of your personal finances, vaccination records and veterinary visits for your family's pets, the addition to your family's house, or something similar.

   Then stretch your boundaries a bit. Write some SQL Server calls, even if you have to create a database emulation (as opposed to having a real client/server environment to work with). The idea is that when you begin work, even if you are initially scheduled for significant amounts of training, then you'll have a leg up on acquiring the skills you need to acquire.

   (One caution, though: try not to acquire "bad coding practices" through your self-study. Make sure that you get a book or two that guides you through the *right* way to program in Visual BASIC, or C, or whatever language you're working with. This way, you won't have to unlearn any bad habits).

3. **DO SOME INDUSTRY RESEARCH**—If you're going to work for the information technology (IT) organization of a bank—or perhaps an IT group within one of the bank's lines of business—then do some self-study about the industry and the organization you'll be joining. Learn about the major IT functions of a multinational bank or a credit card bank or whatever type of bank you're joining. Then, if you'll be joining the consumer organization of the bank (as contrasted with the corporate banking organization), learn about the specifics of consumer (also often known as "retail") banking and the types of loans they offer, how individual credit bureau data is handled, and other practices.

So where do you pick up these skills? The Internet, for one place. Also, ask your hiring manager or the HR representative to recommend material that you can read and study. Then, combining this research with your technology and product background, you might design a small-scale program in (for example) Visual BASIC that creates sample monthly reports on consumer banking activity. You likely won't be right on the mark when it comes to what you actually create. Still, you'll be close enough so that after you start the job certain terms and phrases will be familiar and you'll be fairly comfortable in your new surroundings.

YOUR INITIAL TRAINING

Some companies require you to undergo a formal training program at the outset of your employment. *Usually* (but not always) you'll spend your first days with such a company in an orientation course, after which you will be sent to a project or to your regular job. Occasionally, though, if you're going to work at a consulting firm with an orientation program, you may find your program delayed as you're sent off to a project because the firm doesn't have enough people available to work on that project.

So what can you expect in a formal orientation program? The following list is an overview of the likely goings-on.

WARNING

BEWARE OF SUCH a "work first, train later" situation! The reason for sending you to an orientation program in the first place is so you can be trained in the company's ways of doing business, such as their methodology for developing software. Should you be sent off to a project first you will be behind the curve because you won't have all of the prerequisite training and activities on the project that depend on your skills and knowledge and you could have a rough go ahead of you. You may not have much choice, but if something like this happens to you, you may have your first indication that things may not be quite as advertised at your new employer.

1. **ADMINISTRATIVE ITEMS**—A company representative will assist you with filling out forms for insurance, payroll, registration in the company's time-keeping system, and anything else necessary for working at that company. You should also be instructed in how to fill out time sheets (if applicable) and expense forms so you can be reimbursed for your business travel expenses.

2. **THE COMPANY'S CULTURE AND VALUES**—Some of the "this is how we do things around here" presentations will be standard and can apply to any company: policies about sexual harassment, for example. Other presentations will describe the company's history, its unique position in the marketplace, the culture that's prevalent there and its values, and perhaps some war stories from recent project team members so you know what to expect when you start doing project work.

3. **METHODOLOGY TRAINING**—One of the most important things for any group chartered with developing information systems is to have all of the members of a team singing from the same hymnal or studying the same page of the playbook or marching to the same drummer or . . . well, you get the idea. We'll discuss the ups and downs of working on a

real world development project in Chapter 5; as you'll see, it's important that a project manager (or another leader on a larger project) can give directions to a team member and not have to oversee every moment of that person's work. New employees will (or should) have their work reviewed and receive assistance as required; however, everyone's job is much easier if the entire team—including new employees—is grounded in the appropriate techniques and tactics of the company's way of doing projects.

4. **TECHNOLOGY TRAINING**—If you're going to work at a company that *exclusively* develops software using Microsoft technologies, for example, you may receive boot camp training in those technologies and associated products. Likewise, if the company is making a major shift towards Java development, then new employees may receive rudimentary training in Java programming as part of their orientation program (that is, perhaps followed by additional, more in-depth training).

5. **TEAMWORK EXERCISES**—Now for the sometimes silly side of new employee training. Teamwork is a critical, critical, *critical* attribute of computer professionals in the real world. I can tell you that over the years I've declined to extend job offers to highly qualified "technical experts" because they came across during interviews as people who had had (and would continue to have) difficulty in working as part of a team. So, ideally, a company with a training program tries to ground its employees in teamwork basics from the very beginning.

Some teamwork exercises really bring out the best in people. For example, miniprojects that require teams of six or seven people to gather requirements and produce a small-scale system or design specification or some other type of deliverable in a matter of days can help ground new employees in the basics of what they need to know.

Other exercises, however, border on the silly (at least in my opinion). Creating paper houses according to very restrictive rules, for example, could—in theory—help a group of people start to learn to work together, but I believe that time would be better spent on more productive, technology-based exercises such as the mini-project described above.

However, as a new employee of a company, you have no say at all in the firm's choice of exercises to promote teamwork. So please take this advice to heart: no matter how silly, how stupid, or how much a waste of time any particular exercise seems, go along with it! Don't mutter (or, worse, complain out loud) that your time is being wasted. Think of some of these situations as similar to military basic training: Sometimes you have to do things that seem senseless but it will all be over soon and you'll be in your real job before you know it.

GENERAL DO'S AND DON'TS

Finally, here are a couple of do's and don'ts to guide you in your general behavior with the company . . . not only during orientation and your first days on the job (this information is included here so you don't get off to a bad start!) but also as you go forward.

NO HACKING!

Maybe on your college campus hacking was "cool" (or whatever the equivalent term is these days). Within your computer science department, there was a loose association of students who hacked into sites over the Internet, maybe placed a "harmless" virus or two into software, and did the technological equivalent of sowing their wild oats.

Well, if you were one of those folks, consider your hacking days over. Unless you go to work for a group responsible for network security and part of your job description is to try to find security problems in your company's (or your company's clients') systems, you *must* refrain from any hacking, virus planting, or similar activities. Trust me: Your manager and your manager's manager and your manager's manager's manager will frown on such activity, especially if it disrupts internal system operations—or worse, those of a client of your company—and no matter how skilled you are, you will soon acquire a reputation as someone who can't fully be trusted. (Assuming your employment isn't terminated, that is.)

So keep your "creativity" in check, channeling it towards the software you are chartered with developing. However, if viruses, hacking, and other mischief are really what turn you on about computing, then you really should go to work for a network security group.

NO INTERNET OR E-MAIL ABUSE

The same warning applies to Internet and e-mail within your company. First, have a very clear idea of your company's policy with regards to both of these tools. Can you use company e-mail for personal use (for example, to send and receive messages to friends)? If so, great; if not, then get yourself a personal e-mail account through an Internet service provider and confine your personal communications to that account.

Even if you can use company e-mail for personal use, don't send off-color jokes, large attachments (especially those in questionable taste), and similar material using your company account. If you're sending this stuff either within the company or to someone outside use an Internet gateway.

Likewise, keep your Internet access (should company policy allow you to access sites that aren't related to your work) to sites that aren't questionable or pornographic. Accessing a database of movies or an interesting looking web site that shows up on a list of new sites is one thing; spending your time browsing through offensive sites and downloading large moving image files from those sites is a definite no-no.

Remember: A company's internal information technology (IT) department could, should it choose to do so, monitor your e-mail and Internet access. Keep that in mind when you think whether you should be doing certain activities in your off-hours or during breaks.

CAREER TIPS

TELL YOUR FRIENDS not to send offensive e-mail to your company e-mail account. If you really want to expand your horizons, so to speak, on the Internet, give your personal e-mail account information to your friends for those purposes.

BE PROMPT

This should go without saying: throughout your orientation program, show up on time for all classes, group dinners, and other activities.

DON'T SHOW OFF

Don't be a techno-geek! There's nothing wrong with trying to write the crispest, tightest C code you possibly can, and there's certainly nothing wrong with taking pride in your work. Yet at the same time, you don't want to get a reputation as someone who spends all of his or her time trying to be as "technically elegant" as possible but can't even finish an assignment because you're too busy playing around and experimenting. So try to acquire as many skills as you can and as much expertise in them as possible, but don't do so at the expense of your primary objective: successfully finishing your work and producing deliverables assigned to you.

MAINTAIN SENSITIVITY REGARDING COMPANY INFORMATION

Resist the temptation to call up your college friends and tell them about this really great product you're working on at Company X and how it's going to absolutely revolutionize the Internet search engine space! Or to tell your friend who works at a chemical company all about the project you're working on through your consulting firm employer at another chemical company—the arch-rival of your friend's employer. To borrow from the famous old World War II poster, "Loose lips sink ships." Maintain confidentiality!

CONTINUE TO BE PROFESSIONAL IN YOUR SOCIAL RELATIONS

In Chapter 1, I cautioned against excessive partying or (as we used to call it when I was an Air Force officer) fraternization during a site visit. Well, once you become an employee of a company, the rules relax for you . . . perhaps a bit, perhaps a lot, depending on the company's policies. In this day and age, most companies have given up on the "thou shalt not date any other employee of this company" policy, realizing that when young (and sometimes not-so-young) people spend long hours working side by side, common interests often have a way of leading toward romantic involvement.

Yet I would still recommend remaining as professional as you can in any personal relationships. Avoid getting involved with a direct supervisor. Even if a company doesn't prohibit it, you will certainly be, uh, less welcome by other members of your team or group once that involvement becomes known.

Leave the relationship outside the workplace. Avoid (again, using a term from my Air Force days) public displays of affection in the office. After work, during a company happy hour, sure; on the job, no.

Also, if a relationship ends, don't drag any emotional baggage into the workplace. Don't start unfairly and harshly criticizing your former partner's work quality, for example.

SUMMARY

As you begin the first days of your job, you want to make certain that you have as few distractions as possible so you can concentrate on getting the best start possible. I would recommend using the contents of this chapter as a checklist to do just that: to help make sure there are no unforeseen problems that creep up on you and also to help you get a head start on the technologies and products you'll be using. Likewise, you should review the other portion of this chapter—the guidance and advice for your first days with your new employer and, particularly, to any training and orientation programs—to get an idea of what will be expected of you and what you should avoid doing.

CHAPTER 4
WORK, A LIFE, OR BOTH?

INTRODUCTION

The scene is well known. The dozen or so programmers in one room, the clock on the wall showing that it's nearing 12:00—midnight, not noon—and the pizza boxes and takeout containers strewn all over the room.

But there's a lot you can't tell if you were just to look at a snapshot of that scene without listening in on the dialogue or looking inside those individuals sitting there in front of their PCs:

- Their project could be weeks, even months, late—because of a comedy of errors by management, and the brunt of trying to overcome those errors has fallen on the downtrodden project team. It's 14 hours day in, day out, including weekends, with no end to the workload in sight.

- Or maybe this is a rather rare occurrence: perhaps the second of two nights just polishing up a prototype so the consulting firm where the developer's work can win a multimillion dollar contract. Up until this point the team has worked some long hours—usually eight or nine every night for several weeks—but once the project starts, it's back to a more normal schedule.

- Perhaps these twelve developers *are* the company . . . a small startup firm of people with a couple of years' experience each, who got together and decided to start their own software firm. And further, they all really enjoy what they're doing as they try to develop a snazzy new Internet product.

In this chapter we'll delve into this image of today's computer professional, particularly software developers, as talented, but one-dimensional, young adults who have little if any life outside of work. We'll look at different working environments not only for their respective properties but also how they can indicate where a company might be headed and what that means to your career there.

YES, YOU CAN!

First, let's get right to the point. You *absolutely* can have an appropriate balance between the professional and personal sides of your life. This means that:

- You can have a job where you work "only" 40-45 hours each week, travel moderately (or even rarely), and have a successful career.
- Even if your job has occasional spurts where you have to put in long hours for a few weeks, that doesn't have to become a way of life at work.
- Even if you steadily work 50 or 60 hours each week, you can take time off for vacations or emergencies.
- Even if you're a "road warrior" and work away from home most of the time, your weekends are still your own . . . you can come home on weekends, or someone can fly or drive to meet you and spend the weekends sightseeing.

I hope the idea is coming across clearly. Balance between your personal and professional lives is not a matter of a simple set of equations such as "more hours equals great success; fewer hours equals less success." Or that occasional spurts of long hours and some amount of personal sacrifice can be tolerable if they're only temporary or if you're appropriately compensated (for example, through overtime pay or maybe receiving comp time). In fact, achieving that all-too-elusive equilibrium is more of an art than a science.

So with that behind us, let's see why it's often difficult to find that equilibrium. Once you have that insight, how do you do your best to keep things in balance?

STEP 1: SELF-ASSESSMENT

Yes, again! Just as your first step in finding a great job was taking a look inside yourself, it's essential to understand what your optimal personal-professional balance should be before you can begin correcting any out-of-equilibrium situations. And it shouldn't be any surprise that your optimal balance can be very different than someone else's.

START WITH YOUR PERSONAL SITUATION

Before worrying about the work side, you should first spend some time analyzing your personal life, considering the following:

> **NOTE** **DON'T THINK ABOUT** these questions and others like them in a vacuum; talk with your spouse or partner to make sure that you take his or her feelings into consideration also. You want to come up with an idea of how much strain would occur if (say you're a woman) you begin a new job after graduation that requires you to travel a lot. How would your fiancé feel about that?

- **RELATIONSHIPS AND FAMILY**—Are you married? Involved in a relationship with someone? Do you have children? The answers to these questions (and I hope you don't have to do too much thinking to come up with these particular answers!) then become input into more soul-searching questions such as, "What would things be like if I were to travel four or five days a week for business?" and, "Would it be too stressful if I were to get home after 8:00 P.M. from work every night during the week?"

- **OTHER FAMILY OBLIGATIONS**—Do you have an elderly or ill parent or relative with whom you'd like to regularly spend several evenings a week and one weekend day?

- **PERSONAL INTERESTS**—Do you coach a kids' soccer team? Are you a volunteer at the local museum where you conduct tours on weekends? How would you feel if you had to put such activities on hold for such job-related reasons as long hours or travel?

What you're trying to do is create sort of a calendar in which your personal desires, obligations, and interests are scheduled first. *Then* you can fill in the rest of the calendar with work-related obligations. True, very often you're already in the midst of the job from you-know-where and everything is way out of balance in your life. We'll discuss how to put things back in balance later in this chapter; for now, we'll assume that you're reading this chapter *before* you've made a commitment to a less-than-desirable work situation. This way, you can proactively take charge of (or try, at least) what your professional life should be like before you stumble into it and have to take your chances.

WHY ACHIEVING CAREER EQUILIBRIUM IS OFTEN DIFFICULT

So what's the problem? Why do so many computer professionals (and people in other fields, for that matter) wind up sacrificing so much for their work life . . . and regretting it for many years to come?

First, we need to separate out the "workaholic" from this discussion . . . the person whose life *is* work, who truly has no other interests outside of what happens in the office or under the flag of his or her employer. These individuals consciously choose to craft a life where there is an imbalance between their professional and personal sides. Since it's their own doing we have to assume they *want* to devote the majority of their waking hours, at least at some point in their respective careers, to work.

So let's focus, then, on situations that you might find yourself in where you want to have a life outside of work but find it very difficult to do so.

THE WORKAHOLIC CULTURE

First, we have companies that have a *workaholic culture*. Recall what we just said about workaholics. There are companies that *expect* the majority of employees to subscribe to a corporate culture that is steeped in that behavior. Meetings are routinely scheduled for weekends or 6:00 P.M. or 7:00 A.M., for example. "Face time" (see Chapter 1) is valued as much, if not more, than work produced by its employees. Vacations are routinely canceled by most employees, and remarks such as, "I haven't taken my family on a vacation in four years" are considered badges of honor.

VOICE OF EXPERIENCE

EARLY IN MY CAREER, I interviewed with a startup company that did computer consulting and systems integration work. During the first interview I was told, "We get every other Sunday off (from work)." Several months after I began working there, the company instituted an official policy of a 50-hour work week. The company was a successful one, but it was not one conducive to having a personal life because of the "giving it all for the company" culture.

THE HAZING CULTURE

Other companies have what is almost a *hazing culture* for new employees. That is, new developers are deliberately scheduled for extralong hours on their respective projects, sent on extensive travel, or assigned to a project using new tools and technologies with no training and told to "learn this product over the weekend because you start a new project using it on Monday." The philosophy is that those who can survive and thrive in such high-stress situations will eventually "earn" the chance for a more normal work life . . . and the accompanying rewards (that is, stock options, higher salaries, plum assignments).

RESULTS OF POOR DECISIONS

The key word in the above two discussions is "culture." Whether a company values workaholics or "hazes" its new employees, both situations are steeped in the culture of the organization.

Reasons aside from corporate culture could adversely affect your chances for a good balance between your personal and professional lives. As anyone who has spent even a few years in the real world will tell you, all too often we find ourselves having to put forth superhuman efforts to overcome poor decisions made by a manager. Examples include:

- A consulting company agrees to a client's demands for a lower price and shorter schedule on a project than what was originally proposed . . . and the result is that fewer developers can be put on the team, and the project plan is revised to include weekends and ten-hour days (and in the world of software development projects, official ten-hour days usually mean 14- or 16-hour days!).
- Budgetary pressures cause company executives to institute a hiring freeze despite an increasing workload, requiring you and everyone else there to work extralong hours to perform that work.
- A project manager allows users to add a whole new set of requirements half-way through the design of a new application (this is commonly known as "scope creep") but agrees that the original delivery date will be maintained . . . so guess who is in for a whole lot of redesign work to include the new requirements?

The point is that even in companies where there isn't a deliberate, conscious, and institutionalized effort to overload your work schedule and those of your co-workers, a whole lot of things can happen that result in the same overwork situation, and most of them are due to someone, somewhere making a poor decision. In some situations, that person may not realize that the decision is a bad one until it's too late and then it's up to everyone to pitch in to overcome its effects. Other times, though, the person may very well have a good idea of the effect on you and your colleagues but makes that decision anyway (for example, the scope creep example above) with an attitude of, "Oh, well, I guess they'll have to work extralong hours for a while."

The saying that goes something like, "Poor planning on your part doesn't make a crisis for me" is appropriate here, except that in the work world, the person doing the poor planning, or making the wrong choice, often has the authority to cause a crisis in your world. So not only does your work life become a bit more stressful, but the effects on your personal life can be unfortunate.

SO WHAT HAVE YOU LEARNED?

From the discussion in the sections above, you should now have enough tools to get a pretty good idea of why your life is out of balance regarding your personal and professional activities, should that be your situation. Not to oversimplify matters, but you can probably place yourself into one of the following two categories.

1. **YOU'RE WORKING LONG, HARD HOURS FOR A PURPOSE, AND THE SACRIFICE WILL BE WORTHWHILE**—Maybe it's the financial reward at the end of the rainbow and even though you're away from home a lot and don't see your girlfriend or boyfriend (or husband or wife) much these days, that person is understanding and you don't have any nagging feelings that things are falling apart because of your work. Somewhere down the road things will likely ease up and you'll be better off for it.

or:

2. YOU'RE BEING EXPLOITED—Yes, that is a blunt statement. But if your personal life is being compromised and you have no say in matters; if you're not going to be compensated accordingly for the extraordinary effort you're putting in; and if you have this nagging feeling that should you even slack off one single day you're going to be persona non grata, then there's no other way to put it. Someone is taking advantage of you and your efforts.

TAKING ACTION: THE OPTIMAL BALANCE AND HOW TO ACHIEVE IT

Assume, then, that you've found yourself in one of the situations described in the previous section. What do you do about it?

Yes, you *can* do something to try to get things back in balance. Unfortunately, you may not always be successful (in fact, I'd say that you'll be successful less than half the time in trying to change an out-of-balance situation after it's entrenched).

Still, here are some techniques that you should try.

1. THE TEST CASE—You canceled your last two attempts at vacation because of problems on the project, and you're now in a "use-or-lose" situation (see Chapter 2) with your vacation days. Take that vacation! Go on that ski trip or go to the Jersey shore or go see your parents for their anniversary as you had planned. And then see what happens. If your manager grumbles and makes sarcastic remarks about how much further things are behind since you took that week off, you know that you're probably in a bad situation. Or you might be pleasantly surprised that there are no repercussions, that you receive the raise the following month that you had expected. Your perceptions were not necessarily wrong as to the pressures for conformity to the culture of excessively heavy workload. You simply discovered that you're not necessarily in career purgatory should you actually take a week off to decompress before getting back to the grind.

2. THE GROUP WARNING—Never, never, *never* go out on a limb alone and try to buck the culture and effect corrective actions within a project team or an organization or an entire company. Either find an ally in management (discussed next) or become part of a group effort to "warn" management that the lack of professional-personal equilibrium is causing problems.

3. FINDING AN ALLY—A few years ago I was working on a large government computer system development project as part of a company's team that was subcontracted to a larger company (the prime contractor). Without going into a lot of details, the project was in trouble because of continuous change in direction and an attempt to use technology that wasn't ready at the time for what we were trying to accomplish. Consequently, many of the tasks were behind schedule. One of the people working for me had worked ten hours a day on Saturday and Sunday of Labor Day weekend, but had tickets for a New York Yankees game on Labor Day itself. He went to the game as he had planned and made up the work over the next few days (remember that this was a holiday day that he "took off work"). In a management meeting a week later, one of the project managers from the prime contractor complained to me about this person going to a baseball game instead of working. In my most sarcastic tone of voice, I replied, "Oh, no! He went to a baseball game that he had tickets for on a holiday instead of working!" I then proceeded to point out that he had given up the other days of that holiday weekend, that he had met his deliverable by working extra hard the next few days, and—this is the important part—the reason that he had to work that weekend anyway was because management hadn't fixed problems that we had pointed out a month or so earlier regarding the efficiency of the process of transitioning from one version of our software to the next.

Though I was reprimanded for my sarcasm, we were able to improve the efficiency of the software transition processes and for a little while, at least, the culture in which our team was working improved slightly. So . . . this story serves as an example of finding a higher-ranking ally (me, in this example) to try to effect changes to improve the equilibrium (or lack thereof) situation.

4. GET YOUR RÉSUMÉ UPDATED—If nothing is going to change, you decide that the situation is intolerable, and your first thought every morning is that you hate your job and what it's become, then it's time to move on. See Chapter 15 for a discussion of looking for your next job.

CHANGES CAN OCCUR

Three years from now, the culture in which you work, and the effect of that culture on your personal and professional life, will likely be different. A new manager may be hired; you may move to a new project with a totally different environment and set of rules. Your company may be bought and you'll be part of another firm. Any one of a thousand different things may occur to disrupt (or, for that matter, improve) your equilibrium.

Each time a significant change occurs, I would recommend that you again go through the analysis and study that you've done throughout this chapter so you can set your course of action as expediently as possible.

SUMMARY

I'm assuming my college days were much like your own (even though mine were back when Jimmy Carter was president). Ordinarily, I liked to do things or go places on weekends, go home to see my family occasionally, go to parties Friday and Saturday nights, and sometimes just do nothing during the day between classes. But when a paper was due or there was a big test coming, sometimes I'd study on Saturday night (and go out later, of course!). There was the occasional all-night study session and more than a few late-night group work sessions for class projects. True, I was only actually in class for 15 or 18 hours each week (depending on how many courses I was taking), but as necessary I'd put in the 10, 20, or 30 additional hours for assignments and studying.

So do you see where I'm going? You want your professional life to be something like your college life probably was: a decent amount of personal time and a balanced life but also, when necessary, working late or on a weekend to finish what you had to get done. And that's the balance you should strive for. That's what your work life after graduation can—and should—be like.

CHAPTER 5
YOUR FIRST PROJECT:
WHAT TO EXPECT, AND WHAT TO WATCH OUT FOR

DEADLINE!!

INTRODUCTION

Increasingly, most computer professionals in the early stages of their careers—and a substantial amount of more experienced IT professionals as well—find that they spend the majority of their on-the-job time working on projects. Project work has its own set of rules, guidelines, do's and don'ts, and pitfalls—as well as rewards—compared to other types of nonproject work (such as software maintenance, staffing a help desk, or—later in your career—managing a group of programmers or consultants who are working on many different projects).

In this chapter, we'll talk about:

- exactly what a project is: specific attributes and how project work differs from nonproject IT work
- different types of projects (large or small, application development vs. system development, and the like)
- roles and responsibilities of project team members and what their significance is to you and your career
- what you can expect to happen at a project during different phases
- project deliverables
- how to deal with the many, many types of project turmoil you will inevitably encounter

WHAT IS A PROJECT?

Before answering the question, "What is a project?" let's first look at what type of computer work is *not* considered project work. Then we will contrast project and nonproject work so you have a clear idea of the distinctions.

Nonproject IT work is typically open-ended, without a clearly defined set of very specific tasks and deliverables. For example you begin work in a brokerage's IT department and your job is to maintain and modify a set of applications "owned" by the fixed-income group. Your charge is to field requests for enhancements from brokers and traders, then study code listings and gauge how difficult each change will be, and how much impact it will have. You also receive problem reports (or, more accurately, reports of suspected problems) and you must again look through code listings, try to duplicate the problems on a separate testing system, and see if indeed a problem does exist . . . and then code the changes necessary.

The tasks described as part of the above job are, again, open-ended—that is, you have a generally stated job description of "fix problems and gauge the impact of requested enhancements and modifications." Over the course of several years, perhaps even longer, that job description may stay relatively unchanged. New applications may be added to those for which you're responsible and others retired as they're replaced by new systems. But in general, your day-to-day activities will probably be the same three years from now if you're still in that specific job (unless you're promoted to a supervisory position along the way).

Another example of nonproject work that you could find yourself doing is staffing a company's help desk. You may be hired to be a member of the team responsible for supporting Microsoft Office applications (Microsoft Word, Microsoft Excel, Microsoft Access, Microsoft

Outlook, and the rest of that applications suite) for the entire user community within the company. Your day-to-day job is to field telephone calls and e-mail requests for assistance from users who are either (1) having problems with a particular feature or function, or (2) want to know how to do something that they can't figure out on their own. Over the course of several years, a help-desk role will be relatively unchanged other than adding new versions of software to those which you support, or perhaps shifting your focus to another technology area (supporting a custom-developed inventory management application's users, for example).

You're probably wondering, "So what exactly is project work and how is it different from the jobs described above?" Let's look at some specific attributes of project work.

1. ACTIVITY THAT USUALLY CREATES SOMETHING—Note the nonproject examples described above. Both of the examples (maintenance and help-desk support) are ongoing activities that "operate" on existing technology assets (that is, business applications, the office support infrastructure, and the like). Working in either of those roles, you won't be creating something. In contrast, those who work on a project *do* create something, usually some type of application (more on that later). Further, the "thing" being created (for example, an application to manage the stock portfolios of a brokerage's customers) is broken down into specific requirements and tasks. These might include "create an interface for customers to access their accounts over the Internet" and "produce reports for brokers that list their most profitable customers."

2. FINITE START AND END DATES—Unlike the open-ended nature of nonproject work (where you are consistently performing the same set of tasks as part of your job), a project starts on one particular date and ends on another. By the end date, certain deliverables—an application, associated documentation, and other material—must be completed.

3. WORK THAT IS DIVIDED INTO DIFFERENT PHASES, WITH DIFFERENT ROLES FOR TEAM MEMBERS WITHIN EACH PHASE—Most projects are divided into phases (this is discussed further later in the chapter). You and others on your team may have one role in the early phases of a project while you're collecting user requirements. Then, later in the project, when you are actually developing software, you will be performing a totally different set of tasks.

4. A DYNAMIC TEAM—By "dynamic" I don't mean a great group of flashy dressers who drive sports cars. Rather, "dynamic" in this context means that throughout the duration of a project, the team of which you're a member will likely change. Early in the project, for example, business analysts may be responsible for leading the requirements collection process and be staffed on the project full-time. Later, as software modules are being coded, the business analysts may only be part-time team members or perhaps not even on the project. But the coding staff has now doubled in size, with new team members who weren't part of the project while requirements were being collected and the software was being designed. (We'll discuss the significance of dynamic project teams later in this chapter.)

Conceptually, working on a project in the work world isn't all that different from working on a class project with several classmates in a programming class that you took during college. The finite dates (the date you're assigned the class project and your due date), the clearly defined activity and your deliverables, the dynamic nature of the team in that the group you worked with is most likely different from your group from another class project . . . all aspects of project work should be fairly familiar to you.

DIFFERENT TYPES OF PROJECTS

No two projects are identical, no matter how similar they sound (that is, producing a billing system for one chemical company will be done differently from the same task at another chemical company). In fact, there are actually different categories of projects. Each type of project is discussed below.

LARGE, MEDIUM, AND SMALL PROJECTS

The size of a project is significant not only for the obvious reasons—a large project will have a large team, while a small project may be staffed by only three or four people—but also because the tasks will vary widely between large and small projects (medium-sized projects are somewhere in the middle). For example, a small-scale project with you and three other team members working side by side will (or should) feature almost constant communication within the team as to what screens should look like; coding standards; and hundreds, maybe thousands, of other details. In contrast, a large project may have dozens or hundreds of people, possibly working in different locations (even in different parts of the country or even the world). This large team can't communicate with each other nearly as efficiently or comprehensively as a small project team. Therefore, the project plan for a large development effort will (or should if it is to succeed) include a significant number of checkpoint meetings, architecture and design reviews, advice from outside experts, and other activities.

When you work on a small project, you have a chance to "freelance" a little bit or maybe even a lot. That is, as long as you keep your focus on the problem you're trying to solve and the deliverables you're tasked with delivering, then you can explore your creative side a little bit. Perhaps you can try different coding techniques or ways of solving the same problem and indulge your sense of technical exploration.

On a large project, though, you'll usually need to follow very stringent coding standards—including rigid rules on how you name variables, how your code should be indented, how modules must be named, and dozens of other items—not to mention strict rules about how you test your software and make changes to modules (see Chapter 7). These many rules often are stifling to technologists who tend to be creatively oriented, but in the real world, your capacity to adhere to such guidelines is as important as your technical abilities when it comes to producing functional, maintainable software and systems.

Again, medium-sized projects fall somewhere between loosely run small projects and tightly run large ones when it comes to the importance of standards.

APPLICATION VS. SYSTEM PROJECTS

Should you find yourself in the midst of project work after joining the ranks of computer professionals, you'll most likely be developing some kind of application. For example, there are thousands of different types of business applications: inventory management, customer billing, employee payroll, analyzing sales results . . . the list goes on and on. The platforms may vary—some may be client/server based, others will run on mainframes. The languages and development environments will differ—some will be written in COBOL, others perhaps created by installing a package, as we'll discuss later. Some may be large, others small. But all in all, the project's purpose is to produce something that will be of value to the people paying the bill for its development.

Other applications are scientific in nature: weather tracking, analyzing medical statistics, mathematical research programs, and many more. Still, the operative concept is that the application, when completed, will perform a specific function for those who funded its development.

The opposite of an application development project—either business or scientific, or some other variation such as engineering—is a project that will produce systems software. Operating systems; compilers; database management systems; graphical development environments; a snazzy new, revolutionary Internet browser; a search engine; software to manage devices on a computer network . . . these are examples of systems software.

So what's the significance? Recall the discussion in Chapter 1 about the different paths that business computing (that is, MIS) majors might take compared to computer science majors. This is a *vast* oversimplification, but if you're a business computing major, your background better suits you towards application development projects. In contrast, computer science majors—particularly those whose course work focused on systems software, hardware, and other very technical subjects—may find themselves more at home as part of a system development effort.

Remember, that's an oversimplification. Don't assume that you are destined to pursue only one type of project work, that determined by your academic background. People certainly do cross the boundaries between systems and applications software, and it's my opinion that computer professionals who spend a bit of time in each of these two realms tend to be better rounded and have a broader perspective than those whose careers take place solely in one domain (application or system).

The significance of this discussion, however, is that those of you who find yourselves doing application development work will tend to spend much more time focusing on business requirements and whether software is usable by novice users, for example. Systems software developers will focus their efforts on creating interfaces that can be used by application developers; tuning their software so it performs as quickly and efficiently as possible; and other more "internal" concerns.

TACTICAL VS. STRATEGIC PROJECTS

Some projects are tactical in nature. What this means is that speed is of the essence, and the project team focuses its efforts on creating and deploying a functional product (business functionality) to a community of users as quickly as possible. The code may not be all that elegant, and in fact might not be too maintainable, because of the patchy, sometimes frantic way the software was created. Chances are that the system will have to be rewritten within a year or two because it won't be easy to enhance the software to add new functionality.

But that's okay! Despite what many "experts" will tell you, in the real world it is frequently acceptable to produce a tactical, "quick strike" application. Often organizations with limited budgets or that (as stated earlier) *must* have certain automated capabilities at some just-around-the-corner date are less concerned about all of the "good coding practices" that you were taught in college or your company's training program. What they're trying for is to put functionality in the hands of certain users in the company as quickly as possible.

In contrast, other projects are more strategic in nature. The company may want certain functionality to be deployed quickly, but they also want to be sure that they can add additional features after that first release, then more, and more, all without "breaking" the software. A system's architecture becomes very important; a significant amount of time is spent in the early stages of the project looking at not only short-term needs but also those of two or three years out, and then trying to make certain that the architecture can evolve and scale to meet future needs.

If you're assigned to a tactical project, your charter is usually "go forth and code and produce something: quickly!" Conversely, a strategic project is more a matter of "think . . . think some more...try something . . . see if it worked . . . then go to work." Not surprisingly, tactical, quick-strike projects tend to be smaller than strategic, multiyear efforts. But you could have, for example, a strategic effort with a relatively small team: you won't necessarily find a hundred or more programmers and other support people on every strategic, multiyear project.

MISSION-CRITICAL PROJECTS

Pssst! Want to start an argument among some of the more senior developers and managers at your new employer? Ask any two (or more) of them the following question: "What is a mission-critical project?"

Many different definitions are floating around in answer to that question, and our purpose here is not to say which ones are right and which ones are off the mark (I have my own opinions, as you might guess). Nevertheless, we should briefly discuss the possibility that you could find yourself on a project that is so critically important to your company (or, if you're working for a consulting firm, your company's client), that if your project team is not successful, the results could be dire. The company could be in danger of going out of business or, in the "best case," it will miss tremendous opportunities and almost definitely will not meet its growth plans and other objectives.

Conversely, a project that isn't mission critical could fail (though you obviously don't want that to happen) and, basically, it's not a big deal (though it may be to you and your career—see Chapter 9). The company will just start a new effort or decide that it wasn't worth having started that project in the first place.

Working on a mission-critical project can be a pressure-packed experience. You are more likely to experience the 80-hour work weeks and all-nighters and an impeded personal life in such an environment, compared to a less urgent effort. At the same time, those with career aspirations to get on the fast track as quickly as possible can really make a name by being a team member on a *successful* mission-critical development effort.

CUSTOM DEVELOPMENT PROJECTS AND PACKAGE INSTALLATIONS

This may come as a surprise to those of you just entering the computer profession fresh from college, where coding and software development were emphasized: increasingly, companies are turning to off-the-shelf software packages to meet their business needs.

Don't panic and think that you've wasted all that time learning how to write software and that your entire career future is in jeopardy. Installing application packages is *not* the same as, say, putting a new version of Microsoft Word or a new screen saver on your PC. The world of installing application packages is *not* one in which you pop a CD into your PC and run a setup program and 15 minutes later your software is ready to use.

It helps to look at an application package as a set of building blocks that can be customized, if necessary, to meet the specific needs of a company. For example, you may be part of a project team that is installing a human resources (HR) system from Peoplesoft, a vendor that produces a number of different package modules that companies install in lieu of developing custom software. You and the other members of your project team still need to:

- gather the company's specific HR requirements
- modify the underlying database structure to support any extensions or different, specialized ways of doing certain processes that the company wants to implement
- adjust the software to support those nonstandard requirements
- test the new system
- make sure that the company's network infrastructure can support the new environment
- install software on users' PCs
- write custom software interfaces as necessary
- migrate existing HR data from the HR systems that will be retired after the company's new system is successfully installed

And there are many other tasks, so rest assured, there is *plenty* of work for you if you're working on a package installation project. However, many people who really enjoy coding can find working on a package installation to be a bit too restrictive and not quite what they had in mind for how they'd be spending their workdays. So when you're considering employment options, and the idea of project work seems to be the way to go—at least early in your career—make sure that you match your own aspirations regarding coding (or lack thereof) with the type of project on which a company is likely to place you.

MULTI-COMPANY PROJECTS

Sometimes projects involve people from more than one company. If you work for a consulting company, for example, you could find yourself working side by side with your client's employees on one of their projects. Perhaps, too, you'll work with people from another consulting firm when your company teams up with one of its sometime competitors to win a large project. Consultants also often work with technical support people from vendors (such as a supplier of a database management system).

Maybe your company is working with one of its largest suppliers to create a *supply chain application* for automated reordering and delivery of parts. You and others on your project team may be assigned to work with your peers from the other company (or perhaps several other companies).

Multi-company projects deserve special mention because it is very common to find:

- Methodology clashes—your company develops software according to one set of standards and guidelines, and the company that is your employer's partner on the project uses a dramatically different methodology. Whose approach will prevail? What happens when problems persist past the first few weeks of the project? Beware!

- Power struggles—your company has a project manager who is your boss, and the other company has an equivalently assigned project manager. Which project manager is the "real" project manager? If the other company's project manager assigns you certain tasks that conflict with those assigned by your project manager, what do you do?

- Schedule and assignment clashes—suppose you work for a consulting company and you're assigned to a project at a client site and two programmers from the client are also members of the project team, working (supposedly) under the direction of your company's project manager. By "supposedly" I mean that it's common for those client resources to also be receiving direction from their manager (or managers) within their own organization. It's equally common for them to consistently receive time-consuming tasks unrelated to the project to which they've been assigned. The result: the project schedule begins to slip and the rest of the team has to pick up the slack.

The opposite also occurs in consultant-client mixed teams. You may be one of those client team members. For the sake of argument, let's say that your supervisor within your company is also assigned to the project and the two of you can devote all of your time to project-related tasks. But the consulting company that has won the contract to help develop your system has assigned several of their team members on a part-time basis. However, the other project to which they're assigned starts to run into trouble and before you know it, their 50-50 split between your project and the other turns into 80 percent there—four days a week—and only one day on your project. Sure, that's a matter for the managers of your company and the consulting firm to deal with, but until they do, you can certainly expect some unpleasantness during the work day.

INTERNAL VS. EXTERNAL PROJECTS

If you're working for an IT organization within a bank or chemical company, a consumer products company, a brokerage, or any other company where software development is *not* the firm's primary product, you'll be working on an internal project. In contrast, if you're working for a consulting firm and your work occurs at a client company, you're working on an external project.

The difference here is that on an internal project you are less likely to run into some of the issues discussed above about multi-company efforts. At the same time, IT organizations within companies often are among the most underappreciated, underbudgeted, and understaffed groups.

External projects are often subjected to the multi-company issues discussed above (methodology clashes, power struggles, etc.). Additionally, you could find yourself working in an environment (the client's) that isn't at all like the one that attracted you to your new employer. Everything you learned during your research about your employer's organizational culture, your manager, and other items are negated because you are now spending all of your time working at a client with, shall we say, a less than congenial working environment.

PROJECT ROLES AND RESPONSIBILITIES

Even though early in your career you most likely will be assigned to relatively junior project roles, it is essential that you have an idea of the roles—and associated responsibilities—of those with whom you'll be working. This section presents a brief discussion of the roles typically found on an IT development project.

THE PROJECT MANAGER

The project manager (PM) is the person who is chartered with orchestrating all of the various resources—people, computers, software, budget, and time—to ensure that a project is successful. On small- and medium-sized projects, the PM "lives the project schedule," meaning that he or she not only assigns and coordinates all of the many, many tasks and subtasks on the project but also understands as much as possible about each of those tasks. This means that the PM knows when things are on track or behind, when they've been successfully completed (as contrasted with "supposedly finished" but not really done).

A good PM also needs to have a sixth sense as to how the project is going even without poring over the project plan, status reports, and tons of other paperwork. By talking with people and seeing how their work is going, knowing where the trickiest parts of software development are and being satisfied that that portion of the project is going well, and gauging the mood of the team as a whole, the PM can build an early warning network to catch small problems before they grow and threaten the entire project.

TEAM LEADERS

On larger projects, a PM will often have several people heading up different teams: sort of managers in their own right of various portions of the project. The team leaders and the PM form the overall project leadership team and, ideally, all share responsibility for moving the project towards successful completion (but the PM still has the overall responsibility for project success).

PROJECT ADMINISTRATOR

Another common role on large projects is a person assigned to regularly track all the tasks on the project plan and recalculate how the overall schedule is doing. The idea is that the PM on a large project needs to be in the trenches with various teams and will also be spending a lot of time in meetings. To prevent the PM from being sidetracked by massive amounts of administrative work, the project administrator offloads those tasks and gives summarized status reports to the PM, who is then freed up for more of a leadership role.

THE PROJECT ARCHITECT

Often, the project manager is not necessarily the person most qualified to drive the technical side of the project: choosing hardware and systems software, determining how different off-the-shelf software can best be integrated, and determining the order of development of different pieces of the application. Even technically oriented PMs usually have more than enough to do in managing the many tasks and handling problems, with very little time to devote to the great technology unknowns inherent in most development projects.

These roles fall to the project architect: a senior-level technologist who has been through a number of successful projects in the past, who has a thorough understanding of not only tried-and-true technology but also new products and technologies, and can craft together a workable proposed solution upon which to develop the system or application.

An architect's work is often shaped by certain guidelines that he or she is given. For example, suppose the product mission is to develop an online system through which a company's customers can order products. If the general directions given to the project team are to use traditional client/server technology, an architect will look at one set of tools and products—and an underlying infrastructure—through which to build an environment. If, in contrast, the direction is to build an Internet-based environment, then the architect will use an entirely different set of assumptions and corresponding technologies as the basis of his or her toolkit.

For the most part, the project architect is chief of all technology when it comes to making such choices. Large projects will likely have a team of architects covering different facets of the project, with one designated as the chief architect.

Much of the architect's work is done in the early stages of the project. Sometimes, the project architect will stay with a project through development; other times that person will give way to a more development-oriented technical team leader. An analogy of the latter situation would be an architect of a building who hands over the blueprints he or she creates to a construction supervisor, who is more of a hands-on person.

THE PROJECT QUALITY ASSURANCE (QA) LEADER

Ideally, a person responsible for the overall project quality will be assigned to a project team from the first day. The quality assurance (QA) leader is *not* the same as a software tester (discussed later), though testing software is obviously one aspect of quality. QA should be a day-one activity, from setting standards for documentation and coding (and making sure that those standards are followed) to establishing acceptance criteria among the users, to helping ensure that vendors' candidate products are thoroughly and accurately evaluated.

TECHNICAL SPECIALIST

Certain types of projects require specialists in different technologies to help guide the rest of the team. For example, for a data warehousing project in which the team needs to copy data from eight different applications into a separate database so that users can run reports and do online analysis of data, it would be best to have specialists on the team who understand:

- the different ways in which data in the warehouse is initially loaded and periodically "restocked" and which model(s) are best for each of the data sources
- the tricks of the trade in how to best develop screens and reports that users will actually use
- what database design models work best for the type of reporting and analysis that the system will support

Likewise, a project team chartered with installing a package to support an automated call center system needs to have team members experienced in the package of choice, who know the best features of the package to use and also those to avoid because they don't work well.

THE DATABASE ADMINISTRATOR (DBA)

The database administrator (DBA) is the person responsible for creating, tuning, and loading the database(s) that the applications will use. On smaller projects, one of the team members will usually perform the DBA role in conjunction with his or her other responsibilities. On medium-sized and large projects, one person (sometimes more) is usually dedicated to this role full-time.

THE BUSINESS ANALYSTS

The business analysts generally have the primary responsibility for interviewing users and conducting group work sessions to gather and validate requirements that will be supported when the application is built. Ideally, business analysts straddle the project's business and technology realms of the project. That is, they have enough knowledge about the business operations so they can efficiently and effectively gather requirements, yet at the same time they understand technology and know what is—and isn't—feasible.

SOFTWARE DEVELOPERS

The coders! Finally, we've arrived at the coders! This doesn't mean that of all the people on a project team, the coders are near the bottom of the list in importance. Very often, particularly on small projects, people who are software developers are also the business analysts; a project manager may also be responsible for some software development activities; or a technical specialist also develops software. Even on larger projects with a sizable staff of dedicated software developers, though, it is imperative that these developers:

- adhere to the standards set by the QA leader
- do their best to meet the schedules set by the PM and notify him or her as soon as possible if problems occur
- work under the guidance of the project architect(s), technical specialist(s), and other more senior technologists on the project
- be responsive to errors found by the testers (discussed next) and follow the appropriate steps for fixing code and submitting it for retesting

The software developers will usually be the most hands-on members of the project team, making them the people closest to the actual system being produced. They need to ensure that every one of their activities harmonizes with the overall project direction and the team's assigned mission. The key: teamwork!

TESTERS

In Chapter 7, we'll discuss software testing and other less exciting parts of the world of software development that you most likely didn't cover (or, at best, barely skimmed) during college. Many hot-shot coders don't want anything to do with the process of software testing. Yet any PM or senior manager will tell you that without adequate software testing, any project is in jeopardy: at best it will probably be late and over budget. At worst, it will fail.

So if you're one of those hot-shot coders, please give respect to those assigned to the less glamorous role of testing software. And if you're one of those who is assigned such a role—or if that job was your choice—then rest assured that software and systems testing is not (as some would tell you) a home for wanna-be coders or those who just aren't skilled enough for a software development role. It may not be a glamorous place to be, but it certainly is a critical one.

THE PEOPLE RESPONSIBLE FOR PROJECT OVERSIGHT

The somewhat wordy title of this section actually describes several different roles:

- the person for whom the project manager works
- a senior manager assigned to look after a project and make sure everything stays on track
- a project's sponsor(s): senior executives who make up a committee that oversees a project
- a program manager: sort of a project manager of multiple projects (each with its own PM) that relate to one another as part of an overall company strategic initiative

And there are bound to be others, such as the company's chief information officer (CIO) or, from the business side, a senior executive from the functional area that the project's deliverable will support.

You may seldom see these oversight people; very often they show up the first day for the project's kick-off meeting and are never seen again. Or, alternatively, you might have one of them who constantly criticizes the directions of the PM, and perhaps even counters his or her directions with contrary recommendations or even orders.

CAREER TIPS

WHEN YOU'RE WORKING on a project, you need to be *absolutely clear* **as to your chain of command: from whom you take directions. Should you receive countermanding direction from anyone else, no matter how senior a person, you need to notify the PM or (on a larger project) your team leader immediately and let the honchos fight it out. Whatever you do, stay out of political conflict, especially early in your career.**

WHAT TO EXPECT ON A TYPICAL IT PROJECT

In this section, we'll briefly discuss what you can expect to find at different points on a typical IT project. Methodologies will certainly vary from one organization to another. For the most part, though, you will begin by collecting business requirements, add technical detail in the form of a design, move into development, and then deploy—roll out—the system you've developed. The following paragraphs provide a bit more detail about each of these phases.[1]

REQUIREMENTS COLLECTION

At the earliest stages of any project, your focus should be on collecting requirements from appropriate people—senior business executives, middle managers, and the people in the

---

[1] If you're interested in a more in-depth discussion about what to expect on a software project, one of the other books I've written covers a recommended approach to building a *data mart*—a small-scale environment that will support business analysis and reporting. Consult *90 Days to the Data Mart* (John Wiley & Sons, 1998) if you're interested in studying this area further.

trenches whom the application will most directly support—and then validating and prioritizing the material you've collected.

Some organizations prefer to use one-on-one interviews or small groups as the primary conduit through which requirements will be collected; others prefer larger groups sitting through long (half-day or all-day) facilitated sessions.

There are tradeoffs to each approach.

- Facilitated sessions gather all of the key stakeholders into one room and through a long series of sessions—often lasting several weeks—requirements are offered, discussed, and validated. Very little is overlooked.

- At the same time, many organizations can't—or won't—free up a dozen executives and managers for several weeks due to other business pressures. Then interviews and smaller group sessions, interspersed with other ongoing work, can help to fill in the gap. But it's the responsibility of the project team to ensure that *all* the things that would be covered during an extended series of facilitated group sessions are also gathered, piecemeal, through the interviews.

The actual work product at the end of requirements collection will vary according to the methodology being followed. But in general, the team will have a detailed statement of features that need to be built and as much detail as is known at the time about each of those features.

DESIGN

During the design phase, the focus of the team shifts from a business (or functionality) orientation into the technical realm: but not too much yet. Sometimes design is preceded by a quickly developed prototype through which users can see what portions of their application will look like once the system is fully developed.

But whether or not a prototype is developed, it is important that the team halt their collection and refining of requirements at some point; freeze what they have; and then move forward into designing the technical details of the system. High-level design is an overview of what the system will look like—what major components or modules it will have, the hardware and software, the products that need to be integrated together, and so on. Detailed design takes each of the pieces from the high level and adds substance and content to each piece, the idea being that when development (coding) begins, the developers can closely follow the specifics of the design and have all—or most—of the information they need right in front of them so there is no need to guess, "What does this mean?"

It's important to guard against *scope creep*—additional requirements, changes to requirements, and the like—during design and also later development. Requirements should be frozen at this point; to add new ones or change those that may have already been designed will usually undermine the progress of a project. Of course, if there is a valid business reason for doing so, then going back to reopen the requirements phase may be the only answer. If so, it's important to understand *why* this has to happen. If it's because of a radically new business idea or important change in business operations, then it can't be helped; if it's because important items were overlooked during the requirements phase, then the organization needs to look again at its methodology and techniques and identify its shortcomings.

DEVELOPMENT

This is where it happens if you're a coder: ideas and concepts turn to reality through your software development skills. Even though you may have to revisit a design issue or two, maybe get a bit of clarification about a feature that isn't as clearly specified as the others, for the most part you will be immersed in programming and other aspects of hands-on software development.

Ah, but there's a catch. Remember that program (or perhaps more than one) in one of your college classes that kept blowing up . . . and you couldn't find out why? Remember the all-nighter you pulled trying to fix it, and you finally patched it up just in time to make the deadline? Or maybe you couldn't find the problem and wound up with a C grade? Well guess what: those days aren't over, not by a long shot!

I don't know that any meaningful statistics are available but it's my estimate that you'll actually be coding for only about half of the time you spend in front of a keyboard with a module of software on your screen. The rest of the time you'll be scratching your head, perhaps cussing a little bit, trying to figure out just what the heck is not working that should be, because you've looked over every line of code twelve times and it looks absolutely perfect but just isn't running the way it should. You'll deal with outright errors (that is, incorrect results); abnormally slow—and unexplained—slow performance; software that works fine in your self-contained test environment but "breaks" when combined with modules that other developers have written; and other problems that will make you wish you had decided to major in cultural anthropology.

So get ready because you'll be coding, testing, fixing, coding some more, fixing some more . . . you get the idea.

ROLLOUT AND DEPLOYMENT

When a project team has completed its development work, additional work (often, a lot) remains. Specifically, the application or system that has been developed needs to be deployed—or "rolled out" —to its user community. It's possible, of course, that as with a program that you wrote for a college course, the user community is extremely small: one or two people, just as you and your instructor were the people who had an interest in whether or not your program worked.

More likely, though, dozens, perhaps hundreds—sometimes even thousands—of users will need access to an application. The architecture of an application will usually dictate the type of rollout that the team will need to accomplish. Sometimes, pieces of the application you developed will need to be loaded onto every single user's PC (desktop or laptop), and other pieces will have to be installed onto one or more servers. Such an environment is common in a traditional client/server environment (sometimes called a "thick" or "fat" client/server model, meaning that significant processing power is installed onto each user's PC—the client devices).

A trend in recent years, though, is to develop "thin" client/server applications where users access the system primarily through a web browser and the majority of the processing occurs on one or more servers. Deployment and rollout is, theoretically, easier to do in modern, thin client/server environments because less—perhaps no—actual installation needs to occur on users' PCs. Their web browsers are already installed and working and perhaps they need only a small add-in or plug-in (and these could possibly be downloaded via the company's intranet capability).

Regardless of the application architecture, developers from the project team often find themselves doing more than supporting installation procedures. They may also end up fixing problems that slipped through the testing and quality assurance procedures; checking out incompatibilities on older, newer, or otherwise nonstandard platforms; and even helping to train users.

The point to this discussion, in case you were wondering, is that as a member of a project team, you are likely to be involved in the deployment of the system you developed, if not full-time then at least enough to help fix any last-minute snags. So hold the celebration when you've finished coding. Your job isn't quite done.

PROJECT DELIVERABLES

Here's a trick question. Assume you are a member of a project team and your mission is to develop an application for the Internet through which your company's customers can browse, order, and pay for furniture products. Your best friend from college also works for the same company as you—but in another division—and she is a member of a project team whose mission is to develop an application for the Internet through which your company's customers can browse, order, and pay for knick-knacks, books, and other gift-shop-type items. Here's the question: Will you and your friend have produced more or less the same type of application when your respective teams have finished their development work?

Well, since I said this was a trick question, you should expect that the answer is "no." True, both applications are of the electronic commerce variety, both use the public Internet (rather than a private network), and both have the overall mission to support browsing, ordering, and financial transactions.

But suppose that one or more of the following situations is also true:

- The division of the company for which you work has already deployed electronic commerce applications and what your team is doing is plugging into an existing infrastructure . . . basically, adding a few new pages to a well-established e-commerce environment. Your friend, however, works for a group that is just now dabbling in Internet-based marketing and commerce and everything must be developed from scratch; someone high in the ranks of your company has decided that her organization isn't allowed to tap into your organization's infrastructure.

- Your team is tasked with quickly developing a prototype e-commerce application that must be ready for a test run in a matter of weeks and then will only be deployed to a handful of test customers who must log into the system with special passwords. Your friend's team, however, is chartered with producing what is sometimes called a "bulletproof application"—this means that it has to be extremely secure, totally error-free, able to handle extremely large user communities, and, in general, absolutely guaranteed not to "break."

What this example illustrates is that even though two projects may sound similar—or even identical—one's deliverables might be very different from the other's. One might be a prototype, the other a "real" application. One might be an add-on to an existing infrastructure and *must* be able to run on that environment, while the other might start with a clean slate.

It is, therefore, imperative that you and everyone else on your project team have a clear understanding of *exactly* what deliverables you are chartered with producing. There can be no room for uncertainty or ambiguity; the work processes, quality metrics and requirements, and accompanying results are very different in a prototyping environment than those needed for a mission-critical application.

HOW TO DEAL WITH PROJECT TURMOIL . . . AND SURVIVE!

At some point in your career you *will* find yourself staffed on a computer system development project that will be (to put it mildly) an unpleasant experience. In this section we'll discuss some of the problems to watch out for and, more importantly, how you can deal with and survive them with your career (and your sanity) still intact.

Some of the problems are small-scale in nature: not being able to find and fix a bug in your code, for example. However, these minor problems can quickly escalate into more serious situations, so you must handle them quickly and forcefully.

Other problems are outside your control: interpersonal conflicts between the project manager and the primary contact in the user community, for example. Still, you need to have a clear idea of what you should and shouldn't do in such situations.

THE ELUSIVE SOFTWARE PROBLEM

One thing you should have learned in school is that when you write software, you will usually have problems that far exceed making a syntactical error in your code. Think about the difference between debugging a program that you've written yourself as contrasted with a team effort where you and two other classmates each wrote several modules that you subsequently integrated together. When you had total control over your code and your program was basically an extension of your ideas—and yours alone—of how to solve a particular problem, you could usually locate a problem pretty quickly. When your thought processes and interpretations of a problem are only one-third of a particular deliverable, though, you often have incompatibilities and inconsistencies in some of the less clear portions of the problem that is to be solved.

Now make the jump into a real-world development project where you may have dozens of developers, each responsible for a portion of the application. You are developing a piece that five other people must use as part of their routines, but that piece you're developing is, in turn, dependent on another module of code that one of those five people has developed . . . which in turn is dependent on an interface from one of your own earliest modules from another project.

You get the idea. Often, the problem that you are having so much difficulty in finding, the problem that is causing your software that once ran perfectly to crash every time it's run now, may have its root cause in a portion of the system that is not within your direct control.

89

WARNING

EVEN AS YOU'RE DOING your part for the team, you need to have an up-front, open discussion with your project manager and have some indication of his or her idea of what will happen to your deliverables. Will your personal schedule of assignments and due dates be adjusted to take into consideration your diversion into the team debugging effort? Or will you be expected to still hit your deadlines on time, meaning that you probably have a few 18-hour days ahead of you.

The good news is that on a well-functioning project team, such problems can usually be found through an intensive group effort where everyone pitches in, thoroughly checks out each of their respective pieces of code, and exhaustively searches everything necessary to track down the problem.

The bad news, though, is that such heroic group efforts are almost always time-consuming, with unfortunate results on the project schedule. Now think what happens when you have, oh, a couple of dozen of these mysterious, elusive problems scattered throughout the project.

Before you know it, tensions start to run high as long nights in the office, an occasional (or frequent?) sharp word gets exchanged, and the sort-of-fun atmosphere has been supplanted by a much less congenial environment.

So what should you do? Basically, play follow-the-leader when it comes to any extraordinary hunt-and-seek efforts for problems. If you're told by the project manager that you should drop your work and assist others on the team in troubleshooting efforts, then that becomes your assignment (despite what the project plan has you doing) today, tomorrow, the next day, and for however long it takes to find and correct the problem.

Ideally, your work schedule (and those of your colleagues in the same situation) will be modified because in most situations, you will be unable to make up a week or more worth of work simply by working longer and longer hours each day. Personal productivity tends to diminish after working a certain amount of time, and errors will start slipping into your work.

So in actuality, we're discussing two different types of project turmoil in this section: elusive bugs and other problems, and then also the aftermath of an extended effort to find and correct the problems. In both situations you must look to your project manager for direction but you should also, shall we say, protect your own interests. You don't want to be put in a situation where you devote a week or two to correcting other team members' problems and then be expected to meet your original work schedule as if you had been working on your own assignments all along. Be a team player, but don't be a chump! Point out any such illogical and unfair situations and hope your project manager will either reallocate work assignments (such as offloading some of your tasks to others), slip the schedule, or otherwise help you out.

PEOPLE NOT DOING THEIR JOBS

In the previous section we talked about "heroic team efforts to track down bugs" and similar group efforts. You may, unfortunately, also encounter situations where one or more of the people working on the same project as you aren't pulling their weight. Sometimes it's one or two people who aren't meeting their respective schedules; they're working just a bit too slowly and dragging down the entire project. Other times it's people who aren't working too slowly . . . they're not working at all!

Either way, you are likely to find:

- an unhappy user community and project sponsor because a project is running late

- tensions on the project team (see the following discussion of interpersonal problems)

- the project schedule falling even further behind as disorganization starts to take hold

Basically, you'll find a project that's in serious trouble when all team members aren't doing their job. So what do you do? (Assuming, of course, that it's not you that we're talking about . . . .)

Sometimes, the most prudent course of action is for you and possibly others to pitch in and pick up the slack. For example, a team member may be going through a personal problem and although the person has always been a productive contributor, his or her workload has been slipping for the past week or two. Under the flag of teamwork, you help the person with the work that's behind schedule and then to get caught up with the current tasks. *But:* don't make such a choice without having a heart-to-heart talk with the person you're helping to let him or her know what you're doing and to "encourage" that person to get his or her mind back onto work as soon as possible.

In other situations, a unilateral decision to help someone out isn't a good idea. A team member may be flagrantly doing as little work as possible, or a position on the project team has been filled by someone who clearly isn't qualified to perform that role. Rather than cover for that individual, it's best to put the situation in the hands of the project manager. You should handle such situations diplomatically—through a private meeting with the PM, rather than through an outburst in a team meeting, for example. You *absolutely* have to have all of your facts in order: exact details of missed deliverables that have impacted your own tasks and deliverables and those of your teammates; noting that the person has spent most of his or her

WARNING

SOMETIMES, AS I ALLUDED TO above, the person who isn't pulling his or her weight isn't necessarily someone who disregards project tasks to surf the Internet or skip out on work. It's possible that a person who is on your project team in a role as, say, a lead Visual Basic developer has only rudimentary VB skills with nowhere near the knowledge that he or she should have. Further, that person may have been *explicitly* assigned by the PM into that role with full knowledge that the individual isn't fully qualified for that position.

So be careful—be *very* careful—before going to the PM about the problem. Sometimes, there could be such a shortage of qualified IT professionals that people must be assigned to project positions for which they're not fully qualified. Some people rise to the occasion and through some just-in-time training and on-the-job self-education, quickly pick up the skills they lack. Others just can't rise to the occasion, and you had best make sure that the PM is aware of that (if he or she isn't already).

But suppose the person causing the problem is a friend of the PM. The two of them worked together at a previous employer and the person is, in all probability, exploiting his or her friendship with the PM to get paid for not doing much (or any) work. You're probably in a no-win situation: You can try to talk with the PM about the person, but whose side do you think will be taken? Or you can ignore the situation and hope it gets better, but it probably won't; your own deliverables and the project as a whole will start to suffer. You could try going over the PM's head to a project sponsor, but that rarely works. So take this as a lesson: Not all turmoil you're going to encounter in the course of computer project work can be satisfactorily resolved.

time surfing the Internet instead of working on deliverables; has not shown up for scheduled meetings; and so on.

Even though bringing such problems to light might seem like ratting someone out or tattling, remember that unlike school or extracurricular activities, you're now working in the real world where you and others are paid to do your respective jobs. Further, your personal success is often dependent on whether others are successful; this is particularly true in project settings. Consider that if two or three people cause a project to fail, your own job could be in jeopardy! You have a number of obligations that you need to consider: to yourself, to your employer, and (if you're a consultant) to your company's client. You do *not* have an obligation to protect slackers whose disregard for their own obligations can damage your career, your employer, and your employer's clients.

INTERPERSONAL ISSUES

Sometimes, people just don't get along. That tidbit of wisdom should come as no surprise to you, right? After all, you've probably known people during your school years—not only college, but also in your earlier years—whom you didn't particularly care for. For the most part, however, you probably avoided them. During a programming or systems analysis course in college, for example, it was unlikely that you would decide to work on a project with someone with whom you didn't feel you could work. Of course, it's possible that during the course of a class project, interpersonal clashes might have surfaced, leading to a two-path choice: you or the other person could switch to work with another team, or you both could just grit out the duration of the project.

But jump ahead to the real world where you might find yourself working on a project with one or more people with whom you just have extreme difficulty getting along. Or perhaps you aren't even one of the parties in the clash of personalities: maybe you're a lowly junior team member, but the project manager and the chief architect are always sniping at each other and trying to drag you and the other team members onto one side of the clash or the other.

Unlike college, though, you find yourself living under the shadow of this conflict for eight, ten, maybe twelve (or more!) hours every single day during the week, and perhaps even on weekends, depending on your team's work schedule. Before you know it, you feel as if you're working in the middle of a combat zone and the mission at hand—developing an automated system to meet some set of requirements to produce business value—has shrunk to the furthest recesses of your mind as you try to stay out of the line of fire.

Without going on and on about personality clashes, suffice it to say that during the course of your career you will likely find yourself facing many (or perhaps all) of the following:

- you and a teammate not getting along
- you and the project manager or another senior manager not getting along
- senior members of the project team clashing
- the project manager not getting along with one or more key executives from the user community (or, in a consulting setting, the client)
- the project manager clashing with his or her manager who is one of the project's executive sponsors, the result being that your project's budget is cut, the team is constantly under pressure from the sponsorship committee, or other ominous clouds that distract from the tasks at hand

So what do you do when confronted by interpersonal issues in the course of working on a project? First of all, whenever possible, stay out of the middle of these situations! Particularly when you aren't directly involved (for example, it's the PM and another team member who are constantly clashing), don't take sides, no matter who you think is right. Stay professional in all of your behavior: keep your mind focused on your project tasks, avoid gossiping about the issues when you're with other team members . . . just stay out of it.

When you're one of the people involved, though, take the high ground by refusing to lash out at the other person (or persons) no matter how much you dislike them. If the conflict is the result of other team members not doing their jobs, handle the lack of performance issue accordingly (as discussed in the previous section). If, however, the issues are ones of style; work habits; preferences in music; both being romantically interested in the same person; or other similar points, then for your own sake don't let your work be affected by these matters. I can tell you that, as a manager, I absolutely lose confidence in a person's ability to deliver if he or she gets distracted by personality conflicts. Don't derail your career in this way.

ARCHITECTURAL AND DESIGN GOOFS

So here you are in the fifth week of a 12-week project and the project manager calls an emergency meeting. Stop what you're doing right now, you're told; we have a serious problem.

The PM gets right to the point at the beginning of the meeting: the underlying architecture for the system your team is building has some serious problems. Maybe it's something like too many users accessing a single database at the same time, resulting in poor performance for the user community as a whole. Perhaps it's a "distributed database server environment" in which the contents of four different databases are to be kept coordinated with one another . . . but the modules that were designed to handle this coordination—the ones *you* are now coding—have been found to have some fatal flaws that require everyone to go back to the drawing board and start all over.

Even though by the time you get to the coding portion of your project there shouldn't be any surprises left about the architecture and design of the system you're developing, it isn't uncommon at all for goofs to slip through that put a project in jeopardy. Maybe the architect or the design team overlooked some crucial detail; perhaps they misunderstood the capabilities of one of the products that will be integrated into the system; or perhaps new requirements that the PM was forced to accept have caused such a significant change in the underlying architecture that it can no longer work.

When confronted with situations like these, it's best to play follow-the-leader regarding what you specifically need to do. Most likely, the tasks up next on the project plan that have been assigned to you will be changed: someone else may work on those tasks, while you go back and

WARNING

WHATEVER YOU DO, though, don't openly grumble that "the chief architect sure messed up" or "I can't believe how badly the PM handled all of this; it's all her fault." When projects are in trouble, tempers are usually on a relatively short fuse; you don't want someone's ire redirected at you because you are overheard being critical of the processes and methods that caused the project to now be in jeopardy. Keep quiet; be professional!

rewrite modules that you thought had been completed but now need to be modified. Or perhaps the project halts while you and everyone else on the team go back to redesign the application. Maybe the project is postponed or canceled and you find yourself reassigned to a new project.

PRODUCTS THAT DON'T WORK

Related to architectural and design goofs—but a little bit different—is the problem that arises when a product that the team intended to use as part of the system doesn't work quite as advertised or as anticipated. For example, the team may have selected a snazzy new database capable of handling not only traditional data (numbers, dates, and alphanumeric data) but also images and video. The demonstration went well; the cursory going-over that the PM and the chief architect performed showed no glaring problems. But wouldn't you know it, when you and the other members of the team started using it, you find bugs all over the place causing the product to blow up and consistently terminate the system. Or, perhaps, the product works fine with up to 15 users . . . but with more than that performance isn't only abysmal but data is frequently lost.

Just as with architectural and design problems, unanticipated product deficiencies often send you and the rest of the team back to an earlier stage in the project as you scramble to overcome these deficiencies. And, again, in these circumstances your best bet is to follow the leader, help out as directed, and refrain from editorial comments.

PROJECT TURNOVER

The last type of project turmoil we'll discuss takes place when people start leaving the project for one reason or another. Sometimes it's because a person is leaving the company and decided not to complete his or her work on the project. On other occasions turnover results when the company pulls a team member to work on another project.

Some amount of project turnover is normal and could even be part of the plan. For example, a business analyst who isn't a coder may be involved in the earlier stages of the project but gone once coding begins. However, other turnover, such as programmers leaving half-way through the development activity, will usually cause project problems regardless of the reason for the departure.

So what should you do? Again, follow the directions of the project manager. If the PM directs you to pick up someone else's work in addition to your own, then take a bit of time to (1) see how far that person got on his or her tasks, (2) how "good" the code or design or whatever the deliverables are, and (3) what is ahead in the next weeks in terms of the tasks you'll inherit. Make sure, though, that if you see problems in meeting your own assignments because of this additional work, you notify the PM immediately and seek direction and guidance (which you hope will be a little more substantive than "just try your best"). Or if the person who has left was developing a different part of the system than you are and you aren't familiar with the tools or products he or she was using, make sure the PM knows that. You'd be surprised how many project managers aren't fully aware of the skills (or lack thereof) of each person on the project team, particularly during a very large effort.

SUMMARY

Project work in the real world can be, shall we say, a character building experience. When you work on a project that goes extraordinarily well, you'll feel confident . . . confident to the point of feeling as if there's nothing in the world of computing technology that you can't tackle. Conversely, being on a "challenged" project will make you wish you had majored in English literature and you were teaching high-school classes instead of working with this $%#@$% computer technology!

Regardless of the experiences you have—and like everyone you'll most likely have both throughout the early years of your career—some day you'll look back and be thankful for all of the experiences, including the not-so-positive ones. Keep your wits about you and you'll do just fine.

CHAPTER 6
BECOMING A FIRST-TIME MANAGER OR SUPERVISOR

INTRODUCTION

I actually could sum up almost everything you need to know about your first experiences in managing other computer professionals in a single paragraph:

Before you make any statements to those whom you're managing, issue any directives, or—basically—do anything, think of the boss character in Scott Adams' Dilbert. If what you're about to say or do is something that you could see Dilbert's and Wally's boss saying or doing, then don't say it or do it.[1]

I guess, though, it would be best to provide a bit more detail and substance, so in this chapter we'll put together what might be considered a "survival kit" for first-time managers and supervisors in the world of computing. We'll talk about:

- how to draw on your past leadership experiences
- learning from others
- why learning to delegate is a critical part of succeeding in a managerial role
- how to make sure that your responsibilities and the authority you have are properly aligned . . . and what can happen if they aren't
- some tricks of the trade in managing someone older than you
- the importance of following through with assignments you make to your team members
- how to deal with people who might want you to fail in your new role (and they're out there . . . really!)
- seven key principles of being a good manager

DRAWING ON YOUR PAST LEADERSHIP EXPERIENCES

Have you had any past management and leadership roles? No? Well, are you sure? How about:

- working on the high school yearbook where you were the editor of the Honors and Activities section and were responsible for coordinating the work of three other students;
- the extracurricular activities club in college of which you were vice-president your junior year and president your senior year;
- the semester-long project in graduate school where you were assigned the role of project manager, and you worked with four classmates to develop that Visual Basic application to handle inventory management for a video store; or some other setting in which you were officially or unofficially in charge of other people's work or activities.

---

[1] If, by some chance, you're not familiar with Dilbert then you really should be; Scott Adams, the cartoonist who created the comic strip, really hits a nerve (actually, lots of nerves) in strips with idiotic management practices, especially in high-tech firms. So you might want to check out the web site at http://www.unitedmedia.com/comics/dilbert/ or one of any Dilbert books.

VOICE OF EXPERIENCE

I WAS IN AIR FORCE ROTC (Reserve Officers Training Corps) while in college at Arizona State University. In the fall semester of my sophomore year, I was the commander (president) of an auxiliary ROTC organization that had about 20 members and a dozen pledges (prospective new members, just like in a fraternity or sorority). At the end of each semester the organization sponsored a formal dinner (called a "Dining Out") at a local Air Force base to welcome the pledges as new members of the organization. The student I appointed to the role of operations officer was responsible for planning all aspects of the Dining Out, including identifying and inviting a guest speaker.

Three days before the Dining Out, the operations officer mentioned to me that he hadn't found a guest speaker yet! Panicked, I walked (crawled?) into our advisor's office and, as casually as I could, asked, "Major, do you happen to know anyone who might be interested in speaking at the Dining Out this Saturday?" Exasperated, the advisor mentioned our dilemma to the colonel who headed the group at Arizona State, who contacted a friend of his and presto, instant guest speaker.

Now . . . who was responsible for the predicament and the near-goof? True, the operations officer had let slip something rather important—inviting a guest speaker—but the ultimate responsibility for the problem rested with *me*. That's right, since I was the commander of the entire organization, I should have done a better job in following up on assignments that I'd given people in my organization. It wasn't enough for me to tell the operations officer to plan the Dining Out and invite a guest speaker: I should have tracked his progress according to a project plan and identified that there was a problem long before I was forced to humbly ask our advisor to help rescue us.

True, there is a big difference between being president of the coin collectors' club in high school or being the sports editor on the college newspaper and being a team leader or project manager on an application development effort. But you can learn from your past successes—and, more importantly, your past failures—to help guide you in managing others' work.

This particular incident occurred in December 1977, and almost 21 years later I'm writing about it. Not only has it stayed with me, but I've put the lesson I learned about following up on work assignments into practice ever since. So think back to your own experiences in similar circumstances and try to glean a few important lessons that you can put into practice in your real management role.

LEARNING FROM OTHERS

Here's another story from my past that should say everything you need to know about learning managing techniques from others.

In the mid-1980s, after I left active duty as an Air Force computer systems officer, I worked with a small startup consulting firm that concentrated on government contracting and systems integration. That is, unlike the many consulting companies who provide technology services to large and medium-sized corporations, the firm where I was working did consulting and systems integration for Air Force, Army, Navy, and other government systems.

I was assigned as the project manager of an effort to bid on a contract for an Air Force financial system. Our firm, which was paired with a larger systems integration firm, was competing against other organizations to provide an office information system with integrated word processing, spreadsheet management, database, graphics, e-mail, and bulletin board systems to thousands of Air Force users. We were responding to a Request for Proposals (RFP) in which the Air Force outlined their requirements and we (and our competitors) proposed a set of packages that could be integrated to meet their requirements.

In 1987 the capabilities we take for granted today in Microsoft Office and Lotus Suite and other integrated suites of software were in their infancy. There were a few integrated, all-in-one packages available, but at that time it was the independent packages—WordPerfect, Lotus 1-2-3, and early versions of Microsoft Word and Excel—that dominated this space. Also, the Macintosh had only been introduced a few years earlier, and integrated cut-and-paste operations across applications was primarily a Macintosh function at that time . . . Windows 1.0 had just been introduced and it was, shall we say, somewhat less robust than what the Air Force was looking for . . . but the requirements were written in such a way that only DOS desktop environments were permitted.

We proposed a solution based around an integrated software package for DOS called Enable and added some "bolt-on" software to integrate Enable with a UNIX office system that had e-mail, bulletin board capabilities, and the rest of what was in the requirements. The Air Force organization responsible for acquiring this system was less than enthused with our proposal even though it met the requirements. We were in danger of not being awarded the contract. (If you're wondering how this relates to learning management techniques from others, we're finally at that point . . . .)

The Friday before Fourth of July weekend, my boss contacted me and said that "just to be on the safe side," my team—which consisted of two junior consultants and me—needed to evaluate every other word processing, spreadsheet, graphics, and database package that we hadn't already checked out to see if they might be able to meet the requirements because the Air Force didn't seem thrilled by our proposed solution. And we needed to do this over the holiday weekend and present any alternatives by Tuesday.

Well, I walked into a room at our office where Dave and Tim, my two team members, were and they were talking to the company's director of marketing, a senior-level manager who was about ten years older than me with equivalently more experience. I started telling my team members what I had just been told by my boss. Over the course of ten minutes, my explanation went from a forced calm to a profanity-laced tirade about how ridiculous this assignment was, how impossible it was, how we already had a solution that worked, and so on. I vented my frustration and anger and then went to my office.

About ten minutes later the marketing director walked in and asked me how I was going to proceed. We talked about it and he said, "If it were me, the first thing I'd do is take Dave and Tim to dinner tonight, and over dinner, when we had all calmed down, think about what we had to do, and together come up with an approach so we'd be able to get as close as possible to meeting our objectives."

So, to end this story, we did exactly that: we ate dinner, and decided that we'd pursue a process of "eliminate at first chance" whereby we'd find the first requirement that a product couldn't meet and automatically eliminate it from consideration. (I should note that the Air Force's stated requirements for the system were all-or-nothing: the system had to do everything stated in the RFP or a proposed solution was automatically rejected.) We did work over the holiday weekend and by Tuesday we had come up with one alternative approach that we wound up switching to.

So if you're still wondering what the relevance of this story is, I'll spell it out. My initial reaction to an "impossible" assignment was to rant and rave about how idiotic it was . . . and in turn, demoralize my two team members. My older, wiser compatriot observed my mistake, but he didn't chastise me for it. Instead, he steered me onto a path where I could not only correct the mistake I had made but also was able to think more clearly of a way to complete the assignment.

THE PRINCIPLES OF DELEGATION

One of the most difficult adjustments for some computer professionals as they assume managerial responsibility is shifting from a role of "I am the doer" to "I am the coordinator, and others do." This isn't to imply that every team leader or project manager gives up his or her hands-on responsibilities; particularly on small teams, it is common for a PM to also have some development responsibilities. Even on larger projects, it's important for a PM to be in touch with what is being developed . . . to be able to check out code quality, run software, and help the quality assurance (QA) team member(s) find possible problems, and otherwise avoid being simply a paper-pushing PM.

But when you reach that first management role, you will find yourself assigning certain tasks to other team members, establishing due dates and along-the-way milestones, and periodically checking the progress of their work, but *not* personally doing the tasks yourself.

It's often difficult for talented technologists to watch other, more junior, team members stumble and bumble their way when they're just starting out. The module that you could personally code in a couple of hours before lunch is taking a "newbee" all day, and you see him making all kinds of rookie mistakes . . . why not just step in, write the module yourself, and show the rookie how it's done?

Well, there's nothing wrong with sharing the tricks of the trade that you've picked up. But if

CAREER TIPS

IT'S NATURAL TO GET frustrated when a junior team member isn't proceeding at the development pace that you or other more senior team members could achieve. But it's important to align the tasks assigned to each and every team member with that person's capabilities. Think back to your first project, perhaps a C++ effort, and you were fresh out of two weeks of rudimentary C++ training. Would you have liked having extremely advanced tasks assigned to you that were beyond your limited understanding of C++ and the business application at hand? So make sure that you make appropriate assignments to all of the team members based on what they're capable of producing. "Tether" junior team members to more senior developers and have the senior developers oversee the work of the inexperienced members. Help out when you can and certainly take time to spend with each member of the team—you don't want to be viewed as an out-of-touch PM—but don't adversely affect your own job because you have difficulty delegating tasks to others.

you could just go and code everyone's modules yourself, there wouldn't really be a need for a project team, would there? You could just develop an application all by yourself.

But you have to understand that every time you do someone else's job for him or her, you are most likely neglecting other aspects of your managerial role. For example, the day you spend developing that module might be better spent working with the primary interface person from the user community in developing training plans for the organization's business analysts. So look back at Chapter 5 and the various roles and responsibilities identified on the project team. When you're a project manager or a team leader, make absolutely certain that you not only understand the specific role you're filling and the tasks that comprise that role, but also that you avoid straying from those boundaries.

ALIGNING RESPONSIBILITY AND AUTHORITY

In a perfect world, anyone in a leadership role will have a formally defined and universally understood set of responsibilities *and* formally designated authority to direct the work of others in achieving the organization's objectives.

Alas, the world is certainly not perfect. It's all too common to be stuck in a "king (or queen) of nothing" situation when it comes to your assignment as a project manager or team leader. Or, putting it another way, you're responsible for delivering an application to a group of users, but perhaps:

- of the ten people "assigned" to work on the project, only three of them are reporting to you full-time; the other seven work for another organization and can only help on your project when they're not busy working on other tasks;

- you intend to develop an application according to a particular development methodology (that is, a formal set of phases and activities) that is designed to collect and validate requirements before moving into design and development . . . but any user in the organization is permitted to request new features be added to the application at any time, and you don't have the authority to freeze requirements;

- your team conducts an exhaustive product evaluation and selects Product A because it's superior to Product B, but you're told by your company's executive management that your team must use Product B anyway . . . and you've heard rumors the reason is that your company's vice president of marketing is friends with the person in the same role at the vendor that produces Product B;

- team members regularly rebel at their project assignments, refuse to work the hours necessary to meet their deliverables, and otherwise are definite pains in the you-know-what to manage . . . but every time you attempt to enforce discipline among the team members, they go over your head to your boss, who happens to be a good friend of most of the people you're managing. Your manager countermands your directions and puts the project in jeopardy, which—of course—will reflect badly on you when the project fails.

It's important to understand before you begin any type of leadership job just exactly what your authority is and what you are officially responsible for. You need to get a sense of whether authority and responsibility are properly aligned. If not, then you need to talk with the person who appointed you to the position. Sometimes, realignment can be effected but other times, you may

WARNING

THIS MAY NOT BE what you want to hear, but you need to hear it. Misalignment of responsibility and authority becomes a more serious problem when you get further along in your career. Perhaps you work for a consulting company as a manager and you're responsible for project quality, but you can't control staffing of the projects. Or maybe you're responsible for your group meeting certain training objectives but your budget is slashed . . . and the objectives remain in place. So don't think that as your career moves along and you progress to senior roles that you're less susceptible to misalignment problems. Get used to dealing with them now.

find yourself in one of the situations described above or others like them. Should that occur, your best course of action is to keep an accurate log of misalignment issues and the effects on the project or whatever it is that you're managing. Sure, I know this sounds like a CYA (Cover Your you-know-what) approach. But when you find yourself in a no-win situation, you'd better look out for yourself while you try to do the best job you can.

MANAGING SOMEONE OLDER THAN YOURSELF

Throughout your high school and college years, there is usually a direct correlation between age and responsibility. It's unusual for, say, a second-semester college freshman to be the president of an organization that includes juniors, seniors, and graduate students.

In the real world, though, it isn't uncommon for a person to manage others who are older (sometimes much older) than himself or herself. This is particularly true in the area of computer technology, and has been common since the late 1970s when relatively young entrepreneurs such as Bill Gates, Steve Jobs, Mitchell Kapor (the founder of Lotus), and scores of others demolished the notion that one must be of a certain age to build and manage a company.

Even leaving aside these high-profile entrepreneurs, here are the two realities of computing life with respect to age:

1. **AT THE OUTSET OF YOUR CAREER**—you will most likely be starting out in an entry-level position regardless of your age. That is, if you are 22 and fresh out of college with no prior work experience, you will usually be slotted into an entry-level role . . . the same as if you are 42 and have gone back to college after 20 years in a totally different career field or if you've been out of the work force for years. The dominating factor in your initial level of responsibility is *experience* (or lack thereof), not age.

2. **MOST PEOPLE ADVANCE TO A CERTAIN LEVEL OF RESPONSIBILITY**—then their careers reach a plateau. That is, someone might become an organizational manager within a large bank at the eight-year point in his or her career, but that's as far as he or she gets. Ten years later, the person is still in more or less the same role. Yet here you come (or someone else who is a rising star) and at the five-year point in your career, you could find yourself assigned as the program manager for a high-profile effort . . . and that project manager is now working for you. Responsibility and authority have become irrevocably decoupled from not only age, but also years of experience.

Even in the early stages of your career you might find yourself managing an older person. When I was an Air Force officer, after a year and a half I was assigned as a section chief and was responsible for a group doing systems and communications development. One of the people who was now reporting to me was an older civilian government employee who had been in that organization when I arrived. Fortunately, there weren't any tensions between the two of us; he was given a few areas for which he was responsible and together with the other junior officers who reported to me, we all worked together as a team.

But keep in mind that often, a person who reports to a younger computer professional

 WARNING

DON'T BE MANIPULATED into ceding the authority you've been given . . . it's one thing to put a personal touch on the relationship between you and an older subordinate, but you don't want to find yourself taking directions from someone who is supposed to be working for you. Assume that there's a reason—a valid reason—that you've been made this person's manager. Don't disappoint those who made this determination.

resents the situation. You (the younger supervisor) might personify that person's frustrations at not being able to progress further in his or her career. Those frustrations could be manifested anywhere from subtle feet dragging to open rebellion and attempts to sabotage you.

The key is to set expectations when you assume a leadership role. Have lunch or dinner with that person; try to get inside that person's head to determine how he or she will act in the course of day-to-day business.

THE FOLLOW-THROUGH

Remember the story about the Air Force ROTC Dining Out and how we had to scramble at the end to find a guest speaker? The moral should be clear: after you make assignments of any type, ensure that they are on schedule and completed. Here are some tips:

1. **CONSULT YOUR PROJECT PLAN REGULARLY**—. . . as in at the beginning and end of each day. Know what progress has been made during the day and what hasn't happened that should have . . . and why. Was the team diverted to chasing a software bug, causing delays for some deliverables? Or is one person consistently lagging on his or her deliverables while everyone else is on schedule?

2. **FOLLOW YOUR INTUITION**—After a while you'll know which team members can be managed in a more or less hands-off manner and which ones you need to monitor regularly.

3. **DON'T BE AFRAID TO CHANGE YOUR MIND, BUT DO SO CAREFULLY**—Every manager has to redirect resources at one time or another because of changing priorities, unforeseen circumstances, or other valid reasons. But you don't want to get a reputation as a manager who regularly assigns tasks that are then canceled at your whim . . . those who work for you will usually start delaying work on their tasks as long as possible "just in case that jerk changes his (or her) mind as usual; no point in wasting effort."

WHEN SOMEONE WANTS YOU TO FAIL

Sometimes, being a manager in the real world is like something out of *Melrose Place* (or, in my day, *Dallas* or *Dynasty*). That is, there are people—some of them your peers, some more senior, others who work for you—who would really, really, *really* like to see you fail. Why? Consider:

- the person whom you beat out to receive the project manager position who felt that he or she deserved it more;
- the manager of another project against whom you're competing for funds on a suddenly slashed budget . . . and only one project will be funded to go forward;
- your boss's counterpart in another organization who is competing with your boss for a promotion to executive ranks . . . and who would like to see a project in the other guy's space fall apart.

You get the idea. The business world is not one big, happy, "we're all on the same team" festival of cooperation. So what do you do when you're a manager in a nasty, "I win if you fail" type of environment? Here are some guidelines.

DON'T GO ON THE OFFENSIVE

To be blunt, some people in the business world are very, very good at advancing their careers at the expense of others. I don't mean professional, head-to-head competition; I'm referring to (again) the type of person whose real-life behavior mirrors that of the most sinister characters on television soap operas. Let's hope you're not one of these people (or won't become one). If you're like the rest of us, you'll find it's best to avoid pitting yourself in a "how low can you go?" competition against someone who wants you to fail. More often than not, any tactics you try will be turned against you (sort of a business world version of one child picking on another and when the second one strikes back, the first one starts crying, "He hit me!"). So it's best to avoid the temptation to stoop into that world. Instead, try the following approaches.

DOCUMENT ANY TRANSGRESSIONS AGAINST YOU

When you request a meeting with the manager of a project on which your project depends in part, and you're continually put off, document that (politely) in an e-mail to him . . . with a copy to your boss. Or when the chief architect assigned to your project team—an ally of a peer of yours with whom you don't get along—deliberately disregards your directions and designs a technically elegant but inappropriate (in a business sense) solution, and then refuses your directions to modify the architecture, call a meeting with that person and your boss.

I don't want to make it sound as if every time you have a conflict, you need to go running to your boss. It is best to handle things by yourself as much as you can. However, it also is important to have someone in authority be aware that you are handling a difficult situation that is more interpersonal and political in nature than technical . . . and that you are doing your best to resolve the situation. Should no resolution be possible, you can elevate the issue to someone in authority who is already familiar with the problem and, with luck, less likely to be blindsided by any manipulative behavior on the other person's part.

FALL BACK ON YOUR AUTHORITY WHEN NECESSARY

I'm not a big believer in the "do it this way because I'm the boss" style of management. Ordinarily, you get better results when others buy into the approach that you plan on taking.

However, when all else fails, and you are convinced that you're right and one of your subordinates is wrong and his or her behavior is bordering on revolution and threatens a project's success, sometimes you need to use your "I'm in charge here and don't forget it" card. It's best to turn authoritarian only when necessary. You tend to be more effective when that side of you is seldom seen.

UNDERSTAND THAT YOU MAY LOSE

Right does not always win in the business world. Sorry for the bad news, but that's the way it is. It's entirely possible that someone may decide that your failure is in his or her best interests and no matter how well you document what is happening, it will still happen. Perhaps your boss is less influential or powerful than his or her boss; no matter how much your boss realizes that the other PM is sabotaging your project, nothing can be done. So what do you do? Either regroup or, if things seem irreparable, consider moving on to another place of employment (see Chapter 15).

SEVEN PRINCIPLES OF BEING A GOOD FIRST-TIME MANAGER

It's a trendy thing to present seven principles for this, seven principles for that . . . so who am I to buck a trend? This section contains a brief discussion of seven items that will, if you adhere to them, greatly increase your chances of being a good first-time manager.

1. CONSISTENCY—Be as consistent as possible in what you say or do, such as:

- Treat all team members with equal respect. Don't favor certain people at the expense of others.
- Be consistent in how you formally evaluate team members' performances from one reporting period to another.
- If you're ordinarily pleasant in team meetings, don't be one of those unpredictable managers who occasionally rants and raves just to shake up the troops.

2. CREDIBILITY—A manager who loses credibility has a lot of difficulty functioning effectively. Once people who work for you start to doubt the validity of what you're telling them, you will find yourself the subject of, "so I wonder what the real story is" musing and contemplation that will distract people from doing their jobs. Don't blow smoke at people who work for you about organizational issues (that is, reorganizations), the true state of a project, your own ability to influence staffing assignments, or anything else. If the rumor mill has it that a project's direction is likely to be dramatically changed, don't assure the team solely to calm them that everything will stay the course. If you're uncertain about the state of the project, then a simple "I'll find out what I can and let you know" is the appropriate answer. Being credible with those who work for you doesn't mean violating any confidences, such as when your boss tells you confidentially about upcoming changes. There will also be situations where you will tell your team one thing that you yourself have been told, only to find out later that the company has decided to take the opposite course. So you may have to tell your team that something you had previously told them has changed.

But as long as they don't think that you lied to them initially, your credibility (and your ability to manage and lead) won't be compromised.

3. **REALISTIC TASK ASSIGNMENTS AND DEADLINES**—When making task assignments and establishing milestones and deadlines, think back to your time as an entry-level employee receiving assignments from your manager. Be realistic!

4. **COMMUNICATE CLEARLY**—Written and verbal communications are critical to being an effective manager: Chapter 10 discusses this area in more detail.

5. **BE ORGANIZED**—Sometimes it will seem like tens of thousands of little details clog every business day. It's best to be as organized as possible so you can handle the highest priority items and keep everything on track. Some people function best using old-fashioned pencil and paper. Others can't function without their electronic organizers (like a Palm Pilot). Adopt a style that works best for you and do your best to stay organized.

6. **DON'T LET YOUR OWN WORK ASSIGNMENTS SUFFER**—If your leadership position is a part-time one—that is, you still have development responsibilities—make sure that your own work isn't impeded by your management responsibilities. First of all, be confident that you're not overloaded, between your hands-on and your supervisory tasks. Then plan each day's work to achieve the appropriate balance between these two areas. When you're in a development mode, stay focused. When you're in supervisory mode, try to keep your mind from wandering back to that nagging development problem that you've been trying to solve for two days. Keep all the balls in the air!

7. **DON'T BE AFRAID TO CHANGE YOUR MIND, BUT DON'T BACK DOWN FROM CONFRONTATION**—We touched on this point earlier in this chapter. A good manager changes his or her mind when necessary and communicates those changes to the team. Yet it's important to keep those shifts in thinking grounded in doing the right thing when necessary instead of when confronted by some other person. Your team will respect you for adapting to new circumstances rather than sticking with your original position, even though it may no longer be valid. They won't respect you for buckling to someone else's whims, especially when your shift in position causes them an extraordinary amount of additional and unnecessary work.

SUMMARY

I started off this chapter referencing Dilbert as sort of a one-stop manual for what not to do when you find yourself in a managerial role. Let's end this chapter with a single general guideline that can, I believe, serve you well in determining what you *should* do as a manager.

Most religions have a guiding principle along the lines of treating others as you would like to be treated. If you're not a religious person, think of this principle as a piece of really good advice. What sensible person could argue with this doctrine?

So in the context of decisions you make and the way you act towards people in a managerial role, use this "do unto others" principle in concert with the Dilbert-inspired guideline of what you should not do. With these two simple notions, you should be very successful in leadership roles.

CHAPTER 7
BO-O-O-O-RING!

INTRODUCTION

The computing profession is the greatest! All that time you spend working with the latest and greatest technology, the opportunity to develop cool new applications in classy business settings—that's why you're in this field, right?

Not so fast. If you're still in college and haven't started your first computing job yet, you probably haven't come face to face with the boring side of the computing profession. That's right, boring . . . as in dull, monotonous, wonder-why-you-picked-this-career-field, and so on.

Unfortunately, day-to-day life in the computing profession has many, many ho-hum aspects. And I'm not even talking about endless meetings and other administrative aspects of your job, such as filling out weekly time sheets and expense reports. I'm actually saying that some aspects of developing software and systems are boring . . . boring, but necessary.

In this chapter, we'll briefly discuss some of the many things that you'll almost certainly encounter after you begin working. By gaining a preliminary understanding of these topics, you'll be better prepared when you go through formal training (or even on-the-job training) rather than having to puzzle, "I wonder why I need to worry about that?"

By the way, I just used the word "boring" to grab your attention . . . some of the topics discussed in this chapter aren't all that exciting. But they are part of the world of professional software development and therefore may be of interest to many of you . . . or then again, maybe not. It all depends on your temperament. Some computing professionals choose areas such as configuration management in which to specialize. Even if you're a programmer at heart, you need to have an appreciation for and understanding of the topics in this chapter.

SOFTWARE VERSION CONTROL

So what happens when you decide to make a change to a module that you're working on? You start up your editor (or word processor in text-only mode), make the changes, save the file, and you're all done . . . right?

Well, that *could* be the way you make those changes. But if it is, you're in for some rather unpleasant surprises when you make a large number of changes, try them out and find they don't work, and then decide to try another approach to solving the problem at hand. You could always start up your editor again and try to undo all of the changes you made . . . but how many lines were changed? Ten? Twenty? More? How can you be certain that you've backed out all of the changes that you no longer want in your code?

One way to check is to use a sort of do-it-yourself form of *software version control*. You could create a directory or subdirectory on your PC or the system you're working on called OLDFILES (or something like that); make a copy of the module you want to change and put the copy in the OLDFILES directory. Then, if you need to back out changes, get the copy from there and replace the to-be-discarded file with the now-unwanted changes.

Take it from me (and most everyone who's ever developed software for a large system), it won't be long before you accidentally copy the new file and overwrite the old file; forget which of the seven different versions of the old file is the one to which you want to revert; or otherwise become very, very confused.

A better mechanism, one to which you'll most likely be introduced, is to use a software version control product to manage the different versions of software that not only you, but everyone else on your team, is developing. Keep in mind that very often, more than one person works on an individual module, or at least a portion of a system composed of multiple modules. How about when you and one of your colleagues try to make changes to the same file . . . and wind up overwriting each other's changes because you haven't coordinated your respective efforts (possibly because you didn't even know you were both going to be working on that module that afternoon)?

A software version control product provides an environment in which you can "check in" code that you've completed and tested, with a complete set of information about the author of the code (you), the date and time you checked the code into the system, and other pertinent data managed by the system. Should you or someone else need to make changes at a later time, you "check out" the software (much as you would a book at a library) and if you like your changes, you can check them back in, creating a new version of your code. If not, just discard the file you're working on, and the official version of your code is then what's in the version control system.

How about if you check in a new version but then decide that the changes you made need to be removed? Not to worry. A good version control system allows you to revert to a previous version of the module, effectively wiping out the versions that had been checked in subsequent to the one to which you want to return.

CONFIGURATION MANAGEMENT

Configuration management is often confused with version control, and indeed some aspects of version control are applicable to configuration management. The difference, however, is that configuration management applies to the many different aspects of a functioning system (or one being developed), including:

- custom code
- "library" code (discussed later in this chapter)
- networking hardware and software
- system drivers
- system files (that is, CONFIG.SYS and initialization files, and so on)
- disk and storage systems
- CPU and operating system versions

. . . and pretty much anything else that can be part of a system. The idea is that many systems need to be configurable to run in one of several different ways: stand-alone or distributed, for example, or over a local area network (LAN) in one part of an organization, compared to using dial-up or wide area network (WAN) capabilities for others in the organization. The need for different configurations means that it's very easy for a particular version of an operating environment to inexplicably become nonoperational (that means, it doesn't work, and no one knows why). Maybe a particular driver needed to be activated on desktop PCs but wasn't. Maybe the wrong version of a server database management system is in use. Maybe any one of hundreds of other glitches has occurred, and so the system isn't operating properly.

With proper attention to configuration management, ever-changing environments, even multiple possible operating environments, can be readily (if not necessarily easily) handled. A combination of software and manual processes is used to activate certain modules while deactivating others, select the appropriate communications drivers to use and ignore others, and so on.

Unlike software version control, which is basically an "additional duty" kind of activity, configuration management can—and should—be a full-time job, especially in large systems. The days of the computer operator are fading as less maintenance-intensive systems replace the blinking lights of old (check out some old science fiction movies for an idea of what 1950s and 1960s era computing was like!). But large complex systems haven't quite evolved to the stage where they're considered "lights out" operations (that is, all possible reconfiguring occurs behind the scenes). So it's possible that someone—even you—could be the IT professional in charge of developing scripts and procedures to handle configuration management.

CODE LIBRARIES AND SOFTWARE REUSE

Since the mid-1980s, one objective of organizations that focus on software productivity has been to establish mechanisms by which libraries of code modules can be catalogued, documented, and thus made easily accessible to software developers. The idea is to try to provide a mix-and-match approach to software development rather than having to develop most or all of any new application from scratch.

This idea of *software reuse* has had mixed results, at best, over the past 15 years. Many organizations do have online code libraries where you can locate very common, low-level modules for functions such as printing, string manipulation, character code conversion, and other simple functions and plop them into a program you're writing. However, the software industry as a whole is still struggling to take this idea of code reuse to more robust, higher-level functions.

Here's an example of an idealized environment for code reuse, using an international bank as an example. Most large banks use dozens of applications to do some type of financial functionality, from managing car loans for individuals to establishing and managing large multi-million dollar loans to corporations. At the root of many of these applications, though, there are many *business* functions (not low-level functions such as printing) that are common: setting up a new account, booking a new loan, receiving payment for a loan, sending an overdue notice, forwarding an account in default to the collection department, and so on.

Ideally, a bank that has embraced code reuse would have a common library, accessible to everyone within the bank. Whenever a new application was being developed or an old one replaced the developers could tap into this library of business modules and craft together the ones applicable to their new application, making minor adjustments to the "standard" code if necessary. This way, they need to develop significantly less custom code.

What you're more likely to find in the first few years of your career, however, is the aforementioned library of low-level system functions (if that). Keep your eye out, though, for any major initiatives that your company may elect to pursue in the area of code reuse. First of all, be very, *very* skeptical, because we in the software industry have been trying to establish productive reuse environments for many years with disappointing results.

At the same time, though, it's always possible that major breakthroughs in approaches and technology for software productivity could occur within the next few years.

SOFTWARE DISTRIBUTION

Consider a typical distributed, client/server application with, say, 1,000 users. You and your project team do a phenomenal job of developing that application, finishing several weeks ahead of schedule. Now comes the tedium of installing portions (the client side) on 1,000 different desktop and laptop PCs. Okay, so far. The divide and conquer approach may just do it, with you and the other nine team members each taking responsibility for 100 users. Maybe you can even get some interesting travel out of this!

But what happens when, three months later, your team makes some version 1.1 changes to the application . . . how will those changes get to all of the users? And how about bug fixes and patches that need to be distributed as quickly as possible?

Unfortunately, the discipline of software distribution was one of the major stumbling blocks of the first generation of client/server applications in the early 1990s. The idea of "thick clients" (sometimes called "fat clients") meant that a significant portion of an application was hosted on desktop and laptop PCs. This, in turn, meant that not only was initial loading and installation of that software tedious and time-consuming, but making subsequent changes was often almost logistically impossible.

(And we haven't even mentioned what happens when new employees who need to use the application join the company . . . basically, software distribution is a full-time, ongoing effort in almost any widely distributed system.)

Fortunately, there are several aspects of software distribution that have somewhat lessened the burden, and you'll likely encounter at least one—and probably all—of these models.

First, *automated software distribution* enables new versions of software to be sent over a company's network to all of the applicable client systems. For example, every time a client system tried to make a connection to a server, a version number or a timestamp could be checked; if a more recent version of the client software has been delivered, then the new software (or appropriate portions) could be transferred over the network and any installation/reconfiguration procedures could be automatically started. As you might imagine, incorporating this type of automated software distribution can be tricky and complex, not to mention it doing its share to clog up network traffic when changes need to be distributed.

A variation on the software distribution theme is to require users to log onto a certain site on the company intranet and explicitly download new versions and applicable automatic installation procedures that way. This intranet approach is gaining popularity as more companies install such environments.

Another mechanism, speaking of intranets, is to deploy "thin client" applications in which very little software—ideally, only a standard web browser, perhaps with some plug-ins—resides on the many client PCs within the environment. The majority of the business functionality is hosted on a small number of *application servers* and changes to software can then take place only on those application server machines, rather than every single PC that is part of the environment.

So keep the idea of software distribution in mind when you're working on a development project. If no one has brought it up yet, ask. It's always possible that it's being overlooked and believe me, you don't want to wait until the very end of development to contemplate how to manage software distribution.

SOFTWARE AND SYSTEMS TESTING

Groan! Developing software is one thing, but testing? Testing is the seemingly endless process of finding problems and either fixing those problems directly yourself or referring the bugs to someone else for corrective action.

Interestingly, while I was writing this book, I saw a television advertisement for Microsoft in which several software testers were talking about how cool their jobs were, how they got a chance to work with the latest Microsoft software products before anyone else, and so on. And that's actually a very good attitude to have about testing.

In fact, I believe that software and system testing is actually one of the most valuable activities in any IT organization, and *should* be a valued, heavily rewarded discipline. The problem, though, is that in most organizations:

- testing is done by developers, not other professionals who do nothing but testing;
- project schedules almost never allow adequate time for testing, meaning that those dual-hatted individuals by necessity have to devote most of their time to development;
- at performance review time, success in development is (usually) recognized and rewarded. Success in testing-related activities is rarely recognized as a valuable activity, let alone rewarded.

So all in all, testing is an underappreciated, unloved activity . . . yet an essential one. Even if your organization does not adequately value testing, you'll still need to do some if you're a developer. So you'll find yourself doing:

- **MODULE TESTING**—establishing that the code you've created is correct means more than just getting a clean compile. You need to, as best you can, couple your code to special "stub" code or other testing support code and check out all possible paths through your code and try to determine that these different processing paths are all programmed correctly.
- **UNIT TESTING**—grouping several modules together—yours and possibly those created by others—and performing the testing processes mentioned above.

- **SYSTEM TESTING**—once a complete system has been synthesized, it needs to be tested under real world conditions (or as close to real world conditions as possible). System testing is often done on an "end to end" basis, all the way from client-side actions on users' PCs to checking on network throughput to making sure that database servers and other systems are functioning correctly.
- **STRESS TESTING**—can a system operate successfully at peak loading? Stress testing is designed to load down a system to ensure that it doesn't bog down or "break" under heavy usage.
- **USABILITY TESTING**—even though users may have indicated during requirements collection that they wanted their screens to look a certain way, you may find yourself demonstrating a prototype or an early release of an application to make sure that the interfaces are intuitive and, in general, usable.

STANDARDS

Once you enter the real world, your days of free-wheeling programming are over! Well, that's not exactly true; if you find yourself working for a small company on small projects, you probably won't have to worry too much about coding standards and related guidelines that require you to name variables a certain way, for example.

But in most medium- to large-sized IT organizations, you will find yourself confronted with a mountain of standards for most of your activities. Make sure that you fully understand where you can find your organization's various standards and study them before you begin working on a development project. It's always best to do things right the first time rather than having to go back and change variable names, for example, while you're confronting schedule pressures.

AUXILIARY STORAGE MEDIA

Disks . . . what else is there? Well, maybe CD-ROMs, but that's it, right?

Actually, on real world computer systems you're likely to find significant amounts of magnetic tape, and perhaps optical storage disks, all used as *offline* or *near-line* storage media. If you have a ZIP or JAZ drive for your PC, then you understand the principle of auxiliary storage media. Not all of your data and programs can fit onto your primary storage system (your computer's hard disk), so some content is stored on other devices and loaded when necessary.

When you're working on a development project make sure that you fully understand all the requirements for auxiliary storage. Know that, for example, at the end of each month the database's contents are copied to an optical disk and then erased. Or, in contrast, perhaps there is a weekly incremental backup (that is, only the data that's changed is affected) and a monthly full backup (everything is copied to tape or an optical disk), but the primary database is not affected; new data will continue to accumulate in the database.

In general, it's important to know what capabilities your organization has in the area of auxiliary storage, even for areas outside your project. Are the majority of the organization's data assets stored on disk or do they reside almost exclusively on tape? By understanding these environments you can, when you begin to work in lead architecture and development roles, craft solutions that take advantage of your organization's capabilities rather than contemplate storage management architectures that aren't supported within your company.

EXTERNALLY PROVIDED DATA

Many applications, particularly analytical ones, require the inclusion of data acquired from an external source. Examples include:

- data from credit bureaus about a bank's customer's personal financial information;
- competitive sales data from an industry-specific service bureau, such as those used within the pharmaceutical industry;
- sales data from a "general" data provider, such as Nielsen data (just like television ratings) being used by a consumer product company;
- current stock prices from a service provider to be used in trading applications.

As you're collecting requirements for applications and later designing those systems, get a clear understanding of all external data needs. It's important to note whether your organization is currently using that external data for another application. If so, you may be able to leverage that information without having to repurchase it if it already exists within your company.

SUMMARY

This chapter has presented a brief look at some of the aspects of computing with which you will come in contact once you begin working in the profession. The most important lesson to take away from this chapter is that the work you've done as part of school projects, or even small-scale independent work (for example, creating an application for your family's small single-store business) is significantly less complicated than developing large, complex applications for large, complex organizations. So don't make the mistake of assuming that once you start your first job, you can fully transition your school knowledge and that's all you need to worry about. There is a lot of learning ahead of you, so be prepared.

INTRODUCTION

You thought everything was going along just fine at your employer, a computer consulting firm where you work as a Visual Basic programmer. The number of employees has doubled every year in the two years you've been working there. You've worked on some great projects that have gone fairly well. The company, which is now three years old, is supposed to go public within the next year—according to the company's president—which should make the stock options you received when you were hired worth a lot.

So naturally, you're surprised when you receive an e-mail from the company's chief financial officer (CFO) announcing that because profits have evaporated in the past six months, there will be no bonuses paid for this year, and the company's initial public offering (IPO) is now very much in doubt. And also, by the way, a salary freeze is now in effect, meaning that the raise you were expecting next month won't be coming your way.

Or maybe you work for a company that has created a visual development environment for Java code. The product has received great writeups in the technical press. You've attended several trade shows working your company's booth, and interest from the shows' attendees has been phenomenal. And at the last company all-hands meeting, where there was talk about launching a series of companion products, the company president was lamenting that the company's main problem was not being able to hire new developers quickly enough.

So naturally, you're shocked and appalled when you are called into an emergency meeting one Friday afternoon by the company vice-president of operations and you learn that (1) the company president resigned that morning, (2) 30 percent of the company's workforce will be laid off during the next two weeks, and (3) everyone who survives the layoffs will see his or her salary cut by 20 percent.

There's no way you could have seen either of these situations coming . . . or was there? In this chapter we'll discuss the all-important subject of how to read between the lines and determine your employment situation's *true* state of health and stability. We're not just talking about anticipating losing your job; rather, we'll discuss a number of different scenarios, including:

- early warning signs that the project on which you're working is having serious problems
- a variety of "your company is in big trouble" scenarios and how to see them coming
- ways to detect that the organization that you work for is about to be adversely affected by an impending reorganization
- ways to look at external factors, such as the national and/or regional economy, to try to predict how your career fortunes might be affected

The idea behind this chapter's subject isn't to encourage you to add a healthy portion of paranoia to your daily work life. Rather, my intention is to tell you bluntly that unless you watch out for your own career well-being (and the personal well-being that goes hand in hand with your professional successes), chances are that at some point down the road—perhaps sooner, perhaps later—you'll be caught by surprise by one of the scenarios described in this chapter. Then you'll find yourself scrambling to find a new job for one reason or another. So forewarned is forearmed, as the saying goes: Let's take a look at how to detect those subtle hints and what they might mean.

THE BIG PICTURE: WHY IT'S IMPORTANT

Before we get on with our examples, we need to discuss the idea of the big picture when it comes to subtle clues about what might be ahead. You might be working on a great project with a super team for a company headquartered in a region of the country where the economy is fantastically strong (low unemployment, lots of business growth, and so on). None of that, though, is enough to overcome "dysfunctional" executive management at your employer that, essentially, runs your company into the ground.

Or perhaps your company's executive management is top-notch, and your first year working there has been better than you could possibly have imagined . . . you love your work, which is exciting and challenging. But wouldn't you know it, a national recession takes hold, the stock market plummets, and the market for your company's products and services suddenly shrivels. The company's cash on hand starts to run out, the line of credit is maxed out. The company seems to have no alternative but to terminate a sizable portion of the workforce.

The opposite of the above two scenarios is also true (don't panic: Not everything in this chapter is doom and gloom!). Perhaps the economy is terrible and the market for consulting services in your geographic area is totally saturated. Still, perhaps your company's management is savvy enough to craft a strategy that not only allows your firm to ride out the economic downturn relatively unscathed, but also to be positioned for a return to phenomenal growth once an economic recovery takes hold.

Or maybe your company is doing poorly . . . except for one bright spot, the project on which you're working, a three-year development effort with a client that has contractually committed to funding the whole project. Company management has assured the people on your project team that your jobs are safe, even if the anticipated layoffs elsewhere in the company can't be avoided. They've even offered everyone on your project team a 20 percent salary increase *and* a retention bonus of six months' salary—payable immediately—for sticking with the company and the project.

So the idea is to not only look for early warning signs and clues to what might be coming in the near future, but to process that content along with the other information you've gathered (both good and bad) in the context of the big picture. Some otherwise ominous signs might actually be negated by positive occurrences in other areas.

Also, keep in mind that any situation could change rather quickly, and the hints and clues you pick up could easily be cancelled out by those changes. For example, you might realize that the project that you're working on is being run into the ground by an irresponsible, incompetent project manager, and you worry about the impact on your career of being part of a failed project effort (a subject discussed in more detail in Chapter 9). You update your résumé and prepare to hit the job hunting trail . . . only to arrive at work one Monday morning to learn that the project manager has been replaced by the person for whom you worked on a prior project, for whom you have the utmost respect and confidence.

Or you've now gone through the second straight year of subpar salary increases and no annual bonus because your company is suffering along with most others in a tough economic climate. You love your job, you work with great people, and though you wouldn't otherwise think of leaving, you're finding it increasingly difficult to meet your personal financial obligations. You've been contacted by one of your company's competitors that is doing relatively well despite the economic downturn, and they've offered you a hefty increase over your current salary if you were to go to work for them. You don't really want to—the company has a reputation as a somewhat less-than-pleasant place to work—but your obligations come first, right?

Suddenly, the economy starts improving. Your company unexpectedly wins two large, multiyear contracts and the company president sends a broadcast e-mail message to everyone that special "sticking it out" bonuses that equal the past two years' worth of missed salary gains, along with a special employee stock option package based on seniority, will be forthcoming. The hard times are over; time to look ahead.

So as we review the things to watch out for in projects, organizations, companies, and external factors, (1) remember to keep the big picture in mind, and (2) realize that the situation could change unexpectedly . . . for better or worse.

YOUR PROJECT

You're working 50 or 60 hours every week on your project tasks, and the official word from the project manager is that everything is going along just fine. Certainly you're completing your assignments on time. Shouldn't you just keep your head down, concentrate on your deliverables, and assume that everything on the project as a whole is on schedule?

Well, yes: You *should* devote the overwhelming majority of your attention to your assigned tasks. But in the course of day-to-day interaction, you'll notice a number of different things, such as those described below. Let's go through them and discuss the significance of each.

PROJECT STAFF TURNOVER

You're part of a seven-person team that goes through the first phase of the project (four weeks worth of requirements collection), and you're now half-way through an eight-week application design phase. But on Monday of the fifth week, one of the senior developers is suddenly off the team, replaced by another programmer with whom you've worked on a past project . . . and from what you recall, this new team member is much less talented than the person being replaced. The rumor mill has it that the person leaving the project is being sent to another project within the company.

Then, two days later, the team's technical lead suddenly departs the scene, but this person isn't replaced. According to the project manager, the technical lead is being shifted to the same project that the senior developer went to. The official reason for the lack of a replacement is that "everything on the project is technically solid, so we don't need him anymore."

The sudden change in team composition could actually be a good sign . . . your project might be on track, going so well that the two individuals can be shifted to another project that isn't going so well and only one replacement is needed. True, the replacement developer may not be quite as skilled as the person being replaced. But the project manager will reallocate the tasks. For the most part, it will be business as usual.

However, sudden turnover can also be an ominous sign. Very often, shifting skilled resources away from a project is a sign that the powers that be (such as your company's management) are changing their priorities about your project. Perhaps the people are being

NOTE IF POSSIBLE, try to have an off-the-record conversation with someone leaving a project through a resignation to gather as much information about their perspective of what's what. Particularly if the person is a friend of yours, you can usually get early warning signs that things might be going very, very wrong . . . very, very soon.

reassigned to a brand new project that "is being sponsored at the highest levels of this company," meaning that the focus of the firm's executives will *not* be on the project on which you're working. Keep in mind that in most large organizations, there are dozens of projects on the radar of senior executives. (This is true for companies such as banks or chemical companies where IT projects are underway in support of their business operations, or in consulting firms that are doing work for many different clients.) The truth is that of those dozens (or even hundreds) of projects, some are considered much more important than others. The good news is that if you're working on one of those high-priority projects, and it's going well, then professional life can be very good for you, at least for a while. On the other hand, working on a project from which resources are being siphoned is very often a sign that (1) the project could possibly be postponed or canceled, meaning that you could be reassigned to another effort, or (2) at best, the project will drag on and even if it's successful, no one will very much care.

Another aspect of project turnover is when team members not only leave the project, but also leave the company. Most people try to time their resignations for the end of a project or at least the end of a project phase so as not to disrupt the effort too much . . . sort of an "effort of good faith" as they try not to hurt their soon-to-be-former employer or the friends left behind on the project.

But if people, particularly those in leadership positions (that is, a project manager or chief architect), seem to be departing from a project apparently with total disregard for the work and people they're leaving behind, that could be a sign that they have lost confidence in the future of the project or even the company itself.

SCOPE CREEP

We discussed the topic of scope creep in Chapter 5 as something that might go wrong on a project. Adding a few features that may have been overlooked, even though you might be weeks or months into a project, isn't a major problem. But when the user community or their leaders start questioning a significant portion of the capabilities your project team is developing, the resulting schedule slips and major project turmoil significantly increase the chances that a project could be shelved or started over.

At best, significant amounts of scope creep often dramatically increase your workload (and that of your teammates) as you reopen tasks that were supposed to have been completed and still try to continue forward progress on your project. If unresolved, longer hours → tensions within the project team → project team turnover . . . so see the item above for clues to what might happen then.

UNANTICIPATED DELAYS BETWEEN PROJECT PHASES

If you're working on a project that is divided into multiple phases (requirements collection, prototyping, design, development, as discussed in Chapter 7), the optimal situation is to transition smoothly from one phase to the next with as little delay as possible. This is particularly true if you're working for a consulting firm and project delays might mean that you're not billable for some period of time. When a consulting company sells a project, it usually has an idea of what sort of phase-to-phase transition will occur, as well as any delays, such as those driven by the client company's budgeting process.

But when delays last longer than anticipated, it is often a sign that something might be amiss . . . and the longer the delay, the more serious the situation.

MANDATED USE OF PRODUCTS WITH KNOWN PROBLEMS

Suppose that you've just finished working on a project in which the chief architect and project manager selected a particular tool (which we'll call Product X) to extract data from IBM mainframe files and send subsets of that data across the network to a UNIX platform, where users will run queries and reports. Product X, much to the chagrin of the entire project team, didn't perform as advertised, and in fact was full of problems and features that worked slowly and poorly.

So now, glad that that project is behind you, you get ready to join a follow-on development effort that is just beginning design work, and surprise: Product X has been selected as the tool that will be used for data extraction and transfer. You talk with the chief architect and the project manager and tell them about your experiences, and encourage them to talk with the leaders from that prior effort. They either disregard your input or, worse, talk to the others who "survived" the prior project and then stay with Product X, noting that "the vendor has told us that fixes to the problems should be available in a few weeks."

What are the chances that this new project will see significant problems? Let's put it this way: can you say, "Oh, no! We're in trouble now!" Sure . . . I knew you could!

A SUDDEN SWITCH IN PRODUCTS OR TECHNOLOGIES

Similarly, beware if deep into the project schedule, sudden changes in products or even underlying technologies occur. Say that your team has gone through a ten-week design effort with relative ease, and you're now into the second week of development and Product Y is suddenly scrapped in favor of going with custom code . . . which will take much, much longer for the team to complete its tasks.

Or your team has designed a traditional client/server application based on Visual Basic and a Microsoft SQL Server database running on Windows NT. And now, in the third week of development, all of your work is shelved and suddenly you're directed to redesign the environment using intranet technologies and a browser-based interface.

Now, the purpose of this discussion isn't to note that using a product is better than custom coding (or the other way around), or that intranet-based applications are preferable to traditional client/server environments (or, again, the other way around). Rather, these examples illustrate how sudden changes can impact on the work environment (particularly those that aren't explained with anything but a curt "just make the changes; I don't have time to explain why we're doing what we're doing" reply from the project manager or another member of the leadership team when you ask why the change is occurring).

A SUDDEN EXTENSION IN OFFICIAL WORK HOURS

As we discussed in Chapter 4, long hours are a fact of professional life for most of you in today's computer field . . . but the environment in which you're working those long, long hours can vary dramatically from energetic and friendly to caustic and "I can't wait to get out of here."

An extension like this takes place when the project team is suddenly informed that until they complete the effort, *official* working hours will be extended. This is different than, say, everyone having to put in extra time—possibly a little, perhaps a lot—to meet a challenging project schedule. Rather, the extension of official working hours means that you (and everyone else) are no longer working an official 40 hours-per-week schedule. You are expected to work 45, 50, or perhaps even more hours each and every week, even if you are completing all of your tasks on time.

I'm all in favor of chipping in to help out fellow project team members if you're ahead on your tasks. However: Official pronouncements such as the one above are usually a sign that something is very, very wrong with the project. Perhaps this extension of working hours has occurred in conjunction with one or more of the other warning signs discussed in this section, and therefore just confirms that things aren't going all that well. Or possibly such an announcement is the first indication that some of these other problems are likely to be occurring . . . soon. Whatever the situation, an extension of official working hours is usually a clear indication that a project is in trouble.

HAPHAZARD ADHERENCE TO A DEVELOPMENT METHODOLOGY

In Chapter 7, we discussed different software development methodologies. If, regardless of the variation your project team is *supposed* to be following, everyone is totally indifferent—including the project leadership—to the milestones and project controls of your methodology, it is very likely that work plans will quickly spin out of control. Everyone working on that project will be following his or her idea of what's best, rather than pursuing a coordinated effort in which developers' tasks are interrelated and effectively coordinated throughout the entire project.

LITTLE OR NO TESTING AND QUALITY ASSURANCE AS PART OF THE PROJECT PLAN

I've been involved in many different project situations as a consultant where a client will "push back" on the proposed price and schedule, wanting to see a revised proposal that is cheaper and faster. And before you know it, the management of the consulting company (not me!) and the client have jointly decided that by cutting back on—or cutting out entirely—testing and quality assurance, the cheaper-and-faster objective can be achieved.

Talk about being shortsighted! That makes as much sense as saying that you'd like your oldest child to learn how to play the piano well enough to perform at recitals and public performances, but you don't want to spend the money for professional lessons . . . so you'll simply let your child try to learn by himself or herself, perhaps using some self-study books.

There are certain prerequisites to achieving computer project success, and one of those necessities is an up-front, sincere, from-day-one-of-the-project commitment to quality assurance and adequate testing. If you feel that not enough is being done in those areas, then you're likely to be in for a long, disappointing experience with this particular project.

THE COMPANY

Let's step away from a project-centered view of early warning signs and take a look at items that might lead you to want to skip straight ahead to Chapter 15 (Moving On). Remember, even if everything is going smoothly in your particular project, you could still find yourself with an uncertain career future if other facets of the company's current state aren't in good shape. So take heed; here goes.

AN INCREASE IN RESIGNATIONS, ESPECIALLY AT SENIOR LEVELS

Turnover is a fact of life in any company today. The days of the 30- or 40-year career at one company have faded away (though some senior executives can still be found who have spent most or all of their career with one employer). Statistics vary according to the survey and the time frame at which one is looking. However, it's not uncommon to see turnover at 15 percent or 20 percent *each year* in toay's technology companies.

So what you need to keep your eye out for is when the sudden, sharp turnover rate increases . . . for example, after two or three years of an average 12 percent turnover that has been below the industry average, departures suddenly shoot up to 25 percent of the workforce. The increase could be a one-time phenomenon or perhaps not. Maybe others are seeing the handwriting on the wall (some of the items discussed below) and deciding that their future will be brighter elsewhere.

Even more ominous is when senior people start departing, and not necessarily for bigger and better opportunities (such as the chance to start one's own company, or the chance of a lifetime to become the chief executive officer at another firm). In most of today's companies—technology-focused as well as banks, industrial companies, and other users of technology—senior executives have significant equity (stock) stakes in their firms' fortunes. Walking away from a lucrative—or once-lucrative, as it may turn out—compensation package "to pursue other career options" (as such announcements usually go on the broadcast e-mail) may very well be a sign that this person sees storm clouds coming. True, they may be personal—the individual may not have been selected for a particular promotion—or the person may be clued in to slumping sales, increased tensions in the executive ranks, or other tumultuous situations that aren't generally known throughout the company's ranks.

KEY LEADERSHIP POSITIONS REMAINING UNFILLED

If, after a senior-ranking person leaves, his or her position remains unfilled for a prolonged period, there could be problems brewing. Why? If a company were still on a path of high growth, the powers that be would ensure that operations are disrupted as briefly as possible. Even an interim replacement while an external search is underway is an indication that despite the person's departure, things are pretty much status quo.

But suppose the director of sales for your company departs . . . and isn't replaced? How about your company's director of project quality assurance, the person who oversees QA efforts for all ongoing efforts? If that person leaves and isn't replaced, what does that say about your company's commitment to project quality? Is the lack of a replacement an indication that management doesn't see many new projects coming in the near future, which could threaten the company's viability?

Keep your eye on key vacancies in your company's executive ranks and at other senior levels; the longer positions remain vacant, the more likely those vacancies are an early indicator of big problems ahead.

A CHANGE IN CORPORATE CULTURE

Suppose you joined a company where people worked hard, but the company's management had always showed a great deal of concern for the welfare of all the employees. Pizza and beer on Friday afternoons was a regular event; there had always been two company picnics every year, plus a company-paid holiday party in December for employees and their spouses or guests that everyone looked forward to. All in all, the hours were long but you and your co-workers always had a good feeling about the place.

Suddenly, the pizza and beer parties are no longer. The fall picnic is held, but only one or two of the company's executives show up; the others "have other commitments." Then, in November, it's announced that for this year's holiday party, employees will now have to pay for their spouses and guests . . . the company will no longer be picking up the tab for those people. You attend the party and the atmosphere is . . . tense. That's the only way to describe it. In past years people would all go out together afterwards; this year's party resembles an eat-an-run affair. People seem glad to get out of there as quickly as possible.

The point is this: When the culture of a company changes for the worse, you often have yet another clue that something may be amiss. Just as an individual may react to personal adversity by becoming gloomy and snapping at his or her friends and family, in effect changing his or her demeanor, so too may a company's demeanor—its culture—change in response to corporate adversity. So watch for these changes—some subtle, others more overt—as indicators that problems might be occurring that haven't been officially communicated yet.

PROLONGED REORGANIZATION ACTIVITY WITH LITTLE COMMUNICATION

A company needs to constantly tune its organizational structure in order to remain viable and responsive to rapidly changing conditions in its marketplace. New products and services might be added, with accompanying changes in reporting structures among managers and lead technologists within the firm to respond to these new initiatives. Or perhaps a company decides to make a rather dramatic shift, such as a consulting firm deciding that it needs to add industry-specific focus to its organizations, in response to client demands.

Effective reorganizations are often accomplished rather quickly . . . usually in a matter of a month or two, three or four months at the outside. (Note that I'm *not* talking about all-encompassing, top-to-bottom, bet-the-company-because-we're-in-big-trouble reorganizations such as those in which a multibillion dollar firm is reorganized from top to bottom; rather,

I'm referring to "routine" reorganizations in response to meeting new challenges or trying to take advantage of new opportunities.)

When this type of "routine" reorganization activity drags out, though, a company is often telegraphing one of two things: (1) its leadership is clueless in terms of devising an effective organizational structure to take the company forward, and all of its proposals are met with thunderous disapproval; or (2) there is so much infighting as part of the reorganization activity, as executives jockey for position at the expense of their peers, that the company's future is being swamped by corporate politics and personal agendas. Either way, it's not good!

PLUMMETING STOCK PRICE

As I'm writing this chapter the U.S. stock market and many of its counterparts around the world are reeling from heavy volatility and downturns in the third quarter of 1998. But when I refer to a company's plummeting stock price, I'm not really talking about the price dropping, say, the same 15 percent or 20 percent as most other companies and the stock market as a whole. Rather, I'm referring to a significant drop in your company's stock price, say 30 percent or more, even in an "up" market where most stocks are rising or at least remaining steady.

Very often, the stock market serves as a leading indicator of a company's fortunes, both positive and negative. Sure, the market is (or, more accurately, stock analysts and investors are) quite often wrong. However, I've seen many, many situations where a significant drop in a company's stock price really is a leading indicator for bad things to come: weakening sales, losses instead of profits, and layoffs.

So keep an eye on your company's stock price, even if you don't personally own any stock or options: you can often learn a great deal by what happens out there on the stock exchanges.

WORSENING COMPANY FINANCIALS

Related to a company's stock price (but actually a separate issue, as we'll discuss in a moment) is when a company's financials—revenues, profits, expenses, cash flow, and other measures— take a turn in the wrong direction. Again, you could be looking at a one-time phenomenon as your company shifts its focus to meet new challenges, perhaps by making a significant investment in new technology in preparation for future opportunities . . . or you could be looking at the first signs that problems exist.

The reason you want to look at a company's stock price *and* its financials is that in frenzied, upward moving stock markets (such as most of the 1990s), it's common for a company with a steadily weakening financial picture to still see increases in its stock price, mostly in response to a general ignorance on the part of the investing public with regard to basing investment decisions on financial information rather than on hype and press stories. So dramatic increases in your company's stock price could be a result of a frenzied investment climate rather than based on the fundamentals of your employer . . . and a "correction" (read: free fall) in your company's stock price is just around the corner.

ANNOUNCEMENT OF A VOLUNTARY SEVERANCE OR EARLY RETIREMENT PLAN

More often than not, when a company announces a plan through which people can volunteer to retire early or resign in exchange for a severance package, its next step is going to be the involuntary variety of severance: layoffs. So be prepared!

A SUDDEN SHUTOFF OF EXECUTIVE COMMUNICATIONS

The advent of e-mail and groupware (such as Lotus Notes or the company intranet) has dramatically increased the effectiveness of companies' internal communications, something that most firms have taken advantage of. However, if you suddenly see a shutoff of executive communications through these channels, you could also be seeing the first signs that all is not well in Paradise.

A MAJOR NEW INITIATIVE NOT GOING WELL

Suppose your company has invested heavily in a new venture. Say you work for a software product vendor and last year, the company's executives decided to launch a new line of development tools that aren't necessarily related to the company's core product offerings.

Now, it's a year later and sales of the new tools aren't slow . . . they're nonexistent. Development is way behind schedule and, worse, competitors already have brought their offerings to the market.

Make no mistake: Trouble lies ahead. Expect a resignation or two at the senior levels of the company or, worse, finger-pointing at others as those executives with a Machiavellian style of management posture to save their butts—I mean careers—by shifting the blame to others. (Okay, so maybe I'm a bit cynical, but I've seen this happen!) So watch out for that major initiative that turns into a flop. No matter how well your little corner of the company is going, you'll be affected in some way.

EMPLOYEES SPENDING INCREASING AMOUNTS OF THEIR TIME DOING "ONLINE GRIPING"

When I worked at Digital Equipment Corporation from 1987 until 1991, we had an internal bulletin board system based on Digital's VAXNotes that was sort of like an intracompany version of intranet discussion groups. One of the topics (files) was the goings-on at Digital. As the company's fortunes worsened, I noticed two things happening.

First, the tone of many of the postings regarding the company's strategies and policies was increasingly hostile and sometimes venomous. Second, it seemed that many employees were spending a significant portion of their workday posting messages and replies into that file.

So if your company has a similar forum for discussion groups, watch out for hostility and frequency. When employees are willing to openly post hostile messages under their names, snidely noting their opinions that the company's management is incompetent yet knowing that their careers will most likely be adversely affected by their open criticism, you're seeing a sure sign that things are really, really bad. And besides . . . if these folks are spending all of their time in these online conferences, they're not doing much work!

OPEN DISCUSSION AMONG EMPLOYEES ABOUT LEAVING THE COMPANY

When people start talking openly about other firms with which they've been interviewing; when they start sharing information about corporate recruiters; when they talk about what companies seemed promising at the most recent job fair . . . you know it's all over.

YOUR ORGANIZATION

In case you're wondering why I've included a separate section about hints and clues within your specific organization in addition to those within your whole company, let me share an anecdote from my days at Digital Equipment Corporation.

When I joined Digital in October of 1987, I began working in a group in Colorado Springs that was chartered with developing a suite of tools for designing and managing databases. Our group—Database Tools West—had a sister organization at the main Digital software development facility in Nashua, New Hampshire, that was known as (big surprise) Database Tools East. That group was also working on a set of tools that, together with the ones we'd develop, would complement Digital's database management system (DBMS) products.

One other note before I go on: there was another group in Nashua that was developing different types of design tools, and this group was part of the overall Software Development Technology (SDT) organization, not Database Systems (DBS) as we were.

The first sign that our organization was in trouble appeared about seven months after I was hired when our supervisor met with each of us to discuss our annual raises, as decided by DBS management. He candidly told us that our group had received raises below the averages of other groups (those based in Nashua), even though we were on schedule with all of our work.

The next sign of problems came when our group's assignment was changed to develop only a single tool; the other product development efforts were shelved.

Next, about a year and a half after I got there, our group was disbanded because the powers that be in Nashua decided that all tools needed to use the platform that the SDT tools group was developing, not our own object-oriented platform. Sure, we had done good work, we were told, but the company had taken a new direction with its tool integration strategy.

So, keeping my story in mind, take a look at the items discussed in this section as you try to figure out whether or not you might be working for the "wrong" group within your company, with your career consequently adversely affected.

BEING VIEWED AS "THE OTHER GUYS" WITHIN THE COMPANY

Jumping back to my Digital experience, we were certainly "the other guys" within the tools community at Digital. First of all, we were part of the Database Systems group, not the mainstream Software Development Technology group where most of the tools development was taking place. Next, even within DBS, we were based in Colorado Springs, which might as well have been another planet for a company with the majority of its development activity occurring in New England.

So watch out for signs that, even though your company is going strong and leading the marketplace, and maybe your project is ahead of schedule, you might be in the wrong place at the wrong time. For example, take notice when, at a holiday gathering, a company manager mentions all the organizations who have done such stellar work all year . . . except the one for which you work.

PERSISTENT RUMORS OF YOUR ORGANIZATION BEING MERGED INTO ANOTHER ONE

On the subject of reorganization (as discussed in the previous section), let it be said that every reorganization brings winners and losers. And let it also be said that merit or project success or being a bunch of nice people often doesn't matter one iota when the boxes on the reorganization chart are shifted and merged. Often, corporate politics and friendships and other (you would think) less relevant factors will determine what group gets absorbed into what other group.

So if the story on the company's rumor mill persistently has your group disappearing and becoming part of another, or—worse—being divided up among other existing groups as part of the reorganization, pay attention. Even if the rumors have no substance, you should be concerned because there is a persistent undertone floating around your company that the organization for which you work is superfluous and really doesn't need to exist.

A LOSS OF "OWNERSHIP" OF PERSONNEL AND OTHER RESOURCES

When they (company management) take away your people and your office space and your computers and your membership to the company workout area and . . . Oh, I guess I'm getting carried away. The point is that another warning sign of organizational problems is when new points of control surface in your day-to-day work life, such as:

- Your direct supervisor no longer controls where you are staffed on projects. Someone from another organization now determines the projects on which you'll work, even if they're not in the particular area of interest or expertise for which you were hired.

- You and others in your group are "administratively shifted" into another organization and even though you're told that your day-to-day work activities will remain the same, the first three months paint a different story.

RUMORS OF AN IMPENDING OUTSOURCING ARRANGEMENT

(For those in an IT organization within a noncomputer company, such as a consumer products company or a bank)

One of the major trends of the early and mid-1990s was organizations outsourcing their entire IT functions to a large systems integration or consulting firm such as IBM or Computer Sciences Corporation (CSC). In some of these situations, a company's IT staff was "traded" to the other company where they would, supposedly, continue their jobs with little or no change. In other situations, mass layoffs of the IT staff was the order of the day. Or, possibly, a small staff would be retained to act as a continuity point with the outsourcing company, but those people now have none of the hands-on development responsibilities they once had.

So when the rumors of outsourcing start swirling, pay attention: one way or another, your organization will be affected and most likely, so will you.

LOTS OF OUTSIDE MANAGEMENT CONSULTANTS SKULKING AROUND

Now, I'm not going to go on a tirade about management consultants, because I've spent a good portion of my career doing high-level consulting that combines technology and management advice. But most people who've been in the business world for the past decade or two have had experience with the legions of management consultants who show up, call a lot of meetings and schedule a lot of interviews, and then present results that (big surprise!) recommend further activity by their firm in terms of changing business operations, effecting a reorganization, putting an outsourcing arrangement in place, or some other type of dramatic (traumatic?) change. So watch out when management consultants start showing up.

TRAINING GETS POSTPONED OR CANCELED

Training cuts and cancellations are also a warning of company problems, but more often such cutbacks are slated for a subset of the company's organizations. So beware when training funds are cut and guess who (your group!) is affected by those reductions much more severely than other organizations.

THE COMPETITIVE LANDSCAPE

Here's another set of warning signs and hints that could spell problems for you regarding your company's competitors . . . the current ones and others that show up and cause everything to turn topsy-turvy.

1. **A NEW COMPETITOR ON THE SCENE**—Your company dominates its competitors and is widely recognized as *the* place to contact for whatever product or service it is that you folks produce or deliver. But then, just when everything is looking great for the next five years or so, a new competitor bursts on the scene and targets *your company* as the one it wants to compete with head-to-head. They start nibbling away at your market. They recruit a couple of key executives from your company (as discussed earlier in the chapter). Before you know it, the outlook isn't quite so bright. So even if you're only a few years into your career in the computing profession, pay attention to the competitive landscape. You may not have as much personal responsibility for meeting these specific challenges as do senior executives at your firm, but you can certainly do your part by continuing to do the best job you can do. But just as importantly, you can watch to see how the competitive challenge plays out. Does your company rise to the challenge and prevent the upstart competitor from making inroads, or do things start slowly deteriorating, leading to many of the other changes we've discussed in this chapter?

2. **HEAVY RAIDING OF YOUR COMPANY'S EMPLOYEES BY ONE OR TWO COMPETITORS—** This is basically the same as the turnover issue (above) with respect to company-specific early warning signs. But when you see those who leave headed primarily to a single competitor, you have an early indicator that (1) the pace of defections could increase, and (2)

business could be hampered by this particular company that has targeted your company for employee raiding.

3. A HEAVYWEIGHT NATIONAL COMPETITOR DECIDES TO OPEN AN OFFICE IN THE CITY IN WHICH YOUR SMALLER COMPANY IS LOCATED—One of the hallmarks of the 1990s was the explosion in small consulting and software firms. Most of these firms began operations on a city-specific or regional basis and then expanded their presence, some slowly, others quickly. But as the 1990s progressed, most larger consulting and software firms put expansion plans in place to put offices in cities where they currently didn't have a presence.

Now, if you work for one of those smaller firms, the appearance on the scene of a larger competitor may not be a very good thing for your company's fortunes. Or, possibly, the ties your firm has with clients in your geographic area are so strong that a newcomer really doesn't make much of a dent in your business. But watch carefully what happens over the first six months or so when one of these situations occurs. Watch for defections from your firm or clients who take their business to the other guy. Alternatively, you may see little or no impact, which may mean that your company is really doing well and will likely continue to do so.

4. MAJOR TECHNOLOGY SHIFTS THAT YOUR COMPANY IS SLOW IN ADOPTING—As we'll discuss in Chapter 13, there are some advancements or shifts in the technology environment that turn entire segments of the business world upside down. The Internet is a great example. Only a few years ago it was a curiosity that was still primarily for the academic community, and most of the content of the World Wide Web was online versions of print advertisements. Now, in 1998 . . . well, you *should* have a pretty good idea of what's out there on the Internet if you're in this field!

Suppose, though, that you work for a software products vendor that produces tools designed for business people to build and execute queries and reports. If your company was visionary enough to embrace Internet technologies early, then chances are your firm has fairly strong web-enabled product offerings. That means that as demand increases for these types of environments, you're positioned fairly well for strong growth.

However, consider what might be the state of affairs at your company if you were late adapters of Internet technologies, and only now are scrambling to bring web-enabled versions of your products to market. Your company may see its market share shrink; talented developers may be defecting to more forward-looking competitors; the stock price might plummet; and so on. Before you know it, it's résumé updating time.

The same situation was true in the early 1990s when a major shift from centralized mainframe computing to distributed client/server computing began to take hold . . . there were some early adapters and some late ones, and companies' fortunes rose or fell largely in part because of their early directions on client/server computing.

So watch what's going on out there in the world of general computing. Pay attention to the items we'll discuss in Chapter 13. Just because your company's executives and technology leaders choose to ignore an emerging technology trend doesn't necessarily mean that they're correct. You may catch some early warning signs that many of the other adverse situations discussed earlier in this chapter are on the horizon.

THE ECONOMY AND OTHER EXTERNAL FACTORS

Finally, there are other external factors, many of them economic in nature, that you should also watch as you try to read between the lines and figure out what your professional future might hold. Here's a list.

1. A NATIONAL OR GLOBAL ECONOMIC SLOWDOWN—If you're in your early twenties and a recent college graduate (or you're still in college), then you probably haven't any experienced being in the work world when a recession plays havoc with the American economy and, possibly, that of other countries. But take it from me, things can go downhill very, very quickly. Company problems can be magnified by a weak economy, hastening or even catalyzing many of the situations we discussed earlier in this chapter. So keep an eye on the state of the economy. Slowdowns aren't good, and you should be prepared.

2. A SIGNIFICANT OVERALL STOCK MARKET DROP—Sometimes the stock market takes a nosedive and when you look back, the drop was just a brief interruption of a long-term upward trend. The stock market crash in October 1987; the brief bear market in the summer and fall of 1990 after the invasion of Kuwait; and occasional abrupt—but brief—drops throughout the early and mid-1990s are examples. However, should the market enter a prolonged drop (as may be the case as I'm writing this chapter in the fall of 1998), you might be looking at an early warning of problems are ahead. The most obvious cause-and-effect relationship is stock market drop → economic slowdown → company problems. But even without economic slowdown, it's not uncommon for a stock market drop to adversely affect a company's fate (in effect, skipping the middle phase in the above equation). Consider that many executives have, as we discussed earlier in this chapter, a significant stake in their companies' equity. The loss of a sizable portion of one's wealth, even if "only on paper," can cause some executives to take drastic actions in a frantic attempt to try to influence a stock price recovery. If an executive's decision-making abilities are clouded by concerns about personal wealth, and these concerns overwhelm what is best for a company, everyone could be in for a rough road ahead.

3. A REGIONAL ECONOMIC SLOWDOWN—Here's a variation on the recession theme. I lived in Colorado from 1982 until 1991. At a time when much of the country's economy was booming, the economy in Colorado went through periods that varied from mild growth at best to prolonged economic turmoil at the worst. Why? Here's the abbreviated version of the story.

In the early 1980s, the Colorado economy was hurt by the bust in the shale oil business that occurred after the second 1970s oil shortage. However, spurred by an increase in defense spending in the early years of the Reagan administration, the economy there slowly recovered . . . until 1986, when a dramatic drop in oil prices caused economic turmoil in Texas, Oklahoma, and parts of Colorado. Real estate prices began dropping, and for the next four or five years the Colorado economy basically limped along.

And as you're wondering, "So what's your point here?" it's this: you not only need to keep an eye on the state of the national economy but also the economic fortunes of the region in which you live. Watch out for a weakening economic situation (such as Colorado in 1986) as you're trying to get an idea of the fate of your employer and your career. If much or most of your company's work is based within your region, you could be in for a bumpy road. If, however, a significant amount of your company's business occurs elsewhere in areas with healthier economies, then your firm may be relatively unaffected by regional problems.

4. **YOUR REGION RECOVERING FROM A RECESSION MORE SLOWLY THAN THE REST OF THE COUNTRY**—Watch out for a slower-than-everywhere-else recovery from a recession where you live. Here's another brief personal story. In 1991 I moved from Colorado to New Jersey. Now while Colorado's economy suffered in the late 1980s, New Jersey's boomed. Then the 1990 recession occurred, and after that brief downturn an era of unprecedented growth took hold . . . except in New Jersey and much of the northeastern United States (and also California). It wasn't until late 1993 or early 1994 that the economy in New Jersey got back on the growth curve that the rest of the country was then enjoying. In the meantime, many computer professionals who lived in New Jersey, New York, Philadelphia, and other northeastern cities had their careers disrupted.

(Maybe it's me, moving from one regional recession to another and being out of step with economic health in other places . . .)

5. **REGULATORY ISSUES**—Regulatory issues usually only affect IT professionals working at large companies. The breakup of AT&T in the 1980s, for example, sent many of that company's employees off to the regional operating companies as a result of the divestiture. Around the same time, IBM was under the same type of pressure that Microsoft faced in late 1998. Or perhaps you work for a utility company that is going through deregulation and making significant changes in its organizational structure and business processes to meet these new challenges.

So keep an eye on what's going on in the regulatory climate as it affects your company or industry, if applicable. Try to anticipate the effect of any changes on what will happen to your company . . . and to you.

SUMMARY

Well, I hope this chapter hasn't been too much of a downer in terms of the many, many things that you need to watch out for as you try to anticipate changes in your professional situation. But it's important to understand that even though you should primarily focus your attention on doing the jobs you've been assigned, you also need to use your "professional peripheral vision" to think of various scenarios as they may affect your project, your organization, and your company.

CHAPTER 9

DEALING WITH PROFESSIONAL SETBACKS

INTRODUCTION

This chapter will be a short one . . . mostly because the subject we're going to discuss isn't a very pleasant one. Yet I believe it's necessary to specifically discuss dealing with setbacks, so I didn't want to plop this topic into a miscellaneous catch-all chapter.

Setbacks are a fact of life for nearly everyone in professional life at some point. Sometimes it's a personal situation: performing poorly on a project, for example, or consistently being passed over for promotion for political reasons despite having been a stellar performer. Sometimes setbacks are associated with larger problems: being caught by a massive layoff when your employer faces hard times or as a result of some company directive to "remake the company."

In this short chapter we'll discuss how you can and should confront and deal with different types of setbacks that you'll face, and how to overcome these situations and get yourself back on track as soon as possible.

PERSONAL FAILURES

There may be an occasion or two in your career where you will suddenly realize: "I failed." Maybe the words in your mind won't be quite so blunt; perhaps there will be the nagging fear that you haven't given enough attention to your assignments on a project and consequently, it's running late. Maybe nobody is saying it out loud, but you know what everyone is thinking: if you had put more effort into your tasks the development effort would be on schedule, and the team wouldn't be putting in 20 or 30 extra hours each week to complete the work.

Or maybe you'll be doing a stint as a consultant and you're sent to an assignment at a client. But because you're distracted by personal problems, your work quality suffers . . . and the client requests that your firm replace you with another consultant.

Suppose you decide to give solo consulting a try, or you get together with a few friends and start a software development company (see Chapter 16). The business plan is solid; you start off with a few clients, or you have a lot of initial interest in the product you're developing . . . but within a year you're out of money, expenses are still running ahead of revenue, and it looks as if you'll have to close up shop and go back to corporate life.

I could go on and on, but you get the idea: some situation occurs at a point in your career where you set out to do something—anything from tasks on a project to starting a company on your own—and you aren't successful. So what happens next?

It's all too common for depression to set in, and before you know it you're undergoing a "crisis of faith," questioning your choice in careers, wondering if you'll ever be successful in professional life again, and so on. To prevent a single failure from snowballing into a much more serious situation, here are some suggestions for how to deal with the problem and get yourself back on your feet again.

1. IDENTIFY THE EXACT NATURE OF THE FAILURE—It's easy enough to categorize a failure as "not performing well on a project" or "tried to start a company that failed." But it's important to dig deeper than a cursory description of the situation; you need to very specifically identify exactly what the failure is that you're confronting. For example:

- "I did not complete the modules I was assigned on schedule, which caused the entire project to get behind schedule because other team members were dependent on my having finished my work."

NOTE IT'S USUALLY PAINFUL to verbalize statements like the above, even in your own mind . . . but it's essential that you do in order to proceed with the following steps.

- "After the first three months of working on my own, developing a web site for a client, I couldn't find any new clients."

- "I got into an argument with the client over the system design, and she called my company and asked that I be replaced. My manager told me that I had handled the situation very badly and they almost lost the client because of what I did, and now I'm on a special monitoring plan."

2. **GET TO THE ROOT CAUSES**—So . . . why did the failure occur? After you have verbalized the exact nature of the failure, you need to take a long, honest look at exactly what happened. For example (same order as the bulleted points above):

- "When I first looked at the design specifications for the modules I was assigned, I thought I had a good understanding of what I was supposed to do. But once I started coding, I found out that I had underestimated the complexity of what I had been assigned. I tried to work it out on my own but everything I tried was wrong. By the time I decided to ask for help, we were way behind schedule."

- "The original contract with Client A was supposed to be for nine months, but after I delivered the first version of the web site they decided to hire a college intern and turn over the rest of the web site development to her. I thought I could find other web site development work easily but I was wrong. Every company I contacted already had someone working on their sites, and I ran out of money so I couldn't do any advertising."

- "The client started arguing with me and inferring that I didn't know what I was talking about regarding to the design. I lost my temper and shouted back. Before you know it, I was in trouble."

3. **SEEK OUTSIDE ASSISTANCE AND ADVICE, IF NECESSARY**—The examples above are relatively simple ones, situations where with a little bit of self-insight, you can quickly identify the failure and the root cause by yourself. But suppose that you have a substance abuse problem? Or maybe your personal life is chaotic, such as being in the midst of a divorce or a painful breakup? In these more serious situations—and they do occur—you may need some help before you develop your recovery plans (the next steps). If you feel overwhelmed or unable to get your thoughts together then by all means, get some professional help (and I'm not using that phrase in a cynical way, either). Most large companies have an employee assistance organization, or perhaps your health insurance plan pays for part or all of any necessary counseling. It's not uncommon to feel uncomfortable discussing personal matters with strangers, but sometimes it's necessary to do so.

4. **DEVELOP A SHORT-TERM RECOVERY PLAN**—Whether your particular situation is simple or complicated, you must focus on what you need to do in the short term (the next two to three months) to try to get things back on track as soon as possible. For example (again, same order as items 1 and 2 above):

- "On my next project assignment, I need to sit down with one of the senior team members—maybe the chief architect or the project manager, or maybe a senior developer—and walk through all the specifications that are assigned to me. I need to do some test coding to make sure I fully understand the capabilities of C++ and I also need to make arrangements for someone to regularly check out my work throughout the project."

- "For now, I'm going to give up the idea of working on my own. I'm going back to employee status and I think I might be able to get my old job back."

- "I need help with learning how to control my temper. I'm going to spend some time with a counselor in the company's employee assistance office . . . and I need to clear the air with my manager to let her know that I'm taking responsibility for my actions."

The idea is to look at the root cause(s) you identified earlier and figure out how to neutralize a problem situation; restore your income flow (and self-confidence); make yourself right again with the management of your company; or otherwise, begin to get yourself beyond the failure.

5. CREATE A LONGER-TERM RECOVERY PLAN—Sometimes your short-term recovery plan will only get you back to a point of stability, but not necessarily to where you want to be. For example, the second example (failed self-employment) has a short-term recovery plan of giving up on that idea and going back to an employee status, perhaps at your former employer.

But suppose you still aspire to work for yourself. Do you have to give up on that dream? Definitely not. You can create a longer-term plan that will take you back into a self-employment status, but perhaps:

- You'll wait at least one year so you can rebuild your personal assets.

- Before you try again, you'll develop a formal business plan (something you hadn't done previously) that will include not only the services you'll provide but also a plan for marketing and advertising those services to acquire future clients.

- You'll have the business plan reviewed by other people who can advise you on items you may have forgotten about.

Or, perhaps in the first example, you decide that software development isn't really something you enjoy . . . but you still want to remain in the computing field. Your longer-term recovery plan might be to pursue career broadening of some type, such as moving out of development into a sales or marketing position with a software vendor or consulting firm.

6. WATCH FOR WARNING SIGNS OF REPEATING THE FAILURE—As you proceed through both the short-term and long-term recoveries, you need to be alert for signs that history is going to repeat itself. Are you having trouble again with your latest software development assignment? Do you feel the anger rising within you every time someone asks questions about designs you've put together? Or, in the area of personal problems adversely influencing your work, are you once again abusing the substances for which you've gotten help in overcoming?

If you catch yourself about to slip onto a path leading to another failure, do everything you can to prevent it. If possible, take corrective actions yourself. If necessary, get help.

WHEN YOUR COMPANY IS IN TROUBLE

Sometimes a setback may find you and its cause is nothing that you have personally done, or could have prevented. Suppose the company for which you work has made a serious misstep in the marketplace (for example, introducing a new generation of products that are overpriced and problem-prone . . . and not well received in the marketplace). Revenues and earnings drop, losses mount, and before long you and many of your co-workers are fairly certain you'll be laid off.

Though being caught in a layoff with dozens or hundreds (or even thousands) of other employees isn't quite the same as being fired for poor performance, the end result is the same. You could suddenly find yourself without employment and a paycheck.

Now maybe you're reading this and thinking, "So what? Jobs are plentiful and skilled computer people are in short supply. If I were to get laid off I could find another job tomorrow. So how is this a setback, other than giving me an opportunity to take a vacation for a couple of weeks before I start my next job?"

True, in the late 1990s you would have had no problem moving to a new employer if the company for which you worked failed and you lost your job. But if you were reading these words during the recession of 1990-1991, or the earlier recession in 1981-1982, you wouldn't have been quite so confident about quickly finding new employment. Job loss in slow economic times can have serious consequences: financial, personal, health, and others.

I would strongly recommend preparing for such a situation *today*, no matter how rosy your particular situation seems. Your preparations should include two major areas: finances and skills.

- **FINANCES**—Try to build up savings equivalent to about six months worth of ordinary living expenses, and to pay down your credit cards and similar debt. (Hint: it wasn't uncommon for computer professionals to be unemployed for *a year or more* in the early 1990s, particularly in the northeastern United States and in California, where the recession lasted longer than the rest of the country). You need to devote your energies to finding a new position or pursuing self-employment or other professional matters. You don't want to be sidetracked by financial difficulties.

- **YOUR SKILLS**—If you're skilled in the latest technologies—Java, HTML and HTTP, data warehousing tools, and so on—then you're probably in pretty good shape should you suddenly find yourself having to find a new job quickly because your employer isn't doing well. But if your skills aren't quite as up to date as those of your peers, you could be in for rough going if you suddenly found yourself out of work. The solution: a combination of self-study, training, and a *dedicated* effort to bring your capabilities in line with those most in demand in the marketplace.[1]

---

[1] I discussed this subject of "remaking" one's career in *Downsized But Not Out: How to Find Your Next Computer Job* (McGraw-Hill, 1994). Though that book is intended primarily for those farther along in their careers who are facing disruption, there are some good suggestions about self-assessment and things you can do on your own to make yourself more marketable in the computing profession.

Even if job loss is unthinkable today, don't get overconfident that it could never happen. Even if your company is doing extremely well in a financial sense, you never know when the next round of "business re-engineering" could hit and before you know it, thousands of people are being let go in the name of "process improvement." (Just do a worldwide web search for news clips about layoffs and see how many profitable companies are still regularly pursuing downsizing programs, even in good economic times.)

SETBACKS DRIVEN BY EXTERNAL FACTORS

Your company (and others) can be in trouble because of external factors such as the economy. Again, look back at the recessions in the early 1990s and early 1980s . . . or further back to the inflationary days of the late 1970s or the Great Depression or regular depressions in the 1800s. I'm not trying to play economic historian here. The point is that even though conventional wisdom today (late 1990s) has it that economic cycles have forever changed because of technology and recessions are far less likely to occur than in the past, as I'm writing this, the world stock markets are still down sharply because of economic turmoil in Russia and Asia. I can also state that many companies in all areas of the business world—technology and otherwise—are facing lower profits or even losses for the first time in several years.

So the advice provided above about preparing for company problems, no matter how well things are going today, also applies to external factors such as economy-driven downturns. Get your financial situation under control, make certain your skills are up to date, and always have an idea of what you would do should problems occur.

 CAREER TIPS TAKE A LOOK at the discussion in Chapter 8 about reading between the lines, so to speak, about what's really going on at your company. Budget cuts, canceled projects, resignations, and the rest of the topics discussed are usually good leading indicators that problems are about to occur and you could be facing a setback as a result.

SUMMARY

I received a grade of "D" on the very first test I took during my freshman year in college. After having received almost all A's my entire academic career, this was quite a shock to me. I suddenly realized that my somewhat lackadaisical approach to high school academics wasn't going to suffice in college. So I began studying more for exams, doing reading assignments on time, and otherwise getting more focused about the tasks at hand.

I've also known people whose initial semester results in college were so abysmal that they either found themselves on academic probation or even dropped out of college . . . only to rededicate themselves to their academic studies and eventually graduate with stellar academic records and go on to professional successes in the real world.

Perhaps you've gone through a situation similar to one of those described above during your academic career. If so, you've already had experiences dealing with and overcoming them. You've already overcome some type of a setback and gone on to success.

The point is that in the real world, setbacks do occur . . . but no matter how severe they are they don't have to mark a dramatic downturn in your professional fortunes. The business world is full of people who have overcome being fired from one company only to triumph at another . . . or return in triumph to the place from which they were dismissed. Recessions eventually end, and mass layoffs fade into a tight job market with tremendous compensation possibilities for you and others in the computing field.

So when you find yourself facing a setback in your professional life, take a quick look at this chapter and remember that no matter how bleak a situation looks, you can certainly recover from it and get your career back on track.

INTRODUCTION

Um, you know, communication is, like, really important to your, uh, career.

Okay, okay, I don't mean to be harsh here. I often catch myself uttering a boatload of "you knows" and "ums" and "uhs" when I'm leaving voicemail messages or speaking to people in casual settings. It takes a concerted effort to overcome those long-since-established habits. I'm better when I'm doing formal presentations—mostly because I'm carefully choosing my words even as I'm speaking—but my style is my style, and that's that.

Which, by the way, is what I want to discuss in this chapter: *not* the nuts and bolts, the mechanics, of how to write or how to give different types of presentations, but rather, how to build on your own style and be able to communicate successfully with others in the course of your job, both in writing and verbally.

You've probably noticed by now that my writing style in this book is, shall we say, somewhat irreverent. . . occasional jokes (however bad they might be); a conversational writing style; and, in general, trying to hold your attention as best as I can and doing my best not to bore you.

But if you read a more formal document that I had written—say, a design document or a systems specification—you won't see jokes. The writing style will be much more terse, much more precise; and whether or not the reader is bored would have been at the absolute bottom of the list of important factors when preparing that document. The key, as we'll discuss, is to *thoroughly* understand your audience, *thoroughly* understand the "norms" of the type of document you're writing or presentation you're to give, and then to adapt your delivery style accordingly. Having a toolkit of different communications styles and techniques can, believe it or not, play a key role in your career advancement. Even though we're all familiar with the stereotype of the "computer programming expert" who is a whiz-bang programmer but can only mumble incomplete sentences, is socially awkward, and who lives on pizza and takeout food, it's my opinion that in terms of career advancement, such an individual is at a disadvantage to someone who may not be as technically astute but who can also communicate well.

So read on for some tips and tricks of how to communicate effectively.[1]

WRITTEN COMMUNICATIONS

Developers, take your marks . . . I mean, your word processing software . . . because you'll most likely be spending as much time—if not more—writing as you will coding. Much of what you write will be formal project-related documents (such as requirements, design docu-

---

[1] Several years ago I co-authored a book entitled *The Computer Professional's Guide to Effective Communications* (McGraw-Hill, 1992). That book is now out of print, meaning you can't buy it (so don't worry, this isn't yet another attempt at promoting one of my previous books and trying to entice you buy a copy!). But you can probably find a copy in a local library, so the reason I mention this is that if you want more detailed information about written and verbal communications for computer professionals than I'll cover in this chapter, there's a source for you.

ments, etc.), which we'll discuss next. As your career progresses, you'll also need to prepare briefing-style presentations, which we'll discuss after we look at the project-related writing.

FORMAL PROJECT-RELATED DOCUMENTS

Ideally, every step during a project will be accompanied by just the right amount of documentation . . . not too much, so that it's impossible to sift through thousands of pages to glean pertinent information about your project, yet enough so there are as few ambiguities as possible about requirements, specifications, design, and other aspects of the job.

The following sections present examples of these different types of project-related documents that you will almost certainly encounter soon after entering the computing profession, along with key points for you to note about each.

With regard to the format of these documents, *hope* that you'll be presented with a template for each into which your content can be placed. Maybe your company has a set of standard templates for each of these documents, or perhaps if you're a consultant you'll be conforming to your clients' respective formats. At first glance, the idea of standard templates might appear to be a bit restrictive and confining; you may find yourself worrying more about format than content. After familiarizing yourself with the use of document templates, however, you'll soon appreciate the quick start aspect of, for example, opening up a document template in a word processing package and being assisted as you move from portion to portion that you need to fill in.

So by all means, follow the standards and guidelines that you're presented, and use the material below as your introduction to the different types of documents you'll likely be producing.

Requirements Documents

The somewhat ambiguously titled "Requirements Document" might be more accurately termed *"Business* Requirements Document." True, you may include system-related requirements such as "must run on both UNIX and Windows NT servers" or "the application needs to support both Windows 95 and Windows 98 clients." But for the most part, the primary value provided by a requirements document deals with business needs.

Therefore, keep the idea of business functionality at the forefront of your mind as you write paragraph after paragraph. The idea is to produce a comprehensive document that can be presented to a variety of audiences—senior business executives, business analysts (that is, the people who do most of the real day-to-day work), and also people from the IT organization. After everyone reviews and validates the documents contents, there should be absolutely no uncertainty at all as to what will be designed and developed . . . and, more importantly, *why* an application will be developed (the business value that will be provided).

Perhaps the most important thing you should know about working on a requirements document is that your choice of wording is very, very important. Consider the following two sentences:

The inventory application **must** allow authorized users to make correcting entries to product quantities following physical inventory counts.

The inventory application **should** allow authorized users to make correcting entries to product quantities following physical inventory counts.

The only difference between these two sentences is that the first uses the word "must" while the second sentence replaces "must" with "should." A requirements document that includes the first statement sends a clear, immutable message: The ability for certain authorized users to enter corrective inventory entries is a *mandatory* feature of the application. The unspoken message beneath this sentence is "don't bother trying to deliver an application without this feature. It won't be accepted."

In contrast, the wording of the second sentence is ambiguous about the importance of this feature. Sure, that feature *should* be included . . . but what if it isn't? It that okay or not?

The point is this. If you're writing a requirements document and, referring to your notes from user interviews or group requirements sessions, you see that it's been stated that it's imperative that a certain feature be included, use a word such as "must" to note the mandatory nature of that feature. (Some standards, such as government ones, mandate the use of the word "shall," which is more or less semantically equivalent to "must," at least in terms of being stronger than "should." I prefer "must" because it's a more commonly used word and therefore leaves no uncertainty in readers' minds.)

Some other thoughts about requirements documents are described below.

1. **HIGH-LEVEL VS. DETAILED REQUIREMENTS**—You must have a clear idea of the type of requirements document you're writing, in the context of the intended audience. Requirements documents for senior executives are often best written from a high-level perspective . . . that is, major *groups* of functionality are included in the pages along with some diagrams, sample screens, and other graphic material, as appropriate. In contrast, a requirements document that will serve as the foundation for subsequent design work (and a design document, as discussed later) must be *very* detailed, with as much precision as possible in each statement. At the same time, however, you still want to focus your detailed statements mostly on a *business* context rather than describing user interactions and other system capabilities that will support the business functionality (that is, stay away from business requirements statements such as "the system will feature a start-up icon showing a purple dinosaur, and after double-clicking that icon the user will see a menu that will . . . "). Statements such as that one are more appropriate for a design document, as we'll discuss.

2. **REVISIONS**—Modern word processing software features capabilities to manage revisions within a document (sort of an intradocument version control). Depending on your organization's policies and standards, you may need to track revisions from your first iteration of a requirements document through all subsequent versions of the document until it's "frozen." If you haven't used the revision feature in your word processing software (in Microsoft Word 95, you can find it on the Tools menu), practice using those capabilities *before* you start work on a document as part of your job.

3. **EASE OF REFERENCE**—The template you'll use for your requirements document should feature a standard numbering mechanism for sections, subsections, and (if applicable) paragraphs. If not, then create one for your own use. Why? For ease of reference from other documents, that's why. When you're working on a design document you can refer to specific sections or paragraphs within your design document and study the specific requirement(s) being implemented through a module you're designing and documenting.

CAREER TIPS

USE PLENTY OF DIAGRAMS in your design documents, but also remember that diagrams don't stand on their own, no matter how well annotated they are. A document structure I personally prefer is to intersperse a series of diagrams with appropriately detailed narrative about that particular diagram. Additionally, by using graphical capabilities of your word processing software, you can annotate screen shots with additional information right in the middle of your diagram. This provides further clarity for the readers.

Design Documents

The fundamental idea of a design document is to create a bridge between business requirements (discussed previously) and the code that you'll eventually write. If you and others on your project team do a thorough job in creating and validating a good design document, then software development will almost always go much, much smoother than if you were to just plop yourself in front of a PC screen and start coding.

As noted in the preceding section, design elements should relate to one or more business requirements so it's clear to every reader exactly *why* you're implementing a particular feature . . . the "why" is just as important as the "how" in the context of overall project success.

Analysis Documents

The purpose of requirements documents and design documents is to describe what *will* exist after an application is developed and deployed to a group of users. In contrast, an analysis document describes what *currently* exists.

Often, an organization wants to understand some portion of their current environment before committing to new development activity. Though this statement might sound surprising, consider that any large organization has hundreds, if not thousands, of applications in use, and it is the rare (actually, so far unheard of) executive who fully understands all the interoperability, overlap, and gaps of the technology for which he or she is responsible.

WARNING

ANALYSIS DOCUMENTS then are often the most politically charged type of formal written communication that you will likely encounter in the early years of your career. By all means, make sure that you have a project manager or your supervisor review and comment upon *everything* that you write before you show your document to a client, user, or anyone outside your immediate organization. This caution is particularly true as you identify gaps in functionality, methodology and process deficiencies, or inefficiencies caused by organizational structures. Be careful to focus on these types of details in a rather dry, factual manner . . . an analysis document in which you're pointing out problems is *not* the place for a whimsical writing style!

Therefore, it's entirely possible that you could find yourself working as part of a small team with the charter of documenting the current state of a portion of your company (or, if you're a consultant, your client). Typically, analysis documents focus on the technology that's in place:

- what applications are running, and for what purpose;
- the effectiveness of those applications (response time, network throughput and existing bottlenecks, known problems, ease of maintenance, and the like);
- who uses applications, for what purpose, how frequently, how effective the user interface is.

The key to preparing an effective analysis document is that first word: analysis. During the course of your work, you need to dig deep and go beyond the often superficial—and more than occasionally, incorrect—answers you receive and make certain that what finds its way into your document is *absolutely correct*. Consider that analysis documents are often the first step to upheaval within an organization as it considers a change. Those with a vested interest in maintaining the status quo will jump on any inconsistencies or errors in your analysis document as a means of discrediting your entire analysis effort.

Package Integration Documents

You could find yourself working on a project in which you're doing no custom development, or perhaps only a little bit of coding. Instead, your team is installing a software package for an organization to do, for example, call center management. So instead of spending time working on a design document that will provide the basis for your coding efforts (and those of others working on your project), you might instead create a document that describes the integration of the package you're installing with other applications; the organization's infrastructure; or underlying network and common services, such as code libraries and version control procedures (see Chapter 7).

It's imperative that a package integration document clearly document all interfaces just as a design document would. I would also recommend that as much as possible, you detail interfaces and integration capabilities with *specific components* of the package (for example, a particular module) rather than just the package as a whole. This way, the integration work can proceed smoothly, with as little ambiguity as possible.

Problem Reports

Perhaps your job entails you working on a help desk, or maybe your organization does maintenance and support for applications running within your company. Or maybe your job is to do testing for applications that are being developed. In any of these situations, you will find yourself writing reports of possible software or system problems. Sometimes, you will be the person who will be researching and recommending a solution for these problems; in other situations, you will pass the reports on to others who will be responsible for making those corrections.

Whatever your role, it's imperative that you thoroughly document the problem you're describing. Make sure you note:

- the exact nature of the problem, including any error codes
- as much information as you can about the environment in which the error occurred, including the hardware and operating system on which software is running, details about the networking interface, other software that was running on that machine, any other users (if known) running that application at the same time, and so on
- what happened after the problem occurred (that is, did the application crash but the system remain operational, or did someone's PC lock up? Did the network become clogged?)
- if this problem has occurred before
- if you or a user made a deliberate attempt to duplicate the problem, and if the problem reoccurred

CAREER TIPS

IN GENERAL, it's always a good practice to ask the person to whom you're presenting (or someone who works for him or her) about the preferred format of the material you need to prepare. Some people prefer narrative forms (that is, word processing documents), while others prefer briefing charts prepared in a package such as Microsoft PowerPoint. Keep in mind that many executives have, shall we say, relatively short attention spans. Now I'm not saying that in a derogatory manner; most executives and managers whom you'll be required to brief have lots and lots of things to which they need to pay attention. Therefore, keep your material as brief and tersely stated as possible.

You should also include any other information as pertinent. The idea is that you don't want someone to whom the problem will be assigned to have to guess about any of this information. The more details he or she has, the more likely it will be that the problem will be corrected quickly.

BRIEFING-STYLE PRESENTATIONS

Okay, I know what you're probably thinking: all of the types of documents I've discussed so far are . . . let's see, what's the word I'm searching for? Ah, yes . . . boring! Truthfully, there is little or no room for creativity or self-expression in a design document or a package integration document.

There is, however, a channel for you to put a bit of a personal touch on written material you produce: specifically, documents that will accompany a presentation that you're to give. Later in this chapter, we'll discuss some tips and guidelines for slideshow-style presentations.

But back to the boring stuff . . . some of the material that you'll prepare to accompany your presentation will exactly mirror the content of what you'll be speaking about (specifically, the slideshow material that we'll discuss later). But it's also important to note that sometimes you will need to prepare supplemental material: executive summaries, background papers, and the like.

ELECTRONIC MAIL

You already know how to write and send e-mail, of course . . . in this day of the Internet and information services such as Compuserve and America Online, you've probably been sending e-mail for years.

But there are things you should note about business communications via e-mail as contrasted with your personal e-mail with friends and relatives. The list below presents these guidelines for your reference.

1. **NO FLAMING!**—Even if you want to make a point, and even if it seems like someone is particularly dense and just can't grasp the concept you're trying to get across, don't start writing personal attacks, sarcastic messages, or bitter denouncements of that person, his or her entire organization, and that person's family lineage. Even if someone "attacks" you, be professional (if not necessarily courteous) in your response.

2. **NO SHOUTING!**—PEOPLE DON'T LIKE TO READ E-MAIL IN WHICH YOU'RE SHOUTING AT THEM. JUST IN CASE THE TERM "SHOUTING" ISN'T FAMILIAR TO YOU IN THE CONTEXT OF ELECTRONIC MAIL, IT MEANS USING ALL CAPITAL LETTERS. EVEN IF YOU'RE TRYING TO MAKE A POINT, DON'T SHOUT BECAUSE IT TAKES AWAY FROM THE MESSAGE YOU'RE TRYING TO CONVEY. (ISN'T IT AGGRAVATING READING THIS?)

Instead of shouting, emphasize a portion of your message by *using italics,* **or perhaps putting certain words in boldface type,** *<u>or maybe even using italics and boldface type</u>* <u>*along with underlining.*</u> But keep those highlighted portions short so the piece of your message you're trying to emphasize jumps out at the reader.

3. UNDERSTAND THE "CULTURAL" IMPLICATIONS OF E-MAIL—Consider the simple "return receipt" feature of most e-mail packages. I usually use return receipts on e-mail I send so I know when people receive messages. But I also know when someone deletes a message I sent without reading it (as told to me by the e-mail system). Sometimes that's okay, if a person perhaps read the most recent message in a long string and then deleted earlier, now-superseded messages. But I can also gauge whether someone in my company considers my messages superfluous if he or she deletes them without even bothering to open and read them. That's sort of rude, but I can also use that information as intelligence to learn who may not have particularly favorable impressions of my group's business mission.

4. BE CAREFUL ABOUT REPLY-TO-ALL FEATURES—The good news about e-mail is that it facilitates rapid communications, even across organizational and company boundaries. It's easy to send a message to, say, members of your project team as well as several people from your client for whom your company is working. However, *please* use caution because the all-too-easy-to-use feature of replying to all addressees on a message can be embarrassing or damaging if you inadvertently send a message that's supposed to be an intrateam communication not only to your team members but to others from outside your organization or even your company. Be sure to check the addressee list if you use reply-to-all to make sure that a message is going only to the people for whom it's intended.

5. USE THE SUBJECT LINE ACCORDINGLY—If you want a person who receives a message from you to do something, add something to the beginning of the subject line such as ACTION REQUESTED. If your message is very important, don't just rely on the "very important" feature of your e-mail package. Preface your subject with something like VERY, VERY IMPORTANT—PLEASE RESPOND IMMEDIATELY.

6. FOLLOW ALL INTERNAL COMPANY GUIDELINES—Don't send messages to everyone in your entire company if only certain executives or IT staff members are authorized to do so; don't send off-color material if your company's policy prohibits doing so. In short, treat your company e-mail as a means of business communication, even if you are allowed to use it for personal e-mail.

7. WATCH LARGE ATTACHMENTS—I work at home or in hotel rooms a lot, and it's always frustrating to receive a message with extraordinarily large (greater than a megabyte) attachments. Sometimes that can't be helped; but consider that not everyone to whom you send messages works in an office with a high-speed networking environment. If you can, "zip" (or otherwise compress) large files or only send the material that you *know* someone needs (or has specifically requested).

8. CLEAN OUT YOUR MAILBOX FREQUENTLY—Enough said.

VERBAL COMMUNICATIONS AND PRESENTATIONS

Don't worry . . . I'm not going to discuss voice inflection, hand mannerisms, whether or not you should stand behind a lectern or wander around, and all of those other "how to give a speech" topics. There are many, many references you can consult and classes you can take; maybe you even took a communications or speech class in college.

Instead, we'll spend the rest of this chapter talking about some general guidelines that should help you out as you take your place in front of your boss, your boss's boss, his or her boss, too, and perhaps dozens of other people. I'm not trying to scare you, but instead letting you know that you can expect to find yourself giving presentations to audiences that not only include those who work with you but also senior managers from your company and other organizations, possibly as part of a very, very large audience.

So in regard to general guidelines, here are a couple of points to remember (and again, I promise . . . no boring stuff about when you should and shouldn't use your hands or trying not to say "um" too many times).

1. **KNOW YOUR AUDIENCE, AND TAILOR YOUR PRESENTATION TO THEM**—This expression isn't quite as trite as it sounds, and is in my opinion far more important than (again) worrying about voice inflection and other mechanics. Consider that:
   - Senior executives are human beings, too . . . which means it *may* be perfectly acceptable to put together and deliver a somewhat lighthearted presentation along the lines of the examples I'll show you later in this chapter. The key, though, is to know what an executive in your audience might find funny—or, at least, not offensive.
   - Technical people want to hear techno-babble; business people want to hear about business requirements and functionality . . . right? Well, that's usually correct . . . but make sure you understand the audience's expectations before you prepare a presentation.

2. **KNOW YOUR TIME LIMIT . . . BUT BE FLEXIBLE**—If you have an hour to give a presentation, then you should have around an hour's worth of material . . . not too much less and not too much more. But at the same time, if a speaker before you runs over his or her time and you're asked to try and compress your presentation (as I've been asked to do many times), then you should be able to select certain slides and still get your main point across.

3. **ALLOW QUESTIONS, BUT STEER THE PRESENTATION**—People will ask questions when you're giving a presentation . . . you want them to, anyway, because questions are key indicators that they are at least paying attention to you. But it's up to you to keep the presentation on track. If someone asks a question that you cover later in your presentation, for example, you could either give a quick reply and say that you'll discuss that topic in more detail later, or defer your answer until that later point. It's your choice, because it's your presentation.

4. **HAVE GOOD SLIDES, EVEN IF THEY'RE ON PAPER**—In the next section we'll talk about tips for your slides when you're giving a presentation using a PC. But you could also find yourself doing a presentation in which there is no PC and overhead projector, but rather a dozen or so copies of your slides, one for each of the attendees sitting around a conference room table. Your slides should be of as high a quality as if you were presenting them on a screen, with several important differences:

- They should be in black and white only, *unless* you have a color printer. Don't print black and white slides with gray-shaded template backgrounds, white lettering, or other features that look good on a screen but do nothing but use up a toner cartridge or two in your department's laser printer.

- You can't use sound clips, build effects, and spiffy transitions from one slide to another when you're briefing from paper slides. So you should know *before* you prepare your presentation whether or not you'll have access to a PC and projector or if you'll be using paper.

ONLINE SLIDESHOW PRESENTATIONS

In this last part of this chapter, I'll present a few examples of presentations I've done recently to give you some ideas that you can use in your own briefings.

Example #1

I once gave a presentation to a software vendor's sales conference, discussing how vendors and consulting companies can work together effectively. Below are several of the slides I presented.

First, the title slide (in black and white for ease of reading . . . remember what I mentioned in the preceding section):

**Vendors are from Mars,
Consultants are from Venus**

or:
**Building long-lasting, effective relationships with your data
warehousing consulting partners**

presented by
**Alan Simon, Vice President,
Worldwide Data Warehousing Solutions**

Okay, so maybe the title of the presentation isn't the funniest thing you've seen lately—certainly not Dilbert or Dennis Miller—but it at least drew the attendees' attention to my first slide, and as it turned out, far fewer people headed out to the hallway during my presentation than during others.

I also decided to resurface the "Venus and Mars" theme (from the John Gray series of relationship books, in case that doesn't sound familiar to you . . . though if you're as old as I am you might also think of a Paul McCartney album of that title) at various points later in the presentation. For example, consider the following sequence of slides:

A Consultant's View of Data Warehousing

What we _really_ care about!

Successfully Delivering Projects

Project failure is bad, bad, bad . . .

We _must_ rely on vendors' products in today's IT world

We have _long_ memories . . .
        (companies _and_ people)

We Like Long-Term, Stable Relationships

So who doesn't?

But Sometimes, We "Need Space"

The need for relationships with multiple vendors (even in the same tool space)

Please . . . don't be angry with us!

(Besides, you do it too!)

But We Do Like Stability

Make us happy and we'll keep doing business together

Again, it's not exactly HBO Comedy Special-quality material but as several attendees commented, they paid attention to the message I was trying to get across: how their company and the one for which I worked could be effective partners.

Example #2

In July 1998, I gave a briefing at our organization's "data warehousing summit" in which the people from my organization, plus other data warehousing consultants from around the company, gathered to discuss what had happened over the past year and what the plans were for the next year.

In my keynote presentation, I decided to stress that from a personal sense, I'd been doing the same thing that many of my regional managers had been doing . . . traveling all over the place and working on many, many different tasks, from project work to business development sales calls.

On the slides I've included below, as well as many of the others, I had two features designed to grab the audience's attention: first, a quote (in words) from an appropriate song clip that captured the spirit of that particular slide. Additionally, for some (but not all) of the slides, I added a sound bite via a .WAV file that was *different* than the song clip but served to emphasize the point I was making; as each slide popped onto the screen, the .WAV file added the sound effects. (After each of the following slides, I'll mention the sound clip I used.)

What I've been doing over the last year . . . first, lots of sales calls

". . . to do the show in Chicago; or Detroit, I don't know, we do so many shows in a row . . ."

— *Jackson Browne*

On my laptop PC, there is a .WAV file with a voice that informs you that "your battery is now fully charged." Since I was emphasizing that immediately following the previous year's summit I spent a significant portion of my time doing sales calls, the combination of the song clip and the .WAV file indicated that my personal battery was fully charged, and I was filled with energy.

Project work - enterprise data warehousing scope

"You know I can't sleep, I can't stop my brain, you know it's three weeks I'm going insane, you know I'd give you everything I got for a little piece of mind."

— *The Beatles*

The project to which I referred in the previous slide was one known throughout my organization for the long, long hours (often until after midnight) that everyone on the team (including me) spent meeting the project deliverables during the five weeks we were collecting requirements. I didn't use a .WAV sound bite for this slide; the clip from the Beatles song stood on its own, I thought.

Then more sales calls

"I went from Phoenix, Arizona all the way to Tacoma, Philadelphia, Atlanta, L.A."

— Steve Miller

In addition to the geographical aspects of the Steve Miller song clip—and I actually did go to every city mentioned in the slide except for Tacoma—I used another .WAV file from my laptop, this one saying, "Your battery is running low." Basically, I wanted to get across to the attendees that like all of them, I was running at top speed and I empathized with their situations.

Back to the southwest

"By the time I get to Phoenix. . ."

— Glen Campbell

No .WAV file for the above slide was used; just the geographical reference, indicating that we were doing intensive business development in Phoenix.

> # "What
> a
> long
> strange
> trip
> it's
> been!"
>
> *— The Grateful Dead*

In this slide, in response to the question I posed, "How would I describe this past year in a single phrase?" I used a "typewriter click" .WAV file and built the slide, one word at a time, each word "flying" from left to right (try that in PowerPoint if you've never done it; it's neat). So the slide build went:

(click) What
(click) a
(click) long
(click) strange

. . . and so on. The idea was to emphasize each word. I hoped that most of the attendees would recognize the Grateful Dead song by the third or fourth word and tune in to the slide as it finished building.

There was more in this presentation, but the slides I've shown here give you the idea of what I was trying to do: use a bit of humor with some mild special effects and try to grab the attendees' attention.

CAREER TIPS

#1: DON'T OVERDO use of slides, transition effects, or sound clips. When used sparingly, you can really get some of your key points across; when overdone, it's hard for the audience to distinguish between the major points you're trying to make and other parts of your presentation.

#2: Don't overuse clip art (the graphical figures and symbols that come with most graphics and presentation packages, or that can be purchased separately or downloaded from Internet web sites). Like the special effects discussed previously, clip art can draw attention to points you're trying to make when used sparingly. But we've all seen the "standard" graphics that come with the presentation packages over and over for the past few years, and there's almost a backlash against using the same figures over and over. It's not original anymore; so you're better off drawing people's attentions to your messages rather than using cute graphics.

SUMMARY

It's obviously difficult to discuss written and verbal communications in any kind of depth in only a single chapter. So remember my major points:

- Be prepared to write and speak . . . a lot!
- Be yourself when you write and speak . . . within reason.
- Be clever . . . but don't overdo it.

That's basically it. The rest of the mechanics you can certainly gather from training courses and the many, many books available that discuss written and verbal communications.

CHAPTER 11

WORKING WITH USERS

INTRODUCTION

Your academic training should have provided you with an opportunity to work on a sort-of-real-world development project. That is, not only did you work with others as part of a group but you also determined the specific requirements for what you'd be developing not from a detailed list provided by your instructor, but rather from interviewing other people. Maybe you met with administrators from the campus career services organization and gathered a set of requirements for a web-based environment through which students could register for on-campus interviews. Your group then actually developed a prototype of the application and demonstrated it to the entire staff from career services, gathering comments and feedback from the attendees.

Maybe at the demonstration of the prototype one of the people said something like, "No, that's wrong; there should be a maximum of five companies someone can register for at one time, not ten like you have it there." Did your group make a mistake? Or perhaps did someone else tell you that the correct number—the requirement—was ten? Who is right? Or did your team just guess?

If you recall an experience or two like that described above, then the topic for this chapter will be familiar to you. If not, then I'd recommend paying particular attention to the following discussion.

Why? Because out there in the real world, your abilities to work well with users in various activities will either lead you and others to great success, or could cause you so many problems that you'll regret ever having chosen this field.

There's an expression that I sometimes blurt out in the midst of a particularly "challenging" time on a project when the lines of communication with users are, shall we say, a bit filled with static: "This would be an easy project if it weren't for the users."

I'm joking, of course; without users, what would be the purpose of working on a project to develop something? So let's take it for granted that user interaction is a necessity for project work (that's "necessity," not "necessary evil," by the way . . .).

But on what occasions will you find yourself interacting with users? How about:

- collecting functional requirements for an application
- validating the requirements that have been collected (note: validation is often overlooked, much to everyone's regret)
- demonstrating various commercial products to the users and gathering feedback as to which products seem to be most usable
- showing users the results of early portions of development or a prototype and collecting feedback on the progress to date
- sitting through long, tense meetings in which users complain that their requirements are not being met and the project manager discusses the principle of "scope creep" and why it's bad
- training users
- answering questions for users, either occasionally or (if you work on a help desk) as the primary activity of your job

Basically, it's unavoidable that you'll spend a significant amount of your time working with the people who will use the things you build or support. But consider the opposite: suppose you were to avoid or minimize the types of interactions just listed, in effect working in a vacuum based on best guesses and ill-defined lists of requirements, with no interaction between receiving those lists and delivering an application to the boos and hisses of "this isn't what we wanted!"

In fact, you might find yourself working in an IT organization where the leaders have a philosophy of "we know what the users want better than they do" and you are quickly exposed to the tensions of the long-running IT-user wars. While it's true that some users don't do a very good job of relating the details of their needs and the IT folks have to do some filling in the blanks to flesh out those requirements, the most effective environments are ones in which there is an ongoing, regular dialogue between the user community and the IT organization. Absent these regular communications, inefficiencies creep into the development process and quickly escalate to become major impediments to a company's effectiveness.

COLLECTING FUNCTIONAL REQUIREMENTS

Recall the example I mentioned at the beginning of the chapter about meeting with people from the career services department for a class project. Basically, you do the same thing—only on a (usually) larger scale—when collecting requirements for a real world project.

Note that the heading of this section is "Collecting *Functional* Requirements." For most readers, the type of requirements they will find themselves collecting in the early stages of their careers will be functionally oriented . . . that is, items that, if successfully implemented, will support business processes. Distinguish functional requirements from other types of requirements: performance, system availability, and storage capacity, for example.

Think back to a college days example, if you can recall one, where the instructor tells your team to pick an on-campus department for which you'll do your class project. So your team selects the career services department, you schedule an initial meeting, and the department head says, "You know, we could use an interview scheduling system on the campus intranet."

But then what? Where do you begin? Did you and your teammates just wander back to the computer lab and, based on what you think might be useful, start coding?

Well, I hope you scheduled a follow-up meeting in which you sat down with people from the department and began by asking a question along these lines: "Okay, so what should this interview scheduling system look like and what should it do?"

The question in the preceding paragraph—or, more precisely, a variation of that question customized for whatever application it is for which you're collecting requirements—is probably the most important question you can ask anyone in the course of your real world computer work. That question should catalyze a discussion about *high-level requirements* such as "a member of the career services department needs to be able to enter information about the companies that will be on campus" and "students need to be able to sign up for interviews."

Now maybe the person stating those high-level requirements thinks that's enough for you to go on, but it isn't. Consider:

- Who in the career services department can enter company information. Anyone? Certain people?
- What exact data about the companies needs to be entered aside from the company name? The name of the interviewer? Phone numbers? What else?
- How about the exact interview locations . . . who sets them up? Can they be changed? By whom?
- Is there a limit to the number of interviews for which any one student can sign up?
- Is it the responsibility of students to make sure that they don't sign up for two interviews at the same time, or should the system catch that?

It is *your* responsibility to guide the users. You'll help them along the path, from stating high-level requirements and an overall "mission" for the application to the many, many *detailed requirements* that must be known to be certain that the system will successfully support the processes it needs to.

Be prepared for griping and complaining from users when they suddenly realize that more than just a few high-level statements are needed, that in fact they'll have to give *significant* time and effort if the project is to be successful. In fact, the paradox you'll find yourself in sooner or later is that the users who complain that you're taking up too much of their time for requirements collection will be the first people to complain should you deliver an application that doesn't meet their needs. If they refuse to adequately participate in the requirements collection process and you must use your best guesses to guide you, then (bluntly stated) that's their fault. If, however, you (as a team) didn't bother to seek a sufficient level of user participation in the process, then it's *your* fault.

So make sure that you understand the importance of working side by side with users as early as possible in the development process. If you're the project manager, then it's largely up to you to ensure adequate interaction. If you can't arrange this, it's your job to immediately hand the issue up to your management. If you're a team member who is participating in the process of collecting functionality requirements, then over time you need to acquire a feel for the types of questions to ask and also sort of a sixth sense for the pieces of information that are being left out so you can effectively facilitate the process. It will take awhile, perhaps a project or two, but eventually you'll become pretty proficient at requirements collection activity.

VALIDATING REQUIREMENTS

Just as important as collecting requirements—functionality *or* systems-related (that is, performance, availability, capacity, and the like)—is validating those requirements. Every project will have features and capabilities you've collected that either:

1. are incorrect, possibly because the person who gave you that information was wrong or maybe because you or someone else transcribed the information incorrectly,

2. are incomplete,

3. have changed since they were collected,

4. might still be valid but their priority has changed, or

5. are somehow affected by external factors such as budget cuts, a new networking infrastructure, or a change in management.

So it's imperative that a *formal* review of all requirements be scheduled in which *all users* participate and verify, in writing, that what is on the list of requirements is correct and should be included in the system that's being built. Or, when any of the previous situations (changing priorities, misunderstandings, etc.) occur—and they will—they are noted, discussed, and resolved at that time or as soon as possible afterward.

It's important to keep in mind that validating requirements can often be a tense, confrontational process. If, for whatever reason, a thorough job of collecting requirements was not done and there are gaping holes and serious errors in what has been gathered, the users will often feel as if the IT folks messed up big-time, while the IT folks are likely to vent their frustration at the lack of participation by the users.

So be prepared for some tense times. Whatever you do, don't lose your temper and loudly point out all the times that meetings you tried to schedule were canceled or cut short and how many times one particular user changed his or her mind about the detailed requirements. Keep your temper in check, regardless of the role (project manager or developer) you're filling on this project.

PRODUCT DEMONSTRATION AND EVALUATION

If the project on which you're working might require the use of commercial software products—a report writer through which users will create queries and reports on their own, for example—then it's imperative that product usability be determined for the candidate products. By usability, I mean:

- ease of use
- online-accessible help
- consistency and correctness of answers
- the "bugginess" of a product
- performance and response time

It's important to remember that you should *lead* users through the evaluation process, not make the decisions yourself. You may have your own preferences from past experiences or from what you've learned through your own research (more on that in a moment). Maybe you have contacts at one or more product vendors, such as friends from college or former co-workers. But you need to keep your role in mind and handle your interactions accordingly. Be objective in pointing out both the good features *and* the flaws of all products under consideration. You don't want to get in a position where you're viewed as a biased advocate for one particular product, especially one with obvious flaws.

WARNING

DO YOUR RESEARCH on the Internet and by talking with the salespeople from the vendors, but by all means, make sure you and the users do adequate amounts of hands-on evaluation before making any decisions. Vendors are notorious for, shall we say, "overstating" their products' capabilities. Don't go solely on what you're told or what you read; make sure that you see things with your own eyes and try them out yourself.

Maintaining your credibility as an impartial, open-minded IT professional is important in these situations. It's the users who have to work with the selection that is made, and odds are that some business organization is going to pay a lot of money for product licenses. You *don't* want to be the person everyone points to and says, "There's the person who recommended we buy that awful product that everyone has so much difficulty using!" (Talk about a career-stalling move!)

GATHERING APPLICATION FEEDBACK

No matter how thorough a job you do collecting and validating requirements, there is still a big difference between lists of features and actually seeing those capabilities on a PC screen as part of an application. Maybe your group has developed a prototype through which user feedback will be gathered, or maybe you show the users the results from the first milestone during the development phase. Regardless, you may find yourself engaged in a "show and tell" effort in which users will try out the features and note what they like and don't like; what seems to be missing; ways in which items on the screen should be rearranged; and other changes they would like to see.

As previously noted regarding requirements validation, it's imperative to handle these sessions professionally, no matter how much the spirit of cooperation seems to be breaking down because key users are displeased with what they're seeing. If you're in a position of authority on the project team (that is, the PM), then calmly try to resolve the issues on the spot accordingly or, if they seem to be too serious, schedule a meeting to do so. If you're a developer or other member of the team, follow the lead of your PM; answer questions; volunteer information; and refer to your notes (but be careful not to do a finger-pointing routine).

TRAINING

Training users in how to use a just-completed application can be one of the most rewarding experiences you'll have as a computer professional—showing off the fruits of your labors, if you will—or it can be a totally disappointing situation in which you find out that even though you successfully developed an application, it won't do what the users need it to do.

On the positive side, users may absolutely love what your team has delivered and by being the person training them in how to use the system, you can win yourself some favorable exposure as "one of those IT people who did such a great job." Even if you're not the primary trainer and you're supporting the training classes, make sure that you're responsive to questions about features—including those that might not be included because they were left off as lower priority—and, generally, try to make the training sessions a pleasant experience.

Keep in mind that many of the people sitting in a training class have had nothing to do with requirements collection, requirements validation, or checking out products and prototypes. Very often, an application's success is determined not by its technical correctness but by whether or not it's effectively used as part of business operations. And, usually, training is the gateway to successful application usage.

SUPPORT

If your job entails you working in a help desk setting, you will find yourself in constant communication with users . . . not during development, as in the discussion so far in this chapter, but during systems operations.

It's important to be able to distinguish among the various types of calls (or intranet-delivered support requests) that you'll receive. Some may be rudimentary "how does this work?" or "How do I (do something)?" types of requests. Responsiveness is important, but not necessarily mission critical.

Other communications will be more serious: problem reports, system crashes, unexplained erroneous results, and so on. It's important that *you* not be viewed as a bottleneck in your organization's problem-solving process. Make sure you know all of the policies and procedures of problem resolution and how to get to the right level those items that you can't handle yourself. You should know all of this if you work on a help desk; after all, it's your job! Don't procrastinate in doing what you're supposed to do. Users have long memories and you don't want to be known as the help desk analyst no one wants to get when reporting a problem because you're so slow and incompetent.

SUMMARY

In principle, your interactions with the user community of your organization should be identical to your dealings with your IT colleagues: professional, cordial, and focused on the success of your company.

But it's important to note that over the years—more than 30 years, to be exact—an atmosphere of distrust and animosity has grown up between the IT and business worlds. It's not uncommon for some companies to have totally dysfunctional relationships with their should-be partners. In such a relationship, most executives and senior managers spend their time pointing fingers at each other, trying to place the blame for project failures (or even about-to-be failures; they don't even wait for projects to tank before getting their blame machines going).

The reason I mention this is that very often, junior IT professionals can become casualties in this business-blame war. I'm certainly not advocating that you spend your working days watching over your shoulder (though I would certainly watch out for signs that something may be amiss, as discussed in Chapter 8). You *should*—make that *must*—perform at your absolute peak when working with users. Basically, you want to use your know-how to help them to help you to help them succeed. (Got all that? Read it again if you'd like but basically, you want to work in a spirit of cooperation and partnership.)

CHAPTER 12

GRADUATE SCHOOL: HOW TO DO IT <u>RIGHT</u>

INTRODUCTION

I'm a strong believer that your career success is strongly and positively influenced by pursuing a graduate degree. It's true that there is a certain multibillionaire who dropped out of college and never finished an undergraduate degree, and so the lack of a master's degree (or a bachelor's degree, for that matter) hasn't exactly been a barrier to success. And then there is the newest generation of people who begin companies in dorm rooms and pretty much have their hands full running successful companies and keeping track of hundreds of millions of dollars worth of stock options, so they just don't have time for graduate school.

But for the rest of us—the other (by my guess) 99.995 percent of us computer professionals on whom fate doesn't shine quite so brightly and so quickly—career success often comes about the old-fashioned way . . . you earn it over time.[1] And an important factor in career success is, very often, an advanced degree of some type.

In this chapter, we'll discuss some of the important decisions you'll face as you contemplate pursuing graduate education, such as:

- deciding what your objectives are in pursuing additional education
- the tradeoffs between full-time and part-time programs
- choosing a school and a program
- additional activities, such as teaching and research, that can greatly enhance the quality of your educational experience
- the financial aspects of returning to school
- deciding if a doctoral degree is for you
- re-entering the work force
- executive education programs (looking ahead to later in your career)

THE REASONING BEHIND GRADUATE EDUCATION

It's important to clearly understand your reasoning behind any decision to pursue graduate education. Simply having an idea that "I want to get my master's degree" or "I want to go back to school" may catalyze you into contemplating and planning for graduate school. Still, you run the risk of having a somewhat less than pleasant experience unless you gain some insight into the reasons why the thought popped into your head. Consider the brief discussions in the following sections and think about which one most applies to you.

---

[1] Probably not many of you associate a variation of this phrase with the old Smith Barney commercials from the 1980s with John Houseman, the distinguished actor, saying that "Smith Barney makes money the old-fashioned way . . . they ear-r-r-n it" (he draws out the word "earn" for dramatic effect). I just wanted to mention this anyway because if you happen to be watching Nick at Nite's TV Land some day and they run a retromercial (old commercial) with this particular Smith Barney ad, don't think I plagiarized that advertisement or anything . . . I just believe strongly in "creative recycling with appropriate acknowledgments."

KNOWLEDGE ACQUISITION

Arguably, the "purest" motivation for graduate school is the pursuit of knowledge above and beyond what you currently possess. For example, your undergraduate degree in computer science taught you rudimentary knowledge about operating systems and compilers, and you've spent the first three years of your career working at a large software vendor as a junior member of the team working on a new version of their flagship operating system. You decide that you like this particular area of technology, but you feel you are stagnating in your current job since you're mostly doing testing and quality assurance (QA) functions. You'd like to advance to a more senior role, but you realize that you just don't have the same breadth and depth of experience and knowledge about the latest advances in operating system architecture as the company's senior members.

The answer (or part of it): a graduate degree in computer science at a school with a program that includes several acclaimed courses in advanced operating system architecture and technology. A year and a half or two years later, you'll be armed with additional knowledge that can help qualify you for more senior roles at the same employer or perhaps elsewhere.

Sometimes the objective of knowledge acquisition has an aspect of cross-training. For example, your undergraduate degree might be in a business-oriented information systems program, and you parlay that academic background into several postcollege years working as a systems analyst. You realize, though, that there are many, many aspects of the underlying technologies for the applications you're working with that you don't fully understand. In many ways, you feel as you do when you drive your car but don't know what's going on under the hood. A possible path is to pursue a graduate degree in computer science where you can learn more about the "under-the-hood" aspects of computing: hardware architecture, systems programming and architecture, software internals, and other areas of computing technology that can better prepare you for career growth and success.

Another popular variation of the cross-training approach to education is to pursue a master's of business administration (MBA) degree to augment your technology knowledge and skills with business acumen as you prepare to move ahead into management and leadership roles.

In general, your pursuit of knowledge through graduate education should be accomplished in such a manner that when you complete your course of study, you are as close as possible to the goal of personal knowledge and career progress that you set *before* you begin studying.

VOICE OF EXPERIENCE

GRADUATE EDUCATION with an objective of knowledge acquisition does not necessarily have to result in you receiving an additional degree. For example, you may decide that you'd simply like to take a few university courses to supplement your current base of knowledge. Or maybe you've already received a master's degree and you don't want to pursue a doctoral program, but there are some additional courses you'd like to take. That's what I did. I received my master's degree back in 1982 from the University of Arizona in Management Information Systems, and later, in 1989 while teaching part-time at the University of Denver, I took several graduate courses in artificial intelligence and medical information systems, spurred by the work I was then doing at Digital Equipment Corporation . . . but did not do so as part of a degree program.

CAREER ADVANCEMENT

Closely related to—but different from—knowledge acquisition is graduate education as a means to career advancement. Some companies pay higher salaries to people with advanced degrees or even require an advanced degree for certain positions and won't even consider someone without one, regardless of talent. Just check out the Sunday classifieds and look for positions being advertised with phrases like "master's degree strongly preferred" or "ideal candidate will have an advanced degree in business or computer science."

The reason I make a distinction between the objectives of career advancement and knowledge acquisition is that one could occur without the other. That is, you could earn an MBA degree solely to qualify for a management position at your current employer. Yet, when you're honest with yourself, you admit that in the degree program, you really didn't learn all that much about marketing, finance, and management. But nevertheless, you have that degree tucked safely under your arm and you've "punched your ticket" into the management ranks at your company.

In contrast, you might earn a graduate degree in art history, philosophy, world history or any other area and learn a great deal . . . that has nothing to do with your chosen profession and does absolutely nothing for your career advancement. So is a "career advancement degree" better? Not necessarily . . . thus the need for understanding what you're seeking out of additional education.

Sometimes, you might enroll in a particular degree program to fulfill a particular career ambition, and this degree is a necessity (or very close to it). Suppose you'd like to work in the international organization of a large corporation and work your way up the ladder through the international ranks. Earning a degree in international management from a well-known program such as Thunderbird (in Phoenix, Arizona) may be the means to achieving your objective . . . without such a degree, your company might not consider you for such an opportunity.

CAREER REORIENTATION

Maybe you work at a bank and your undergraduate degree is in finance. You've spent the first four years of your career acting as a liaison to a group of IT folks who develop and maintain applications for your organization. You've decided that computer technology is more interesting than finance, and would like to switch your career direction.

One way to do that is to earn a master's degree in a technology-oriented program and then start looking for a position as an applications developer or systems analyst. A "natural" transition strategy would be to enroll in a business-oriented MIS program (but that isn't to say that a computer science master's degree isn't also a possibility).

THE FULL-TIME AND PART-TIME OPTIONS

Perhaps the toughest choice you'll have to make about an advanced degree is whether you should enroll in a full-time study program or work on your degree on a part-time basis, perhaps in the evenings and on weekends. Which option is better for you?

The answer is that always-popular "it all depends." Depends on what, you'd like to know, right? Read on.

FULL-TIME PROGRAMS

First of all, let me state that I'm biased towards pursuing full-time graduate study, if at all possible. It isn't so much the classes you'll take and what you'll learn (at least on the surface). You can take a course in database technology in a full-time program just as easily as on nights and weekends.

Rather, the big advantage to being a full-time graduate student is the opportunity for additional learning *outside* of the classroom, through teaching and research. (This is discussed later in this chapter.) You might take three or four classes every semester—say 15 hours of class time every week—but spend another 30 hours weekly doing advanced research in your area of specialization or teaching classes and polishing your presentation skills. All in all, being a full-time graduate student can be a rewarding experience for more than just the classroom knowledge you acquire.

The tradeoff for most people, though, is the financial impact of not being in the workforce during that time, something we'll also discuss later in the chapter. Very often, it's impractical for someone to drop out of the workforce for several years, given personal and family obligations (though, as we'll discuss later, options exist today using the Internet and other networking technologies to keep some real world income flowing while you're in school).

THE PART-TIME STUDY PROGRAM

Working on your master's degree on a part-time basis can give you the best of both worlds. You can still earn your salary—while performing your regular job—and at the same time take courses in the evenings and/or on weekends. Some companies permit you to take courses during regular working hours if you make up the work time through a flexible schedule.

And best of all, most employers will pay part or all of your tuition and other educational expenses (such as books and lab fees). So wouldn't part-time graduate study always be the best option for you?

Well, the primary downside to such a program is that you will find your schedule even more packed and overloaded than usual in today's fast-paced business climate. Imagine working your usual ten- or twelve-hour days and adding six, eight, maybe even ten hours of class time every week or two (more on that in a minute), plus time for doing reading and programming assignments and . . . ah, you get the idea.

So think very, very hard about the commitment of time and energy and the effect on *both* your professional and personal life. Do you travel heavily, meaning that your classroom attendance will be sporadic? (The good news is that many schools now offer programs over the Internet or other correspondence-style formats, so travel and graduate school are not necessarily as incompatible as in the past.)

Take a look at the format of degree programs you're considering. Some schools offer traditional classroom meeting times of, for example, one night each week for three hours, lasting ten weeks. Others divide courses up into smaller "chunks" and offer three hours once a week for only five weeks. Still others opt for an intensive every-other-week format: Friday evening, all day Saturday, and a half-day Sunday, every other week.

YOUR INSTRUCTORS

Often, you have no say whatsoever in who your instructors are. Particularly if you're enrolled in a part-time degree program, you often find only one section available for a course in which you want to enroll, so your instructor is whoever has been assigned to teach that course for that semester or quarter. You have to hope that the

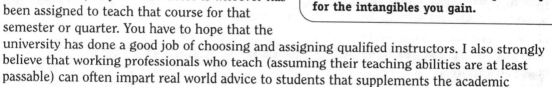

THOUGH IN THIS DAY of the Internet and videoconferencing it's conceivable that you could enroll in a program in which you actually never set foot in a classroom, I'd recommend trying to select a program in which you have at least some personal contact with your instructors and others in your classes. Keep in mind that group projects can be tough for people who never actually meet in person, and the results are often superficial at best. Maybe I'm old-fashioned, but I have a preference for classroom-based education, primarily for the intangibles you gain.

university has done a good job of choosing and assigning qualified instructors. I also strongly believe that working professionals who teach (assuming their teaching abilities are at least passable) can often impart real world advice to students that supplements the academic aspects of their course work.

At the same time, there's something to be said for enrolling in a full-time computer science degree program at Stanford or Carnegie-Mellon University or another prestigious school and having instructors who are world-renowned academicians, and maybe even have won a Nobel Prize. Maybe they don't quite have that "from the trenches" perspective that a part-time instructor has, but you can certainly argue that you'll receive a world-class education from such individuals.

So don't automatically assume that if you're enrolled in a part-time program your instructors will be inferior to those teaching as part of a full-time degree program. At the same time, don't assume that just because you're enrolled in a full-time program, you'll unfailingly take courses from world-renowned, excellent instructors. Consider that some very bright people have, shall we say, a bit of difficulty in communicating their knowledge in classroom settings (no different than an undergraduate program). If possible, use the same professor selection techniques you used as an undergraduate.

SELECTING THE RIGHT SCHOOL AND PROGRAM FOR YOU

The operative words in the title of this section are "for you." Let's leave aside the part-time vs. full-time decision for the purposes of this section, realizing that some schools only offer one or the other option.

So what have you decided about your motivations for working on a graduate degree? Recall our discussion earlier in this chapter about different reasons and the importance of understanding *yours*. Is your passion database management systems (DBMSs) and you want to learn as much as possible about the inner workings of DBMS products? Then consider

CAREER TIPS **BUILD ON THE KNOWLEDGE** you've already gained from your self-assessment exercises, as discussed in Chapter 1. If you've decided that you're more of an application development type than a systems programming and internals type, then concentrate on MIS or an MBA program.

programs with a very strong emphasis—maybe even a formal concentration—on DBMS technology. Have you decided to pursue an MBA because you want to do complicated financial applications for a Wall Street investment bank after earning your degree? Then concentrate on getting admitted to a top-notch MBA program at Stanford, Wharton, or another top-tier university that is a recognized gateway into the Wall Street financial community.

Don't just assume that any old university or any old program will do. You may be geographically constrained—say you can't relocate and there's only one major university within an hour of where you live—but you can still decide whether you should study computer science or management information systems, for example.

TEACHING AND RESEARCH ACTIVITIES

Earlier in this chapter, I mentioned my belief that classroom educational experience is enhanced by such outside work as teaching and research. I was fortunate that when I was in the MIS graduate program at the University of Arizona, I spent a year as a teaching assistant (I taught COBOL programming, data structures, and a course on the role of computers in society), and then a year as a research assistant in which I did early research into computer-aided software engineering (CASE) tools. When CASE was popular in the 1980s, my experience working with that area of technology was very helpful in landing me at Digital Equipment Corporation where I was initially a CASE tool developer. I moved on to distributed database management systems, which were the precursor to data warehousing. Maybe this is a bit of a stretch, but I think that my graduate school research into CASE led me to my emphasis in data warehousing, which is the area I've emphasized in recent years.

So if you've made the commitment to earn your degree on a full-time basis, look into teaching and research as activities to enhance your academic experience. You won't be sorry.

FINANCIAL CONSIDERATIONS OF FULL-TIME GRADUATE EDUCATION

In this section, I'll briefly touch on some of the items you need to consider should you decide to leave the work force and enroll full-time in a course of study. Basically, these are the same items you need to consider for an undergraduate program, so nothing should be a surprise to you.

1. **YOUR SAVINGS AND INVESTMENTS**—Take a good look at your savings and investments and see if you have enough money to fund your stint in academia.

2. **OTHER FINANCIAL RESOURCES**—Assistance from parents and other family members (including your spouse); scholarships; grants . . . start early in determining other financial resources that may help you.

3. TUITION COST—As you probably remember from checking out schools before your undergraduate years, tuition costs vary widely from one school to another. How expensive will the place you've chosen to attend be?

4. LIVING EXPENSES AND FAMILY OBLIGATIONS—Where will you live? How much will it cost? Is your spouse earning enough to cover living expenses? How about your children? Make sure you put together a budget that will cover the entire time you're in school and a few months afterwards so that you don't run into financial problems.

5. ON-CAMPUS INCOME OPPORTUNITIES—The good news about being a teaching assistant or research assistant is that you get paid to do it. Check out other opportunities also available on campus.

6. OUTSIDE EARNING OPPORTUNITIES—
There's always part-time computer programming or consulting (see Chapter 16) as a means to earn money during graduate school. And as I briefly mentioned earlier, the era of the Internet gives you unprecedented channels through which you can earn income from consulting; electronic commerce (for example, selling "things" over the Internet); remote contract software development; or other services.

WARNING **BE CAREFUL** not to overload yourself with revenue-generation opportunities (consulting or programming assignments, and the like) to the point where you compromise your education and learning. You've decided to attend school full-time for a reason, and one of the tradeoffs is that you'll be spending significantly more time each week working on your assignments and other academic matters. Trying to fully replace your regular work-world salary through alternative channels *may* be possible, but the chances of overload are pretty significant.

OTHER POST-GRADUATE EDUCATIONAL OPPORTUNITIES

This section will discuss other educational paths you might consider at some point after earning your master's degree, specifically a doctoral degree and, later in your career, attending an executive education program.

THE DOCTORAL DEGREE

If your career aspirations are to be a university professor, or if you've decided that you'd like to focus on research-oriented work, you pretty much need a doctoral degree. In the case of teaching, nearly all tenure-track positions at universities require a doctorate. For research, many companies with formal research organizations want the leaders in those groups to have doctoral degrees (it certainly doesn't hurt).

You also have probably run across people in the business world who have a Ph.D. (or equivalent doctoral degree) but who've chosen "regular" career paths rather than research or academia. Certainly, should you decide to (and have the resources to) study for your Ph.D. after finishing your master's degree, you won't be hurting your career at all. But before committing to the time and additional expenses of a doctoral program, make sure that's something you really want to do.

EXECUTIVE EDUCATION PROGRAMS

Later in your career, after you've already arrived at the executive ranks at your place of employment, you may have the opportunity to attend an executive education program. These programs, typically sponsored by major universities, are intended to broaden the knowledge base of senior executives in such areas as international management; the latest management trends; how to manage very large organizations; and related subjects. Essentially, you might look at a program of this type as an MBA enhancer through which even executives who already hold MBAs can update and build on their academic backgrounds with information necessary to assume additional senior leadership roles.

REENTERING THE WORK FORCE

Take a look at the discussion in Chapter 1 about looking for a job after college. Basically, all of the same items apply. You may recall, too, that I noted several points where someone with prior real world experience—such as a person about to receive a graduate degree—should build on that experience as part of the job search.

SUMMARY

No matter what path you choose—full-time or part-time, MIS or computer science or an MBA—the responsibility for getting the most out of a graduate degree program lies with you. As with most other aspects of your career, the more proactive and insightful you are about the choices you make, the more likely you are to have a rewarding experience. Conversely, should you haphazardly enroll in any old program just to get a set of initials that begins with "M" for your résumé, you may be in for a disappointment. So pay attention. Do your homework and plan ahead.

INTRODUCTION

Here are a couple of items that I occasionally ponder:

- In the mid-1980s, Ada (the emerging Department of Defense standard programming language) burst on the scene, then fizzled. Later, in the late 1990s, Java was introduced and it sizzled . . .
- The OS/2 operating system has mostly faded away, while Windows NT gains more prominence as time passes . . .
- The Internet is one of the most popular, pervasive technology movements today . . . but why didn't Videotext (circa 1980) take off like the Internet has?

It's not important if you've never heard of, or only have a passing familiarity with, Ada, OS/2, and Videotext. The important point is that some languages, technologies, products, and architectures not only catch on, but become extremely popular and widely used, fueling a generation of application development and product creation (not to mention resulting economic growth). Other areas, even those that are technically sound, fizzle, flop, and fail.

Why? And, more importantly, how does this affect you and your career? In this chapter we'll discuss this aspect of the fizzle-or-sizzle question to better prepare you to take advantage of opportunities that come your way and, just as important, to avoid traps that can cause you to waste a lot of time and energy learning about technology areas that never pan out.

KNOW WHAT'S OUT THERE

So how do you even learn what's out there before trying to predict if it will pan out? I strongly recommend that any computer professional at least be familiar with the names and terms that float around, whether or not your job currently requires you to work in that area. For example, if your area of specialization is data warehousing, you should have a pretty good idea of the major database management system (DBMS) products and front-end query tools and other products related to that discipline. But you should also have at least a cursory knowledge of asynchronous transfer mode (ATM) and frame relay from the networking world, the lightweight directory access protocol (LDAP) from the directory services realm, the Java programming language, Active X, and so on.

Basically, you want to establish a passing familiarity with these terms and phrases and at least know the area of technology to which they apply (for example, understanding that Java is not a DBMS product and that the initials "ATM" aren't only for an automatic teller machine at the bank). How do you do that?

- Spend a significant portion of your time on the Internet and browsing periodicals.
- Engage in some "geek talk" with your colleagues and share knowledge among yourselves, picking up little tidbits along the way.
- Learn what the growing trends are in technology areas related to *and outside of* those with which you're currently working. For example, if in the mid-1980s you spent most of your time programming in dBASE III+ (the most successful of the earliest PC-based database packages),

you should not only have been aware of the rise of Clipper and FoxPro—the then-up-and-coming PC databases that challenged dBASE in the marketplace—but also local area network (LAN) technology, which radically changed the face of PC-based applications by making multi-user applications much more robust than single-user, single-machine applications from the early days of PCs.

- Watch for words and phrases that seem to not only appear frequently, but make their way from the technology press into mainstream media. For example, client/server computing was very much a technology-focused approach in the mid-1980s, but by the late 1980s publications in the business world and in the general media were touting client/server computing as a major wave of the future . . . and they were right.

- Watch out, too, for overexuberance and what seem like too-good-to-be-true statements in all media forms (technology, business, and mainstream). With client/server computing, much of the media discussion predicted the imminent death of the mainframe at the hands of networks of PCs. First, while we certainly have many client/server applications running today, the early days of client/server computing were filled with extremely high (more than 80 percent) project failure rates. It took a long time for the underlying technology and methodologies to catch up with the hype. Second, client/server certainly hasn't meant the death of the mainframe computer at all . . . look at how well IBM has done in recent years in moving mainframe computers into the world of distributed computing.

YOUR CURRENT ROLE GUIDES WHAT YOU NEED TO DO

So how important is all of this, anyway? Shouldn't you just keep your attentions focused on becoming the best Visual Basic or C++ programmer that you can, and when new technologies take hold, you'll eventually find yourself working with them?

For many of you, this "don't-bother-me-now" philosophy may indeed be the best approach, especially in the earliest stages of your career. Do you really have to worry, for example, about whether or not relational databases that are extended to also store multimedia information (voice and video, for example) are really ready for prime time? Maybe not. If your focus and attentions are on an extremely narrow area of technology—say software development in Microsoft-centric environments—then perhaps your attentions are best served by learning as much as you can about Visual Basic, the latest version of Microsoft SQL Server, and other products and technologies in that space.

Yet what about jumping onto new technologies quickly? Consider Java, for example. If you're focusing all your efforts on Visual Basic, should you also learn Java even if you won't be using it right now? I'd argue that you should make the time to at least learn the basics of Java so you can broaden your horizons and, possibly, give yourself more career options. The technology world is famous for its rapid shifts that embrace new approaches and new technologies and leave other areas in the dust. Consider the growth of the Internet. If you had poked around with web browsers in the early days when there really wasn't much on the Internet, you had an advantage over your peers who perhaps didn't start working with HTML, HTTP, and other Internet technologies until recently.

The take-an-early-look approach is hardly foolproof. Consider the story of the Ada programming language. Back in the early 1980s, the U.S. Department of Defense, concerned about the many different languages in which its systems were implemented, decided to standardize software development on a single programming language as quickly as possible. The leading languages of the time (COBOL, FORTRAN, BASIC, C, and others) were rejected for one reason or another, and a new language was developed that eventually became Ada. The language would be standardized. Compilers would be certified by the Department of Defense; and all those in the defense community, military and contractor alike, would shortly be working in the same language on all platforms. (Or so the story went . . .)

So far, so good, especially for those who jumped on the Ada bandwagon very early, even before vendors had built compilers and the language was ready to use. Consider that this was all occurring in the early 1980s during the Reagan administration defense buildup, and defense spending was booming. Those who set themselves up as early practitioners and "experts" in Ada, even those with only a few years of real world experience behind them, quickly became the gurus of the Ada world to whom people flocked for advice. After all, Ada was mandated as the language of choice, right?

To make a long story sort of short, a number of factors—some technology-related, others external (remember the lessons of Chapter 8?)—caused the entire Ada movement to fizzle. Regarding technology, most of the earliest certified Ada compilers were, shall we say, "challenged" in terms of taking advantage of the language's more advanced capabilities, such as multitasking. The compilers were buggy; many Ada systems were implemented in the earliest client/server systems that had their own problems from immature networking and workstation technology. The list goes on. Many defense organizations began to request waivers from using Ada and before long, the standard language had become just another option in the pool of implementation languages. By the early 1990s, Ada was still being used . . . but often so were C, COBOL, and other languages.

On the external side, the mid-1980s brought about a sudden slowdown in defense spending, meaning that armies of Ada-trained programmers soon found themselves looking for employment outside the world of military and defense applications. Despite the belief by early Ada proponents that the Ada language was so robust that it would soon become the de facto language of choice for commercial software development, that never happened. C, C++, Visual Basic, and COBOL were preferred.

So, what's the lesson here? Simply this: if you had been a software developer in the early 1980s (as I was) and had decided that the Ada language was something you should learn—and quickly—because it was the wave of the future (as I did), you may have learned a tool that helped you for several years in your career . . . but stopped after Ada faded from the scene. In contrast, if you had decided that the C language had more potential for the long haul and had concentrated your efforts on learning C (as I didn't) you would have gained a skill that years later would still be a viable, valuable asset in your personal toolkit.

Going back to the question I posed at the beginning of this section: how important is it for you to anticipate major new technology and product trends? The answer: it all depends on your time frame. If you're thinking short-term—what can I learn that will be valuable for the next year or two, even though it might be outdated shortly afterwards—then the answer is that it's not really important to look at longer-term trends. Just focus on what's hot at the moment, learn it as quickly as possible, use it if you can, and then move on.

However, if you want to try to build a career around a particular area of technology, then you do need to look at longer-term trends and their viability (and we'll discuss some tips and tricks later in this chapter) and, essentially, make a bet as to what you should invest considerable time in.

Now, consider yourself pondering the same question later in your career, perhaps when you're an independent consultant: is anticipating these trends important? I would answer, "absolutely." For example, if you had around ten years of experience in 1994 or 1995 and were an experienced application and system architect, deciding that Internet technologies would be usable in the application world would have given you a tremendous advantage over late adapters who perhaps felt that the Internet was just a fad for online advertising. You might have noticed that the word "Internet" was popping up all over the place in the media. Perhaps you started hearing the term "intranet" and read about companies that were deploying inside-the-company, smaller-scale internets and were not only using them for bulletin-boards and e-mail but were dabbling with "thin client" systems built around web servers.

And as you study all of this, and you read that 80 percent (or some other high number) of Fortune 500 CIOs stated in a recent survey that they would deploy at least one intranet environment in the coming year, perhaps you decide that this Internet stuff is here to stay for a while. And eventually, as I'll discuss later in the chapter, you learn that Microsoft has decided that Internet technologies are something that they believe is an overwhelming trend and they're making major investments in the area.

So armed with all of this information, you decide to proactively reorient your skill base by learning as much as possible about Internet technologies. Before you know it, you're a member of the most popular club in the computing world, those who are using Internet technologies for intranet application development, extranets (cross-company intranets), electronic commerce, supply chain applications, and many other business application areas.

TIPS AND TRICKS

Okay, you may be thinking; let's say for the sake of argument that being proactive about major technology trends is something you should do. But how? How can you avoid a situation like that described earlier about the Ada programming language, one in which even though you learn the language and maybe do a project or two, it will fade away and you'll have wasted your time?

Here are some tips and tricks for trying to figure out if something is for real or not. Keep in mind that these tidbits aren't 100 percent guaranteed, but by noting them you'll have a better idea of the viability (or lack thereof) of the many areas you might be pondering over the next five years.

BE CAUTIOUS OF STANDARDIZATION EFFORTS

Since the early 1980s, the information technology world has been hallmarked by numerous standardization efforts whereby different companies (usually hardware and/or software vendors) attempt to develop a common set of interface mechanisms through which their products can interoperate. Standardization picked up steam towards the end of the 1980s with the birth of the "open systems" movement, and many computer professionals tried to gain an edge in the then-tightening job market by proactively embracing some of the emerging standardization efforts.

Those who chose to invest their time and energy in one area in particular—the Distributed Computing Environment (DCE) model of the Open Software Foundation (OSF)—were rewarded when companies began to implement DCE-based applications in the early and mid-1990s. At the same time, another standardization effort of the OSF—the Distributed Management Environment (DME), for distributed systems management—faded quickly from the scene.

Still another competing open systems standardization effort was underway at the time, led by AT&T and built around trying to achieve a common UNIX platform (that organization was called UNIX International, or UI). UI efforts eventually converged with those of OSF.

So the point here is to think carefully about embracing a standardization effort as one in which you want to invest a significant amount of energy and time. Sometimes you get lucky (as in getting involved early in OSF DCE), but more often than not you'll wind up learning a lot about voluminous sets of specifications that themselves wind up never being implemented.

Be especially careful of efforts that *don't* involve one of the major companies in the computing industry (IBM, Microsoft, Oracle, Sun, etc.). The IT world in the past decade is littered with standardization efforts that involved 10 to 15 smaller software firms who attempted to band together and develop common interfaces and platforms in what is often, in hindsight, a last-ditch effort to build together a presence in their particular area of the computing marketplace that they were unable to do on their own. Between the intercompany politics and disputes, plus—very often—the lack of a solid business case, these types of standardization efforts aren't usually worth devoting a lot of your time to *unless* you work for one of those companies and your primary job is to represent your company and work with your counterparts from the other organizations. At least then you can always make contacts that could lead to a new job if the standardization effort—and your company—fails.

KNOW WHAT CAN BE DONE TODAY . . . AND WHAT CAN'T

As much as possible, you should have an idea of the technological validity—or lack thereof—of new products or computing models. Going back to the 1980s again, many vendors spent tens of millions of dollars trying to develop products in the distributed database and artificial intelligence spaces. Looking back at those times with the always-perfect 20-20 hindsight, the infrastructure and base technology (that is, network throughput, processor power and speed, disk capacity, etc.) were grossly inadequate for what the vendors were attempting to do. Jumping ahead to today, though, both of these areas are making comebacks in the emerging areas of virtual data warehousing and data mining, respectively.

So you should try to understand as much as possible about the inner workings of areas in which you're interested to try to determine whether or not they're viable. This is why it's so important to understand not only your areas of primary career emphasis, but also to have a broader understanding of related areas (networking, operating systems advances, languages and development environments, etc.). You can then better gauge whether or not a particular area of computing technology, one that really sounds like something everyone would want, is really likely to happen.

MATCH TECHNOLOGY AND PRODUCTS TO A SPECIFIC BUSINESS NEED

As you read about new technologies and products, try to envision *real* business needs for which they might be useful. Consider the Internet and web browser technology. Before web browsers appeared on the scene, the Internet was primarily the domain of highly technical IT professionals who moved from site to site through command-line interfaces. When browsers first appeared on the scene along with HTML-based graphics, one could easily envision the World Wide Web that we know and love today even though that might be several years off, particularly the emerging area of electronic commerce.

Looking back almost 20 years though, the idea of videotext was very similar to today's basic web technology. So why didn't videotext grow dramatically like web technology? There are several reasons, one of which was technological immaturity and another the need for specialized equipment rather than "ordinary" PCs (remember that the late 1970s and early 1980s marked the birth of the PC, which was nothing like we have today in terms of capacity and performance power). But more importantly (in my opinion), there was never a clear business "mission" for which videotext could be used, which prevented companies and individuals from making large investments in that technology (unlike the Internet and electronic commerce).

WATCH WHAT MICROSOFT AND IBM DO

When IBM and Microsoft choose to embrace technologies, that's often a sign that there is something real that you should pay attention to. Consider the Internet and Microsoft's intensive (though some would argue belated) investments in rearchitecting their products into Internet-enabled offerings, or IBM, which embraced Java, to many signifying the "legitimacy" of that language. The big guys may not always be correct, but you can often take a lead by what they do.

SUMMARY

In the earliest days of your career in the computing world, this chapter may not have much significance to you. I fully realize that many of you may respond to this chapter's discussion with a few yawns. But eventually you'll find yourself at, as a popular song (circa 1998) might put it, "another turning point, a fork stuck in the road." The trade press will feature headlines screaming about revolutionary new technologies and products; your company may ask you whether or not you want to assume a new role in which you'll be focusing on new areas. And you'll have to decide whether or not it will be in *your* best interests to invest of your energies in some new programming language, or a new model for database management, or a new world-wide networking system that will challenge the Internet, or who knows what else. Unfortunately, you won't have a crystal ball that will tell you whether you'll jump into a hot new area and energize your career, or if you'll engage in a colossal waste of time. Still, if you follow the hints and tips presented in this chapter, you can slide the odds a bit in your favor as you decide.

INTRODUCTION

And suddenly, you find yourself working for the Wicked Boss of the West. ("Are you a good boss? Or a bad boss?") Your work days seem endless; you find yourself cringing every time you see that person walking your way, certain that yet another explosive tirade is about to be directed your way.

Or perhaps your boss isn't necessarily a tyrant . . . just incompetent. Group meetings last forever and never accomplish anything. On Monday you get a set of tasks that more often than not gets changed on Tuesday . . . and again on Wednesday. And then, to top everything off, you keep getting below-average salary increases (and no promotion, either) each time your performance is reviewed.

Like it or not, you will probably find yourself working for the boss from you-know-where at some point in your career . . . actually, change that to "at several points." In this chapter, we'll talk about these types of situations and what you can and should do . . . and also what you should *not* do.

But be forewarned. Much of the advice in this chapter is going to be along the lines of "stick it out" or "read Chapter 15 about looking for your next job." Because your boss is your boss . . . I know that's a statement of the obvious, but I'm trying to say that sometimes, there isn't much you can do other than pack it in and move on. Don't expect every tyrannical or incompetent boss to get his or her comeuppance and be relieved of a managerial role. Likewise, don't expect someone with a confrontational and ill-tempered style of management to suddenly realize that he or she should really adopt a kinder, gentler approach to dealing with employees.

But on that note, let's talk about this not-too-pleasant topic.

WHAT MAKES A BAD BOSS?

Actually, let's start this section by asking the opposite question: what makes a good boss?

Here's a relatively short answer: look at the seven principles of being a good manager that I included in Chapter 6. As a refresher, here's a list (without the accompanying discussion):

1. CONSISTENCY.

2. CREDIBILITY.

3. REALISTIC TASK ASSIGNMENTS AND DEADLINES.

4. COMMUNICATE CLEARLY.

5. BE ORGANIZED.

6. DON'T LET YOUR OWN WORK ASSIGNMENTS SUFFER.

7. DON'T BE AFRAID TO CHANGE YOUR MIND, BUT DON'T BACK DOWN FROM CONFRONTATION.

If you find yourself working for someone who consistently exhibits these characteristics in his or her interactions with you and your co-workers, then congratulations . . . and for your sake, hope that person remains your immediate boss for a long time.

But let's look at the flip side. Imagine that you work for someone who is disorganized; who buckles under pressure from his or her counterparts and consequently causes perpetual havoc in your work life as your assignments gyrate all over the place; and who constantly postures to place blame on you and other subordinates when problems occur, even though the fault really lies with you-know-who.

So a bad boss is more than just the tyrant, someone who frequently loses his or her temper and makes work life miserable. A bad boss could actually be someone with a pleasant demeanor, with whom you get along personally . . . but is doing such a poor job that *your* career progress will be compromised. Therefore, as we'll discuss in the next section, it's important to size up the situation so you know exactly what you're dealing with before you seek advice and try to figure out what you should do.

SIZING UP THE SITUATION

Sometimes, having a bad boss is a serious situation . . . and sometimes, it's not. How do you tell the difference? In this section, we'll look at some of the ways you can determine how serious the situation is.

WHAT IS YOUR STATE OF MIND?

First and foremost in your analysis of the situation is *your* state of mind. Do you toss and turn at night, thinking about the offenses of the day and worrying about what's going to come tomorrow? Do you wake up each morning and your first thought is usually, "I hate my job" (perhaps punctuated by a colorful adjective or two)?

Or is your psyche relatively unscathed? Do you have a few tense moments with your boss every couple of days that, once they pass, fade from your mind? It's important to take a step back from the situation at hand and really think about the effect on your life and mental health. (Also think about your physical health . . . stress-related ailments, for example.) By concentrating on coming up with an answer to the serious-or-not question about your state of mind you're on your way to sizing up the situation.

ARE YOU GETTING YOUR WORK DONE ON TIME?

All things considered, outside of your interactions with your boss (alone or with others, such as in endless meetings) are you getting your work done on schedule? Do you find yourself having to frequently backtrack because of your boss's actions, to tasks that you thought had been completed, resulting in you being constantly late in completing your assignments? If so, then your situation is more serious than if your work is progressing on schedule.

ARE YOU BEING TREATED APPROPRIATELY
AT PERFORMANCE REVIEW TIME?

How have your raises been . . . on par with or better than others, or lagging behind? Have you been passed over for a promotion that you should have received either because your boss didn't put you forward for one or perhaps he or she did, but was overruled by others within your company? You need to determine if your financial and career progression is suffering because of your boss's behavior or lack of clout within the company.

WHAT DOES YOUR BOSS'S BOSS(ES) THINK ABOUT HIM OR HER?

You might be guessing here or trying to read between the lines, but do you think your boss is respected by his or her direct manager? By other executives within the company? If the behavior and mannerisms of a problematic manager seem to be out of line with the philosophy and culture of other executives, changes could be coming soon, possibly including your boss being relieved of supervisory responsibilities (as discussed later in this chapter). Conversely, if your boss is considered one of the company's rising stars despite dysfunctional behavior with his or her subordinates, then it is unlikely that any behavior or organizational changes will be coming your way any time soon.

HOW LONG HAS YOUR BOSS BEEN IN THE JOB?

Is your boss a long-timer in the position he or she currently holds or relatively new in that role? A problematic manager who is new to the role could possibly (you hope) be yanked rather quickly for poor performance or behaving in contrast to the company's culture of employee relationships, while someone who is a long-timer may be relatively immune to being pulled. Though, in times when a company needs to retrench through layoffs or radical reorganization, long-timers might find themselves relieved of their positions one way or another if new senior management comes in. So there is not an immutable relationship between employment longevity and someone being entrenched in a position where he or she is wreaking havoc for you and your co-workers.

WHAT DO YOUR CO-WORKERS THINK ABOUT YOUR BOSS?

We'll cover the topic of what you should and shouldn't discuss with others about your problematic boss in a little bit. But chances are you've been picking up scuttlebutt from others about their experiences, if any, with your boss. Do others have the same problems that you're experiencing? Do you find yourself sitting in on conversations that are open gripe sessions about your boss's nastiness and/or incompetence? Or is it possible that you and you alone are experiencing the unpleasantness that has caused you to pay particular attention to this chapter? You want to get an idea of whether or not you're in this situation alone (or, perhaps, if maybe you're being overly sensitive to normal interactions, which is always possible). When we discuss resolution strategies, one of your options is to fight it out . . . and whenever possible, you don't want to do this alone.

HAVE THERE BEEN ANY CONFRONTATIONS YET?

And speaking of fighting it out, have you already tried to resolve the situation in a manner that has resulted in you confronting your boss about the problems you're facing? If so, what happened? If changes for the better occurred but didn't last, then you have a bit of ammunition on your side . . . anyone who attempts to correct his or her performance only to backslide is, by default, acknowledging that his or her behavior has been problematic. You can use this to your advantage if another confrontation occurs.

Or possibly you tried to effect changes by talking out the situation with your boss, only to be told that you don't know what you're talking about and, by the way, your working life is about to get even more unpleasant because obviously you can't stand the pressures of the real world and by the way . . .

You get the idea. Take stock of all past attempts at resolving the situation, including occasions when another executive intervened on behalf of you and your co-workers and tried to set things right. This way, you'll have some idea of what you might expect should confrontation be ahead of you.

IS THIS ONLY A SHORT-TERM SITUATION?

Perhaps your bad boss situation is with the project manager for the development effort to which you've been assigned, and you'll only be working under this PM's directions for the next two months. A short-term situation such as this is different than having a problematic "regular boss," that is, your manager for whom you'll be working for . . . well, who knows how long.

SEEK ADVICE...BUT BE CAREFUL!

One of the things you should do is try to figure out the breadth of the situation you're facing. Maybe your manager has taken a dislike to you for some reason, and all of his or her wrath is directed at you and you alone. Or possibly the boss from you-know-where is universally loathed by everyone in your organization, and when you're all together you can talk of nothing but the tirade of the day.

Whichever situation better describes what you're facing, you should probably seek advice from others about ways to handle the situation. So chat with your brother or your sister or another family member. Ask them what they'd do in your situation.

But you can probably guess that you should also seek advice from those who might have some particular insight into the personalities involved in your situation, such as your co-workers or maybe others who've worked for him or her in the past (maybe they've moved to another organization or left the company).

So by all means, speak to those who can shed some light on your experiences by comparing them with their own. You'll be able to find out if your situation is unique or shared, plus all kinds of other interesting little tidbits that can help you decide what course of action to pursue (as discussed in the next section).

But be careful! The last thing you want to happen is to confide in the wrong person and worsen the situation. Perhaps, in response to a "how's everything going for you?" question, you'll discuss the gory details of how much you dislike working for your boss with someone, only to find out that person worked with your boss at a previous employer and the two of them are relatively good friends. Asking such a person a question such as, "What should I do about this ogre?" is, shall we say, not a great idea.

So I would recommend letting others take the lead as you gather information about the situation and others' experiences. Don't volunteer too much information until you're absolutely certain that your conversations will be kept confidential.

RESOLUTION STRATEGIES

So after you gather all of the information you can and talk with a few trusted confidants about their experiences, what should you do next? Basically, you're now at a turning point where you need to take one of several paths. What are those paths, you ask? Read on!

TALK IT OUT

Sometimes the best course of action for you is to go behind closed doors with your boss—or to lunch, perhaps—and lay all your cards on the table, so to speak. You go through your prepared speech and list of grievances, noting the five times in the past two months where your boss has exploded and started screaming at you when you brought a design problem to his or her attention. And of course, your boss casts his or her eyes downward, a contrite look on his or her face, and admits the past transgressions and promises never to do them again . . . and offers you a raise as a token of good faith in the process.

Yeah, right! More likely, human nature takes over and when confronted by your observations of his or her less than stellar behavior, your boss will become defensive, deny your accusations or, worse, say something along the lines of "So what's the big deal? This is the real world and if you can't hack it, go find some other profession, because that's the way it is." And from that point on, your work days will be even more stressful and unpleasant than you could possibly have imagined. Basically, you'll be labeled as the group's whining complainer. You might as well skip right ahead to Chapter 15 and read up on moving on to your next employer.

The only time I'd recommend the heart-to-heart, talking-it-out strategy is if you're working for a friend, perhaps one of your co-workers who has been promoted to a management position, such as the project manager for the project on which you're working. Maybe that person is under a great deal of stress in his or her new role and has been snapping at you and others on the team and making some bad, bad decisions about handling problems on the project. You may have some success in "managing up" and providing this person with some candid observations; possibly, he or she isn't even aware of the effect of his or her behavior and performance on team morale. But be careful and prepare yourself for a very unfriend-like reaction, because your friend may hold the view that once promoted to the managerial position, he or she has left you and the others behind in developer-land while moving on to bigger and better things. But hey, it might be worth a try!

FIGHT IT OUT

At last, we get to the staple of *Melrose Place* and the mini-series . . . going head-to-head against your boss in a battle that pits right (you) against might (your boss) in a winner-takes-all confrontation for the heart and soul of your company. You line up allies in this battle, such as a manager from another organization who dislikes your boss, and then you "take it upstairs" to your boss's boss and pour forth your laundry list of his or her failures. Of course, right will win out over might; you won't find yourself tilting at windmills.

To repeat my response from the previous section . . . yeah, right! More likely you'll wind up slinking away after being accused of corporate mutiny, lucky to hang on to your job. If (referring to the previous section) your boss is likely to turn defensive if you were to try to discuss your perception of his or her deficiencies in management style, imagine what his or her reaction will be when you bring his or her boss into the picture and, basically, try to begin a mutiny. Justified or not, your days are numbered if you lose.

So am I saying that you should never fight it out? Not exactly. If your work situation is so egregious that there is no way you'll remain working in that environment and you've already started entertaining offers to jump to a new employer; if the majority (or even all) of your colleagues feel exactly as you do; and you're positively, absolutely, definitely certain that your "cause" is justified, then go for it! You may lose the battle but what does that matter? The war has already been lost, and you've already put your transition strategy into motion in terms of looking for a new job. But you never know . . . your boss's boss may only have been waiting to get some confirmation of his or her own opinion about your manager's incompetence or offensiveness. Once faced with the potential loss of an entire project team or much of an organization, he or she might be spurred into action and remove your boss from a position of authority.

STICK IT OUT

Then there's the "stay the course" option . . . just ride it out, putting up with the occasional outbursts or project schedule gyrations. Or should you?

After doing your homework and talking with others, after answering the first question on p. 192 ("What is your state of mind?"), and after really, really thinking the situation through, you could possibly see yourself bearing with the situation . . . giving yourself a little "It's only a job! It's only nine or ten hours every day!" pep talk every morning and again during lunch.

So when should you consider sticking it out? You might consider this option when you're learning a lot and in your mind, that knowledge and experience outweighs the discomfort and other problems with which you're dealing. After all, this is the real world, and sometimes you need to make tradeoffs.

MOVE TO A NEW JOB

You could decide to move on, either within your company or to a new employer. Leaving the company is always an option and as I've mentioned several times, you can always flip ahead to Chapter 15.

Also, resist the temptation to "unload" during your exit interview with someone from the Human Resources (HR) organization—or perhaps another manager at the company—about the *real* reason you're leaving, and how a company so idiotic to keep your manager in a position of responsibility is doomed to failure, and so on. Don't burn your bridges. You might find yourself rejoining your about-to-be-former employer at some point later in your career, for example, or possibly label yourself as a vindictive frustration-venter who doesn't work and play well with others . . . and have that label follow you to future employers.

Another option, particularly in a medium-sized or larger company, is to switch to a new job *within* your company. I would strongly recommend building on the knowledge you have about the state of your company and other managers there. Chances are you either have first-hand knowledge about how other managers behave and their abilities (or lack thereof), or you can tap into

WARNING

DON'T MENTION your boss's ineptitude or behavior as your reason for leaving when you're interviewing! That may be the primary reason but interviewers are often concerned about an applicant who gives such reasons for leaving (I know I am when I hear something like that) and wonder if you're a chronic complainer who may not be worth hiring, no matter how talented you might be. Stick to a more neutral story like "I'm looking for more challenging opportunities than I now have" or something along those lines.

the internal scuttlebutt and find out the inside scoop from others at the company.

HOPE FOR DIVINE INTERVENTION

Or maybe you don't do anything . . . and things wind up resolving themselves. Your boss is transferred or relieved of his or her position by an enlightened company executive. Perhaps retirement is the order of the day, or maybe your manager decides to screw up some other company and leaves before you have to.

So how do you know if you should just stay the course and wait for something wonderful to happen? You can't. Maybe you go on your instincts or a hunch; perhaps when tapping into the company rumor mill you get a feeling that resolution could actually be around the corner without you having to do anything on your own.

Typically, a wait-and-see approach is an interim step towards one of the other courses of action. Maybe things will resolve themselves in the meantime, or maybe not.

> **CAREER TIPS**
>
> **MAKE A GRACEFUL EXIT** from your current position should you opt to move to a new job within the company. Pick an appropriate point to switch positions, such as the completion of a project or maybe a phase of a project at which a replacement can step in for you. *Don't* pick the day after you begin your new position to run into your now-former boss in the company cafeteria and say something like, "Now, let me tell you what I *really* think about your managerial abilities!"

SUMMARY

Think back to the worst instructor you had during your college years. Perhaps it was a teaching assistant who bumbled through the assignments, barely covering the material that you needed to learn to pass the exam. Or maybe it was that calculus professor who, you were certain, took a perverse pleasure in seeing how many students in the class could score under 30 percent on each exam. Maybe it was the professor who actually yelled at students who were called on and didn't know the answers to the questions he posed.

So what did you do? Maybe you dropped the class, or transferred to another section at a different time that was taught by a different instructor. Maybe you and your classmates got together and went to the department chairman to complain about your instructor. Or perhaps you just stuck out the class because you had to get those credits to graduate on time, thinking that it's only another ten weeks . . . another nine weeks . . . eight more weeks . . .

Working for the boss from you-know-where in the real world isn't all that different than being in a class with a less-than-wonderful instructor. You figure out what's going on and what your options are; you talk to others. Then you pursue some course of action that will either lead, you hope, to the situation improving, or you embark on a personal exit strategy.

It would be great if every person in a position of leadership and authority for whom you find yourself working is a talented, articulate, and even-tempered individual who helps you grow technically and professionally in these formative years of your career and afterwards. But you *know* it isn't like that at all, so be prepared to deal with less than desirable situations regarding the person for whom you work.

CHAPTER 15
MOVING ON

INTRODUCTION

The chances are good, *very* good in fact, that within the first five years of your career, you will change employers at least once. A great opportunity might present itself where you can learn the most popular new technologies, get a bucketload of stock options and a 20 percent increase in salary, *and* get your first supervisory responsibilities. Basically, you get that "offer you can't refuse," and you're on your way.

Or, going back to our discussion in Chapter 14, relations with your boss become so untenable that leaving your current employer in search of greener work pastures seems to be your only option—if you want to retain your mental health while remaining a computer professional.

Maybe your company is experiencing difficult times and, after going through the exercises in Chapter 8, you decide that things there look so ominous that you had better start looking for a new employment opportunity. Or perhaps you've totally missed those warning signs, you're suddenly laid off or downsized out of a job, and you find yourself scrambling.

In this chapter, we'll discuss the items you need to consider when you're proactively contemplating a change in employment, including:

- exploring the opportunities that await you
- interviewing (always a challenge when you still have a real job to do!)
- discussing compensation expectations with prospective new employers
- determining how you'll be affected financially if you leave
- making the decision to actually leave
- timing your exit
- how to tell your employer that you're leaving
- what to do if your employer "counteroffers"
- what to do—and not to do—in your last weeks with your employer
- preparing for any lifestyle changes, such as relocation
- whether or not you should take some time off before starting your new job
- the option of going out on your own

We've actually discussed some of these topics in the first two chapters of this book in the context of seeking your initial position as a working computer professional, so I won't repeat that material in any detail (though I'll point you to some of those discussions, as appropriate). Rather, we'll focus our discussion on the most important items specific to *changing* jobs.

SO WHAT'S OUT THERE?

The time frame in which you're thinking about moving on will very much determine the breadth and quality of opportunities that await you. In tougher economic times, many organizations have hiring freezes in place. Then, no matter how qualified you are or how desperately that company needs your skills, the job pickings can be slim and job searches can go

NOTE IT'S ESSENTIAL FOR YOU to fully understand that most headhunters are paid by the employers. The good news about that is that working with an employer-paid recruiter doesn't cost you anything. If you go to work for a firm with which they set you up, great. If not, you're under absolutely no obligation to them. However, just like a real estate agent who shows you a house but really contractually is working for the seller and whose commission is paid by the seller, the executive recruiter's primary "allegiance" is to the employer when it comes time for salary negotiations and other facets of placing you in a job. So be careful of what you discuss with an employer-paid executive recruiter about items such as your salary negotiating strategy (what salary offer you'll really accept even though you're going to ask for more, or the other offers you have through other channels). The recruiter might be your "business partner" but he or she is "family" to the companies being represented.

However, some recruiters require *you* to pay money up front to them. The "good news" is that these types of recruiters represent you, not the employer; the bad news is that you could be paying a significant amount of money for assistance with a job search that could lead you nowhere. I'd strongly recommend sticking with employer-paid recruiters and just being careful about what you discuss with them.

on for a while. In contrast, times of economic growth such as most of the 1990s will result in an abundance of opportunities and many offers coming your way. Basically, this isn't any different than the time frame when searching for your first job.

Regardless of the state of the economy, you have a number of channels open to you through which you can locate these potential opportunities . . . again, very much like the channels discussed in Chapter 1, with a few differences. Specifically, you won't be using on-campus recruiting as your primary vehicle for your job search now that you're already a working professional. You can use the Internet and referrals, of course, to hone in on those companies that are a good match for your background, skills, and aspirations. Newspaper classified ads are now more appropriate for you given that you have some experience behind you.

You also now have an additional resource that may be of benefit: professional recruiters, commonly (and "lovingly") referred to as *headhunters*. These people essentially act as brokers between you and other job seekers and potential employers, screening candidates (such as you) and setting up interviews with companies for which they believe you would be a good fit for openings they have. The headhunter receives a fee for successfully placing you with a firm if they set up the interview (the fee is usually a percentage of your starting salary or, perhaps, your total first-year compensation, including bonus).

Sometimes you'll come in contact with recruiters through ads they place in the Sunday computer employment classifieds or through postings on computer job web sites. Other times, you might find yourself contacted by a recruiter who is looking for certain skills for one or more client companies, and through some information source has determined that you may be a likely candidate for one of the positions. Maybe, later in your career, you'll have a reputation in a specific technology area through a conference presentation you've given or an article or book you've written. Or maybe the recruiter simply got your name from a mailing list to a technology-specific periodical or from a company phone book that "just happened to come into his or her possession."

Another channel you can tap into is job fairs . . . large gatherings of many different potential employers in the area in one hotel or convention center room for an entire day or two. *However,* make certain that your current employer doesn't have a booth at that particular job fair if you're trying to keep your job search secret. If they do, you will probably find yourself stammering an ineffective, unbelievable explanation for why you happened to be wandering around with a stack of résumés in your hand, waiting in line to talk with hiring managers and recruiters from other companies.

So look, look, and look some more at the opportunities that are out there, and don't hesitate to field inquiries as to your willingness to consider a new opportunity. When you find something that strikes your fancy, it's time to start . . . interviewing!

CAREER TIPS

AT SOME POINT in an initial conversation with a recruiter who initiates contact with you, ask him or her how your name was acquired. It doesn't make much of a difference in the conversation with the headhunter but it does give you an idea of whether you're acquiring a reputation in a specific technology area or if you're simply one of the many people on a mass contact list. Should you proceed through an interview cycle with an opportunity facilitated by that recruiter, you may find yourself in a better bargaining position at negotiation time if you're being sought as an expert than if you're simply a mailing list candidate.

HOW TO INTERVIEW WHILE YOU'RE STILL WORKING

Interviewing for your second job (or your third or your fourth or . . .) isn't all that different from interviewing for your first, but you should be aware of a few key variations to the process and the content of those sessions.

THE BASICS

First, let's talk about the interview sessions themselves. Depending on how long you've been plying your trade in the computing profession after college, the questions asked of you will focus increasingly on what you *have* accomplished rather than on what you are capable of accomplishing. That is, expect to field a lot of questions about the development projects on which you've worked or the types of problems you've solved while working on the help desk or whatever your current job is. Also expect a decent amount of "drilling down" to additional details of some of those questions: what specific modules you've coded and how long they took; the trickiest bugs you encountered and how you solved them; and so on.[1]

Something else that will be different from interviewing while in college is the process that you will follow. Whereas interviewing was a very open process in college because the natural

---

[1] You might want to check out some of the sample interview questions in *Downsized But Not Out: How to Get Your Next Computer Job* (McGraw-Hill, 1994), a book I wrote a few years ago in the midst of the downsizing frenzy. The latter part of that book includes different types of interview questions, an analysis of what an interviewer is trying to learn about you, and ways in which you might answer the question . . . plus questions for you to ask.

step after completing college for most people is to find a job, interviewing while you're currently employed is *not* something that you want widely known.

An exception might be if you're caught in a major downsizing effort and your soon-to-be-former employer is sponsoring outplacement services through which they have contracted with an employment agency to help you and the others being laid off to find a new job. In these situations, your current employer certainly is aware that you will be looking for a new place to work. Another exception is one I've experienced when I was leaving the U.S. Air Force after my service commitment had been completed; I had already submitted my separation papers so it wasn't any secret that I would be seeking a postservice job.

So follow these simple guidelines to prevent unwanted complications and unpleasantness as you plan to move from one employer to another:

- **BE CAREFUL IN WHOM YOU CONFIDE**—Tell friends and family members that you're considering looking for a new job and certainly seek their advice about any of their own experiences with your candidate new employers. Maybe you can tell a few close friends with whom you work, if they've already confided in you that they're thinking about leaving. But be careful. If word of your job search gets back to your boss or to company executives, things could become rather unpleasant at work . . . or perhaps not, as we'll discuss later in the context of dealing with a counteroffer.

- **DON'T DO ANYTHING INTERVIEW-WISE ON YOUR CURRENT EMPLOYER'S TIME OR MONEY**—Do your interviewing on your lunch hour or comp time or evenings, or maybe on weekends. Or take a vacation day or personal day for interviewing during regular business hours. If you need to travel to another city for an interview, make arrangements with the company with which you're meeting to pay for the travel. Don't concoct a business trip that, conveniently, takes you to the city in which you need to be for the interview. Don't make long-distance calls from your company's location or that of a client and stick them with the bill. And speaking of telephone interviews, try not to conduct telephone interviews from your work location or at a client's office; you never know what can be heard outside of a conference room or office, even if a door is closed. Find a pay phone in a nearby hotel or shopping center (and keep your eyes open to make sure you're not overheard), or handle those calls from home.

- **BE CAREFUL ABOUT WHAT YOU TELL PEOPLE WITH WHOM YOU'RE INTERVIEWING**— You'll be asked questions about why you're thinking of changing jobs, and other questions about your current employer. Be certain not to violate any confidences related to your company's internal policies or situations or those of your employer's clients and customers. There is nothing wrong with answering a sensitive question from an interviewer with "I really can't talk about that because it's a confidential company matter."

- **DON'T MENTION TOO MUCH ELSE ABOUT YOUR JOB SEARCH**—Try not to divulge too much about the other places where you're interviewing. A recruiter with whom you're working will know where he or she has placed you for interviews, obviously . . . but that recruiter doesn't need to know about opportunities you're exploring through another recruiter or those that you're checking out on your own. Don't tell a company where you're interviewing that you're also talking with their archrival. Basically, pretend you're playing poker and you don't want anyone peeking at the cards in your hand.

- **DON'T BAD-MOUTH YOUR EMPLOYER**—There is nothing wrong with talking about the project on which you're working being canceled and therefore, you're looking for a new challenge elsewhere. It's also acceptable to mention that your job responsibilities have changed as a result of yet another reorganization and you feel it's in your best interests to move on. But avoid the temptation to vent your frustration about your boss, reciting the complete list of your manager's incompetence (see Chapter 14). Don't mention that it's universally thought within your company that the firm's executive management is way, way out of touch with the reality of what's going on in the trenches and they're running the company

WARNING

BE PARTICULARLY COGNIZANT of what you say if you are invited to an interview lunch or dinner, particularly if you're encouraged by the person with whom you're meeting to have a drink or glass of wine or beer. Take a look back at the cautions in Chapter 1 with regard to site visits; they also apply to interviews in social settings.

into the ground because they're spending all their time jockeying for power. You get the idea. Keep your employer's dark secrets out of the discussion and focus instead on why *you* would be a valuable addition to the other company's ranks.

WHAT SHOULD YOU SAY ABOUT COMPENSATION?

One other topic I need to address is what you should or shouldn't say as part of the interviewing process about your current and desired compensation.

Your Current Compensation

First of all, you should try to avoid divulging your current salary and other aspects of your compensation package, if at all possible. The reason is that some employers have a philosophy (if not a formal policy) of offering up to X percent above any prospect's current salary to entice him or her to come work there. Keep in mind that most positions have a salary *range,* not a fixed salary, and that range can be rather substantial from the low end to the higher side (maybe as much as $50,000 at some companies, particularly at senior levels!). If they want you to come work there and know that you're currently making, say, $50,000 and their philosophy is to offer 20 percent "jumping incentives," then you would probably receive an offer around $60,000 . . . even if the salary range for that position is from $55,000 to $85,000 and, conceivably, they'd be willing to go as high as $70,000 for people whom they really want.

So particularly if you're underpaid at your current employer, try not to let below-market compensation hinder your chances to get caught up as part of your job change.

But suppose that the HR person or the hiring manager really persists in asking you about your compensation. Rather than proceed with an awkward "I'm just not going to tell you!" position, you might as well divulge the information. *But—and I know some people don't agree with me—don't lie!* I strongly recommend *against* adding a few thousand dollars to your base salary or saying you have a 20 percent bonus when it's really 10 percent. Why? You'd be surprised how commonly known compensation information is within the recruiting community and at companies that hire computer professionals. Many companies do extensive compensation surveys to ensure that their salaries are in line with market rates, for example. Or, more directly, the company may have already interviewed several of your co-workers who are at the same level as you, and they aren't going to buy that your salary is 50 percent higher than that of every other junior developer at your current employer.

Basically, the chances of you being able to pawn off a bogus salary or compensation package aren't very good, and if—make that when—caught, you could find an otherwise good job opportunity vanish because of your dishonesty. I know that some people would advise you to add a few thousand dollars, or maybe more, to the figure you give people but I'd strongly recommend against doing that. You'll be better off in the long run focusing on your *desired* compensation package as a key aspect of your negotiating strategy.

Your Desired Compensation

Here's another caution: don't make your desired or expected compensation the key part of your job discussions. That is, avoid asking a question such as "What does this position pay?" or "What is the salary range for this position?" for as long as possible while you focus on job responsibilities, training, job location, and other facets of the position.

And even later, I'd also recommend against giving a hard number that denotes your desired compensation. If you say you'll be happy with $65,000 and the company is willing to pay you $75,000, how much do you think they'll offer you?

There are some subtle differences in interviewing if you're initiating a job search as contrasted with you just minding your own business and finding yourself actively recruited by a company that has targeted you for your skills (or some other reason) as someone they *really* want to come work there. I say subtle differences because for the most part, the process you'll follow will be pretty much the same. However, you want to shift the tone of the interview sessions to *you* being sold on why that company is such a wonderful place to work that you should leave your present job, even though you haven't been on the job market. (You may have already initiated a job search, but you don't need to let a company that is recruiting you know that!)

You can assume that you already have one foot in the door, so to speak, when you go to an interview if you're being recruited. But at the same time, the more senior the level for which you're interviewing, the less likely the certainty of an impending job offer is. A company may be seeking dozens of skilled Java developers, for example, and if you have that background and accomplishments then as long as salary negotiations go well, you will probably receive an offer even if others whom they're interviewing may be just a little bit better than you. But if you're being recruited for a senior management position running a business organization and there's only one position to be filled, you need to sell

CAREER TIPS

I RECOMMEND ANSWERING with a generic "I'm looking for a good opportunity" as you continue to avoid answering that question. Or, if pressed, here's an approach that might work well.

Tell the person that you're considering different types of opportunities, such as (these are only examples . . . tailor them to your particular situation):

- with a startup that has a large part of the compensation in stock;
- with a consulting firm that includes overtime pay as part of the package;
- with a Fortune 500 firm with an "ordinary" salary plus bonus opportunity; or
- a sales opportunity with very large upside in the commissions structure.

So, basically, because these opportunities are so different from one another in terms of the way the compensation is structured, it's really an apples-and-oranges situation. That means you don't have any kind of "magic number" as far as your desired salary.

yourself to the company (if you're interested in pursuing the position) just as much as they need to sell themselves to you.

SHOW ME THE MONEY (PART 2)

Take a look at the discussion in Chapter 2 with the same title as this section header. It all applies: base salary, stock, bonus, benefits, and so on.

However, you also need to consider factors such as the financial implications of leaving your current employer, as discussed in the next section. If you will be foregoing your bonus because you're leaving before it's paid, for example, then you want to seek a signing bonus that will compensate you as much as possible for that lost cash.

FINANCIAL IMPLICATIONS OF LEAVING

Let's pick up where we left off in the previous section. You know the time frame at which any bonus payments for which you're eligible will be received, and you also know your employer's policies on partial payments (or not) of targets met throughout the year.

So now, here comes an offer at another company that you decide is one you want to accept. They (the new employer) would like you to start on October 1, and you know that your company won't be paying bonuses until January 31 of the following year, and you should be receiving $10,000. Does changing jobs mean that you have to forego this bonus?

Here's a simple way of handling this situation, or trying to: ask for a signing bonus from your new employer equal to, or—better yet—more than the lost bonus amount from your current employer. If they really want you to come work there, those terms should be agreeable to them.

 NOTE

THE MORE THE AMOUNT of your expected bonus, the less likely it is (but still not impossible!) that the entire amount will find its way in your signing bonus . . . but you can always try!

You also need to consider the following items:

- **RETIREMENT VESTING**—If you're vested in your company's retirement plan at, say, the ten-year point, you probably don't want to resign nine years and ten months into your tenure there if that would mean that you'll lose your retirement benefits.

- **UNUSED VACATION POLICY**—You don't want to leave three or four weeks of vacation behind if your employer's policy is to *not* pay for any unused vacation when an employee terminates. So use up your vacation days (perhaps for interviewing days) to prevent leaving behind a significant amount of time away from work.

- **STOCK OPTIONS**—What are your company's policies on unexercised stock options? Do you have to execute them before you give notice or else lose all of them? Or is there some period of time—a few months, perhaps—after your termination date in which you still can exercise those options? How about unvested options . . . what happens to them? Is the current market price above your strike price? Would your prospective termination date be within a few months of becoming vested for a large batch of options?

I know this is a large number of questions but the point is that you need to *carefully* analyze the possible scenarios for your stock options and what you could be giving up by leaving at various times, depending on vesting information and pricing. You probably want to think twice before leaving a company for a $15,000 increase in salary . . . and leaving behind $200,000 in likely (though not guaranteed, if the market price were to drop) stock profits if you were to stay put for another few months.

- **SIGNING BONUS PAYBACK**—As discussed in Chapter 2, signing bonuses often come with a payback period, meaning that if you leave your employment during that time (usually one year) you may owe back a prorated portion of the bonus. As with any regular bonus you might be foregoing, try to get a signing bonus from your new employer that includes money you can use for paying back your first signing bonus from your current employer.

DECIDING TO LEAVE

Changing employers is, believe it or not, a traumatic experience even if you're really looking forward to making a change. Even in very subtle ways, the routines of your life will be affected and if other parts of your life start to become problematic, you no longer have the "comfort" of your workday routine to fall back on.

So really, *really* think through any job change. Even if you've definitely decided that a job change is in order, you may be considering which of several opportunities is the one for you. Use the job attribute chart discussed in Chapter 1 to help you decide among opportunities.

But also, you need to make a *conscious* decision that you want to leave your current place of employment. Don't just drift into a job change. Write down or speak out loud the words, "I want to leave my company and change jobs" to formally establish that you want to close out that particular chapter of your career.

TIMING YOUR EXIT TO YOUR ADVANTAGE

We already discussed the financial aspects of deciding when to leave earlier in this chapter. You should also consider nonfinancial aspects, such as where the project on which you're currently working is with regard to progress. Will you be relocating to Denver just in time for ski season? To Southern California in time to escape the frigid winters of Minnesota? To Vermont just in time for leaf-watching season?

Think about whether or not you want any time off between jobs—sort of a mental refresher—or if there are other things going on in your life at the same time, such as getting married or other personal matters. Unless you have to find a job quickly because you've been laid off and financial needs dictate doing so as expeditiously as possible, time your changes to *your* advantage.

CAREER TIPS

SOMETIMES YOU MAY NOT HAVE total freedom in setting a start date . . . having to be available at the beginning of a project for which you're being hired, for example. But usually, an employer's flexibility is a good indicator of what it will be like working there.

GIVING NOTICE AND PREPARING TO LEAVE

Most likely, you already have experience in giving notice to an employer . . . from summer jobs, part-time employment in high school or college, perhaps even positions with firms where you held a nontechnology position before you decided to get into the computer field. So you should know the basics, such as:

- the standard policy of giving two weeks' notice before your actual termination date
- submitting a written notice of resignation in addition to verbally telling your manager or a company Human Resources (HR) person
- stating a reason of some type for your resignation, even if it's a generic "I'm moving on to a new opportunity"

As discussed in the next sections, though, you may not have experience dealing with counteroffers and some realities of your last few weeks with a full-time employer in your chosen profession.

 WARNING

I STRONGLY RECOMMEND AGAINST giving notice before you have formally accepted an offer. It isn't unheard of for a company to suddenly withdraw a written offer for some reason, such as an internal hiring freeze or finding another candidate whom they feel is more suitable for the position. True, it's unethical but it does happen. They could always try to do that after you've accepted an offer but that's less likely to happen than someone calling you up before you've accepted the offer and telling you that "uh, there's a problem here." At least if you've accepted the offer you can argue that you've already given notice, that you've made a number of decisions based on accepting that offer, and so on. Which brings us to the main point: make sure that you *do* accept an offer, and have a confirmation from the company in hand that your acceptance has been accepted (so to speak) before you give notice.

THE COUNTEROFFER

It isn't uncommon for your manager, when notified of your intention to resign, to present you with a counteroffer to remain in the company's employment. This usually occurs two or three days after you give notice, possibly after consulting with his or her boss and others at the company. The counteroffer may contain one or more of the following items:

- an increase in your salary
- additional stock options
- a promotion
- an immediate cash "retention payment"

The intent of the counteroffer is to convince you to change your mind about leaving. But I always have had one question about counteroffers that no one has ever been able to answer satisfactorily: if suddenly a company is willing to pay you, say, $65,000 instead of $60,000 after you submit your resignation, shouldn't you have been receiving that higher salary all along? Why should you have to make plans to leave in order to receive the money you deserve?

Obviously, you need to evaluate a counteroffer on its own merits but if it were me, I'd be concerned if an employer suddenly decides to pay me $10,000 or $20,000 more, or dump a bunch of stock options on me, because they—supposedly—now have a better idea of my worth to the company. In my opinion, that's a bunch of you-know-what. A company that wants to take care of its employees does so along the way, not only when they're about to depart.

Besides, many counteroffers don't even come close to matching the offer you've decided to accept. I know of a person who decided to leave his employment for a salary that was almost double what he was making, and his current employer's counteroffer was a 10 percent increase and some stock options. It wasn't surprising when he said thanks, but no thanks to the counteroffer.

Finally, the same is true of your current level within your employer. If they offer you a promotion as part of the counteroffer, shouldn't you have been at that higher-ranking position all along?

YOUR LAST WEEKS WITH YOUR EMPLOYER

Here are a few simple guidelines for what to do and not do during your last weeks with your employer . . . the period between the time you give notice and your last day of work.

1. **KEEP DOING YOUR JOB**—Even though the clock is now running until you're gone, continue to do your job. Don't slack off; you don't want to leave your friends with whom you're still working having to cover for you because you're not doing your job (remember you're still being paid). Work on a transition plan, if possible, with someone who will be replacing you or picking up some of your tasks.

2. **WATCH YOUR EXPENSES**—If you're in a job that requires you to travel, I'd recommend that you watch your expenses while you're on the road in those past weeks, especially if you're paying for them out of your pocket before being reimbursed. You never know when the finance department could decide to reimburse you a little bit more slowly than current employees, or decide that expenses such as phone calls or part of your meals are suddenly nonreimbursable. If you must travel and pay for those expenses, keep the amounts you're spending as low as possible (don't pick up the tab for the entire project team at dinner, for example. Let someone else do that).

3. **WATCH WHAT YOU SAY**—Don't go skipping through the hallways and telling everyone you pass how glad you are to be leaving this slime pit. Don't pick this time to badmouth your boss for the incompetent ogre he or she is (in your opinion, anyway); wouldn't you be surprised to find him or her following you to your new employer six months later and even though you don't work directly for that person anymore, you now have an enemy in your new company's executive ranks? Basically, keep your opinions relatively quiet.

4. **BE CAREFUL ABOUT RECRUITING OTHERS**—Check out your employment agreement. If you're prohibited from recruiting others to leave with you, then *don't do it*! Even if you're not contractually prohibited from doing so, I'd recommend waiting until after you leave before you start collecting and forwarding résumés. If you want a reason for waiting, consider that many employers have referral programs whereby you can pick up several thousand dollars per person if they hire the person you refer. Wouldn't it make sense to wait until you're already at your new employer so you can cash in on placing your friends?

5. THE EXIT INTERVIEW—Some companies insist on conducting a formal exit interview for those who are leaving. I would recommend against using the exit interview as a channel to vent months or years worth of frustration. Be professional. If you have constructive advice about ways to improve project quality or improve retention for those that remain behind, share those points. They may not make a difference (and most likely won't), but at least you can leave with dignity and some words of wisdom behind you.

PREPARING FOR LIFESTYLE CHANGES

If you're relocating . . . if your travel schedule will suddenly change from none to four or five days each week . . . or if other changes in your lifestyle will be occurring as a result of your job change, then prepare yourself as thoroughly as possible.

Talk to others who may have relocated from near where you live to your new location and learn what went well and what didn't for them. If you haven't traveled much before for business, then find out the tips and tricks of how to do so with as little turmoil as possible.

Basically, be prepared so you can concentrate on the new job challenges ahead of you.

HOW ABOUT GOING OUT ON YOUR OWN?

In Chapter 16, we'll discuss aspects of leaving your employer not to go to another salaried position but rather going out on your own as a consultant or starting some other type of company. So flip ahead to that chapter if that option is of interest to you.

SUMMARY

With luck, you'll find yourself moving from your first employer to another because you are presented with an opportunity that you just can't say no to. But even if things haven't turned out as expected, you can still make a positive job change with as little turmoil as possible, as long as you follow the guidelines presented in this chapter and use some of the material from earlier chapters to help in your transition.

CHAPTER 16
GOING OUT ON YOUR OWN... OR MAYBE NOT

INTRODUCTION

One thing that can be said about the computing profession, no matter how stressful and frenzied it may seem at times: it does offer numerous opportunities for entrepreneurial-minded individuals to embark on some type of self-employment venture. In fact, I believe that it was the coming of the personal computing industry in the late 1970s and early 1980s that fueled much of the economic prosperity the American economy and others around the world have seen in recent years, and a significant portion of that prosperity was fueled by entrepreneurs in the information technology business. (Can you say Microsoft? Apple? Lotus?)

So don't be surprised if at some point relatively early in your career you find the going-out-on-your-own whispers getting louder and louder. In fact, I started my own initial entrepreneurial ventures back in 1982, only about six months after completing graduate school. True, I was an Air Force officer at the time, and I began consulting on a moonlighting, part-time basis, but I've floated in and out of ventures such as solo consulting for much of my career . . . and chances are that you will, also.

In this chapter, we'll discuss some of the most important items you should know if you are seriously considering some type of entrepreneurial adventure. We'll talk about not only self-employed consulting, but also deciding to start a software company. Consider, though, that our discussion in this chapter will, by necessity, be abbreviated. Numerous books and other reference sources are available for you to consult for more detailed information, including my own *How to Be a Successful Computer Consultant: Expanded and Updated* (McGraw-Hill, 1998), which is an expanded and updated (big surprise, given the title!) version of the first book that I wrote back in the early 1980s and that has been updated every couple of years since then.

WHAT ARE SOME OF YOUR OPTIONS?

There is a big, big difference between deciding that you're going to become a self-employed computer consultant and, for example, starting a company with the intention of developing commercial software products. In this section, we'll discuss some of the options you might be considering.

AN OVERVIEW OF BEING A SELF-EMPLOYED CONSULTANT

It's relatively easy for a computer professional to become a self-employed consultant, or possibly to get together with one or two other people and form a small consulting firm. The news reports these days (late 1998) speak of persistent shortages in information technology (IT) talent across the world—a shortage that gets more serious by the month. This means that pretty much anyone with any technical aptitude and a bit of business acumen can set himself or herself up as an independent contractor and take a crack at self-employment. True, this situation could abruptly change, as it did in the early 1990s during the last recession, but for the most part, let's assume that self-employed consultant is a viable option.

But should you go down that path? Basically, why consider being a self-employed consultant? Perhaps you're already doing consulting work as an employee of a consulting firm and you do some simple math:

"Hmmm . . . if I'm being billed out at $100 per hour and I'm working at least 50 hours per week, that means that the company is making $5,000 a week, $20,000 a month from my work. But my salary is $60,000, which means I gross $5,000 every month. Why should they get the extra $15,000 from my work?"

Now before everyone starts rushing off and quitting jobs to set up shop as consultants, you need to consider some additional factors above and beyond the simple mathematics above. How about when you're not working on a project—"on the bench" (or "on the beach") in consulting-speak—as an employee? You still get paid, and the company is still paying your salary. How about the time it took to find the engagement on which you're working, and the people at the company who did so (the sales person or account manager, for example), who need to be paid also? How about your bonus and benefits?

So maybe the margin between the revenue your labor generates and the actual cost of your labor isn't quite as great as $15,000, after all. But still, you think to yourself . . . even if I work an average of only 100 hours per month to allow time for marketing and training, and bill at $90 per hour on my own, that's still $9,000 each month working on my own which could work out to over $100,000 per year . . . certainly more than I'm making now.

So armed with this information, you start seriously looking into the world of solo consulting. But before going too far, it's time for a little self-insight and self-analysis. The following list, excerpted from *How to Be a Successful Computer Consultant: Expanded and Updated* [1] gives you an overview of things to consider.

1. **WHY SHOULD I CONSIDER BEING A CONSULTANT?**—One reason: control over your work life (such as the chance to pick and choose among project options and work on the ones that are the most exciting and challenging). Another reason: to get your feet wet and begin to learn about marketing, financial management, and other aspects of running a business so if you decide to stick with the self-employment path, you can try to expand your business into a larger firm. Another reason: the potential for greater financial reward (though accompanied by greater financial risk).

2. **WHY WOULD A CLIENT WANT TO HIRE ME AS A CONSULTANT?**—As discussed previously, there is, at least today, a rather severe shortage of qualified information technology professionals in most areas of the business world. Consider the once-forlorn COBOL programmer who, according to conventional wisdom in the early 1990s, was as much of a dinosaur in the world of modern computing as the people who used to hard-wire computers to do programming back in the 1940s. But wouldn't you know it, here comes the Year 2000 (Y2K) problem (or at least the awareness of the problem, considering it's been around for years), and suddenly COBOL programmers are in high demand to work on Y2K projects.

So sometimes the need for consultants is just a matter of simple supply and demand economics. But even when supply and demand are in greater balance, other factors will likely continue to drive consulting opportunities. For example, many IT organizations embarked on outsourcing programs in the early 1990s (see Chapter 8 for a brief discussion of this

---

[1] See Chapter 1 of that book for more discussion of these items.

trend). The more outsourcing, the greater the need for consultants to supplement the work being performed by the primary organization that will now take over IT operations.

Additionally, demand for certain skills occasionally causes a frenzy to hire consultants with particular expertise. For example, at the time of writing (1998) areas such as data warehousing and business intelligence, anything to do with the Internet, and Java programming are particularly lucrative for consultants as business organizations struggle to "spin up" on those areas.

So in answer to the question posed earlier (why a client would want to hire you), the simple answer is that you have something to offer them that, for some reason, they can't readily obtain from their internal staff.

3. ARE THERE DIFFERENT TYPES OF CONSULTANTS?—Absolutely, and it's imperative that you market yourself and seek opportunities at a level appropriate to your background and skills. I believe there is a three-tier hierarchy that features:

- on the lowest level, consultants who are skilled developers with expertise in one or more programming languages and technologies and who most effectively function in an application development setting;

- in the middle level, consultants with a broader set of expertise than languages—networking and communications, how to migrate data from one environment to a more modern platform, and different ways to interconnect distributed pieces of an application, for example— and who can serve as program architects or in other senior capacities; and

- at the top level, the "superstar" consultants who might be past chief information officers (CIOs); who can successfully do management consulting in addition to technology consulting; who can help an organization establish its next generation of architectural standards; or who perhaps are internationally renowned in a particular area of the information technology world for their expertise.

So make sure that you decide what level is most appropriate for you as you dabble in the world of consulting. Chances are that in the early stages of your career, the lowest of the three levels is the one in which you'll be most successful based on your accomplishments to date.

4. WHAT ARE DESIRABLE CHARACTERISTICS OF A SUCCESSFUL COMPUTER CONSULTANT?—Here's a short list (and keep in mind that these are also desirable characteristics for *any* computer consultant, whether self-employed or not):

- Understands the general principles of a client's business and proposes solutions that are sensible in both a business and technological sense.

- Deals well with people in all kinds of settings, even tense and hostile ones.

- Integrity.

- Objectivity.

- Ability to solve difficult problems.

- Communicates well, both verbally and in writing (see Chapter 10).

- Self-confidence.

- Creativity.

- Ambition.
- Appropriately skilled in hardware and software technology.
- Knows where to find the answers to particularly tough problems.
- Is successful at marketing and selling, financial management, and other aspects of running a business.

Wow! That's a lot of background and knowledge. So before heading out on your own, make sure that you can handle all of these areas with confidence. If not, then perhaps you need a bit more seasoning, working for a consulting firm and rising up through the ranks. This may be a lower risk career option (for now, anyway) through which you can still do well by yourself.

STARTING A CONSULTING COMPANY

Explicitly setting out to start a consulting company is a different proposition than going into that profession by yourself or with one or two others. Unlike the scenarios we previously discussed, where you find a series of engagements and possibly, slowly add one or two employees or other independent contractors over time to help you handle the business, an explicit goal to start a consulting company means that you go for the big time as soon as possible.

An interesting phenomenon occurred in 1997 when senior executives from a large international consulting firm left and, armed with millions of dollars of investment capital, formed another consulting company called AnswerThink, which then proceeded to purchase a number of other smaller consulting companies and grow very, very quickly.

Even if your plans for quickly building a large consulting company aren't quite so ambitious, you still will be going down a different path than setting up shop as an independent contractor. Most importantly, the technical expertise and consulting skills that you hope will fuel your company's growth will have to come from a much, much broader pool of expertise than just you. In fact, your role might have little to do with actually delivering consulting services; perhaps you'll be in charge of marketing or sales, or maybe you'll be the chief technologist and spend most of your time setting the company's technical direction.

You could take the path of trying to build a firm that specializes primarily in placing one or two people at client companies in a staffing supplement capacity. Commonly known as "body shop" consulting firms, these organizations not only hire full-time employees for these assignments but very often act as brokers between independent contractors and client opportunities, pocketing the difference as company profit.

Or you could try and build a company that specializes in project consulting rather than staffing supplement . . . arguably a more difficult proposition, considering that you'll be competing with the big guys in the consulting profession. But some firms have been fairly successful—particularly in booming economic times—in carving out niches on a regional basis and then expanding until they become established.

But the most important thing to note is the dramatic difference between trying to make a go of it on your own as an independent consultant and, on the other side, trying to build a larger consulting firm. Make sure you put appropriate plans in place so you don't wander down a path that will result in your venture not being successful.

STARTING A SOFTWARE COMPANY

Way back in the early days of the personal computer (early 1980s), starting a software company was a relatively easy thing to do. Now this doesn't mean that every software company was successful, or even that many of them succeeded. But back in those "frontier" days it was easy for one or two people to write a rudimentary DOS or Apple II program in Basic or dBASE II or TurboPascal (all early PC development systems), place an ad in *Byte* Magazine, and sell enough copies to fund development of a new software program. Customer support? Nah, it wasn't necessary. Bug fixes? It was the customers' problem; after all, what did they expect for $29.95?

But then came the Macintosh and Windows 3.0, and the much more complex graphic development environments. Suddenly simple command line interfaces weren't enough. Memory and disk capacities expanded dramatically on PCs, meaning that software functionality could be much more robust than only a few years earlier.

And of course when PC software, which had been single-machine stand-alone products, needed to operate in a distributed client/server environment on a local area network, the products became even more complex.

Finally, as the industry matured, the need for marketing and advertising increased dramatically. Basically, software development became a game for serious players only (other than perhaps rudimentary "shareware" programs).

So enough of the history lesson . . . the point is that if you're seriously contemplating starting a company with the intention of producing commercial software products, then you're going to need help . . . either early, as in assistance with development, or later, when it comes time to take your products to the marketplace.

The advent of the Internet and electronic commerce has changed the landscape a bit in terms of reducing, or at least reallocating, the cost of entry into the commercial marketplace. How dramatic the changes will be isn't quite clear yet, but it's important that, if you decide to check out the software vendor business, you thoroughly research how e-commerce can benefit your venture and what strategies make sense in the Internet era.

BECOMING A RECRUITER . . . OR SOMETHING ELSE

Here's a different approach: perhaps your entrepreneurial venture is to become a recruiter, placing other computer professionals in positions with corporations much as you may have been placed in your current job. I mention this option not so much to suggest that you become a recruiter as to point out that setting out on your own doesn't necessarily have to be in any kind of traditional software or systems development sense. There are many different paths you could take, such as starting an Internet/electronically-distributed technology newsletter; writing computer books (as I did on a full-time basis for a while); starting a PC repair business; or possibly even some other option that we can't even envision today.

So keep your eyes open and watch out for opportunities that might present themselves.

SOME OF THE ESSENTIALS

There's no way I can cover the topic of building and running a business in other than a cursory manner within the confines of this chapter. So this section will present a brief discussion of some of the major items you need to consider. For further information, check out sources that discuss the essentials of business building.

THE BUSINESS PLAN

The business plan is the vehicle through which all of your strategies and tactics can be organized and presented for several different purposes. First and foremost, by putting everything down on paper you can find holes in your plans that you may have otherwise overlooked. Your business plan should be a living document, meaning that you consult it frequently, update it as necessary, and, basically, *use* it.

Additionally, your business plan can serve as the mechanism through which you secure investment capital or other financial assistance to help your company get off the ground or, later, to grow. If you'll be asking for potentially millions of dollars in investment funds and/or financing available through a loan or line of credit, the people who control that money will want some idea that they'll be making a sound investment or their loans are secure.

So your business plan needs to be a thorough discussion of the many items[2] you need to keep your eye on when running a business, including:

1. **A COVER PAGE**—containing your company's name, contact information (address, phone number, e-mail address, web site, etc.), and the date of the document

2. **AN EXECUTIVE SUMMARY (OR INTRODUCTORY SUMMARY)**—that explains the major points presented in the pages of your plan

3. **A TABLE OF CONTENTS**—which is particularly important for lengthy documents (make sure to include page references for the sections)

4. **COMPANY BACKGROUND**—such as when your company was founded (or if it is just being created now), the primary services and/or products you'll be offering, information about you and the company's other principals, current customers, the way your company will be organized (that is, a sole proprietorship, partnership, or corporation) and other pertinent information

5. **INDUSTRY INFORMATION**—that discusses the area of the marketplace in which you're concentrating (consulting services, PC personal productivity software, or whatever), who the current leaders are in that industry, and the like.

6. **MARKET RESEARCH AND ANALYSIS**—about the specific market you're targeting: overall size, trends, the portion of the market you realistically think you can capture

7. **YOUR MARKETING PLAN**—that discusses strategies, promotions, pricing, advertising methods, and other promotional means

8. **WHAT PROFESSIONAL ASSISTANCE**—your firm requires (attorneys, accountants, etc.)

---

2 See Chapter 6 of *How to Be a Successful Computer Consultant: Expanded and Updated* (McGraw-Hill, 1998) for more details.

9. A GENERAL OPERATIONS PLAN—that covers roles and responsibilities, staffing levels, methodologies, geographical areas in which you'll be operating, and other aspects of business operations

10. APPLICABLE RESEARCH AND DEVELOPMENT—programs that are essential to business operations and your firm's viability in the marketplace

11. A TIME SCHEDULE—that presents major milestones and decision points and various scenarios of outcomes

12. A THOROUGH AND UP-FRONT RISK ASSESSMENT—noting factors such as being too far ahead on the technology curve or having to go head-to-head with a heavyweight competitor

13. A DETAILED FINANCIAL PLAN—that covers anticipated earnings and expenses, cash flow, additional investment phases, etc.

As I mentioned earlier, it's very important for you to prepare a business plan even if it's only for your own uses rather than as part of seeking business funding. By organizing your thoughts on paper, your chances of success increase, even if you're functioning as an independent consultant.

FINDING CLIENTS AND CUSTOMERS

Let's focus a bit on one aspect of the business plan: finding clients and customers. For purposes of this chapter, we'll discuss doing so as an independent consultant rather than as a larger consulting firm or software vendor, since you're more likely to be heading off on your own as an independent consultant during the first five years of your career.

One way to find clients is to work through a larger consulting firm as a subcontractor. Basically, they find a client that needs, say, a Visual Basic programmer for a six-month project. They collect résumés of people with all kinds of technical skills, interview those individuals, and select the most promising or talented folks as potential subcontractors. So along comes this Visual Basic assignment, which happens to be your particular area of expertise. They send you off to an interview at the client's location; the client checks out your skills and decides if they'd like to engage you for their project; and if that happens, a contract is put in place between the client and the company through which you're working and another contract is drawn up between the company and you. Basically, the company acts in a middleman capacity. Once you're working at the client's, your interaction with the consulting company will probably only be to pick up the payments owed to you.

You might try the subcontracting channel for your first few consulting engagements, but eventually you should try to graduate to

WARNING

THERE ARE MANY, many details you need to know about this type of subcontracting relationship, from noncompete clauses to payment arrangements. Basically, read the agreement you're given very, *very* carefully and if you see things you don't like, such as being paid only once a month and with a one-month lag after you bill the consulting company, then you should probably take your business elsewhere.

finding engagements on your own. Basically, why should a middleman be part of the transaction? Wasn't that one of the things that attracted you to consulting and out of the full-time workforce?

Start establishing a reputation for expertise in a particular area. Suppose it's the area of data warehousing. You might:

- get involved in users' conferences for the tool(s) in which you have greatest experience, perhaps giving a presentation or taking part in a panel discussion
- give a presentation at a local breakfast or dinner meeting for a group in which data warehousing is a topic of interest
- write articles
- get involved in Internet-based discussion groups

Basically, try to build a reputation that will lead people to seek you out to provide consulting services to them rather than you having to scramble all the time to find consulting engagements.

STAYING CURRENT

In most of the career-oriented books I've written (including all four editions of *How to Be a Successful Computer Consultant*) I've included a chapter that discusses how the reader can keep himself or herself current in this fast-changing world of computing technology. Some of the most important items include:

- **FREQUENTLY CHECKING OUT CONTENT ON THE INTERNET**—This obviously wasn't one of the suggestions back in 1983 when I started writing, but today, this is certainly at the top of the list. The Internet has revolutionized the distribution of knowledge and is much, much more efficient than magazines or trade papers for those with the usual crazy schedules that most of us have.

- **COMPUTER AND BUSINESS MAGAZINES AND PAPERS**—The above paragraph isn't intended to imply that magazines and newspapers are now obsolete, having been supplanted by the Internet. Subscriptions to technology-specific periodicals, or general ones such as *Computerworld* and *Datamation,* can give you a pretty good idea of what's going on in terms of what companies are pursuing different technologies for their applications and infrastructure, and how well they're doing . . . or not.

- **BOOKS**—Want to learn Microsoft Windows 98? Java programming? The latest version of Oracle or Microsoft SQL Server? You can learn a lot from the many, many books that are available. This way, you can teach yourself how to program in Java or Visual Basic, for example, and check examples out on your own PC.

- **CLASSES AND TRAINING**—In addition to any self-study (as discussed above), formal training—ideally company-sponsored through your employer but later, on your own, as an investment in your own professional development—is desirable.

- **GRADUATE SCHOOL**—Chapter 12 discusses different approaches to graduate school. Certainly, additional academic work can help increase your knowledge base as well as make you more marketable, whether on your own or in a corporate setting.

ATTRACTING AND RETAINING TALENT

I just wanted to mention the importance of being able to attract and retain talented individuals to help you build and grow your business. This is particularly true if you're trying to establish a viable software vendor or project consulting company. The industry is littered with the remains of numerous companies that at one time seemed promising but for one reason or another faded from existence. At the same time, there are other companies that initially succeeded, struggled, but came roaring back under the guidance of a visionary CEO or chief technologist.

So here are three items that you should keep in mind as you try to make a go of it in the tough, competitive business world:

1. **DON'T BE AFRAID TO SEEK TOP TALENT**—This might seem like a statement of the obvious, but you'd be surprised (or maybe not) how many people are reticent about bringing people equally as talented into their companies, fearful of not necessarily being the "numero uno" technology whiz any more or worried that having a take-charge second-in-command person might mean being purged out of a job at one time. You will have a very, very difficult time achieving any kind of lofty objectives if you are the only talented person in your company.

2. **RECOGNIZE THAT YOU'RE GOING TO HAVE TO PAY FOR TALENT**—Going hand in hand with seeking top talent is realizing that one way or another, you're going to have to pay for those individuals. These are very competitive times in the marketplace for high-quality technologists and business managers, and you won't be able to keep someone happy for long if you establish an environment where you and perhaps only a handful of others are the only people who will earn a lot of money when your company is successful. Whether through lucrative bonus plans or stock options or a combination of both, you want individuals who have as much of a stake in the company's success as you do. Otherwise, you will have trouble attracting these talented people to work with you and if one of them somehow stumbles in, he or she probably won't last long.

3. **KEEP TALENTED PEOPLE CHALLENGED**—Money isn't everything, obviously. Talented computer professionals usually want to be challenged. Just think of yourself. Would you rather work on a development project to create a revolutionary new systems management product or do routine maintenance and bug fixes on a 30-year-old inventory control program? Would you rather grow a business organization or be in charge of a small group of entry-level people working at the help desk, where your "managerial" responsibilities consist of checking the staff members' time sheets? If you can't keep people happy through new and exciting work, they'll find it elsewhere.

SUMMARY

This chapter is only an abbreviated discussion of the lengthy topic of being a successful entrepreneur in the computing profession. For further information, get on the Internet or head down to the library or a bookstore and do your homework.

APPENDIX A

SAMPLE RÉSUMÉS

In Chapter 1, I mentioned that, as you prepare your résumé when seeking your first computing job, you should focus on content rather than worrying about the type of paper on which your résumé and cover letter are printed. The same holds true for preparing to change jobs (Chapter 15).

But as I also mentioned, there are many, many different views on what exactly that content should be. Therefore, let me give you *my* perspective, that of a hiring manager, in both scenarios: an entry-level IT professional and someone at the four- or five-year point in his or her career who is looking to change jobs. The sample résumés in this appendix are ones that would cause me to pay attention and want to speak further with someone about his or her qualifications.

Sample Résumé #1: College student nearing graduation seeking first full-time position

Cheryl Lawson
12 Columbus Avenue
Pittsburgh, PA 15201
(412) 555-1037

Education

Degree: Will receive B.S. in Computer Science from Penn State in May, 1999. 3.6 GPA (3.9 in computer science courses) through December, 1998.

Computer Science Courses: C programming (2 courses); database management systems; introduction to operating systems; data structures; Internet technologies; independent study in data warehousing

Project Work: Currently working on senior class project as part of five-person team, developing data warehouse for campus administration office. The application will be used to analyze patterns among school applicants (geography, demographic information, high school academic records, etc.)

Work Experience

Computer Center Lab Assistant: Summer, 1997 and Summer, 1998. Worked 30 hours per week assisting summer school students and others on campus to solve programming and systems problems.

Zip's Records and Video: Part-time job during high school, 1994–1995. Responsible for cash register and inventory management during working hours.

Personal Information

- Willing to relocate.
- Interests include golf, tennis, and other sports.
- References available upon request.

DISCUSSION OF PRECEDING RÉSUMÉ

It's very important to view your résumé as sort of a balancing act. On the one hand, you want potential interviewers to single out your résumé among the dozens, perhaps hundreds, of those that they'll be reviewing. Therefore, you should put as much real world stuff in your résumé as possible, including (from this example) school projects on which you're working and the classes you've taken that are applicable to the hottest areas of today's technology. (**Hint:** independent study courses look great on your résumé because they show particular initiative on your part in going beyond the basic degree program at your school).

At the same time, though, you *don't* want to overstate your experience and qualifications because the people with whom you'll be interviewing will easily be able to determine whether or not you've really gained the experience you have claimed. So don't claim credit for data warehouse project work if, for example, you only spent a few days studying the basic concepts of data warehousing and the class project on which you're working has nothing to do with that area of technology.

And be prepared to describe the details of not only your project but also your role. Are you the project manager? The person in charge of collecting requirements? The person in charge of evaluating products? Whatever your role is, be prepared to describe exactly what you're doing.

Some other items about the above résumé:

- **GRADE POINT AVERAGE**—After you've spent five or six years in the profession, few people will really care about your grade point average in college. But while you're still in school and seeking that first job, your GPA is one of the key factors by which someone will determine whether he or she wants to speak with you about employment opportunities. Therefore, I'd recommend including both your overall GPA and also your GPA within your major (computer science, in this example). If you haven't graduated yet, include your most recently calculated GPA and update it as applicable at the end of each quarter or semester.

- **OBJECTIVE**—You may not have noticed that I did not include a specific objective in this sample résumé. It's my opinion that if you include a specifically stated objective such as "desire to work with major software vendor as a C programmer" or "desire to work with Internet technologies in support of electronic commerce applications," you risk limiting the opportunities that will come your way during your job search. You may have a few jobs in mind that would be at the top of your list, but suppose no opportunities surface in electronic commerce? Or perhaps you have the opportunity to interview with a major software vendor, but they would like you to do Java work? I'd recommend avoiding a specific objective statement. There's no point in limiting your opportunities.

- **OTHER WORK**—Early in your career, your noncomputer jobs (such as working in a record store) can tip a competition for an open job slot your way if they show you've had the initiative to hold a part-time job during school, or perhaps a full-time summer job. After the first few years of your career, though, you can eliminate that information.

- **PERSONAL INFORMATION**—Some people claim that you shouldn't include any information about your personal interests (golf and tennis, in the example) because they show you have interests outside of work. My opinion is that including this information, particularly while seeking your first job, certainly can't hurt and may even cause a potential interviewer with the same interests to take special notice of your résumé.

You should mention if you're willing to relocate, and I'd recommend not putting references directly on your résumé. Wait until they're requested.

Sample Résumé #2: Developer with four years of experience seeking to change jobs

Martin Elbert
16 La Vista Ave.
Tucson, AZ 85715
(520) 555-7611

Experience
1995–Date

Senior Business Systems Developer-XYZ Corporation (Phoenix, AZ)
Most recently was senior developer and team leader (three-person team) for successful implementation of customer retention tracking system using three-tier client/server technology (C, Oracle 7.3, and custom-coded distribution transaction processing manager). Earlier roles included serving as lead for testing and quality assurance for a contract management application; developing Oracle 7.3 stored procedures for product quality tracking application; and developing configuration management and version control procedures for my entire organization.

1994–1995

Computer Center Consultant-Arizona State University (Tempe, AZ)
As a college senior, worked 25–30 hours per week assisting university computer center customers with problem resolution, research, and other tasks as necessary.

<u>Education and Training</u>

B.S., Arizona State University, Computer Information Systems (College of Business Administration), 1995. 3.54 GPA.

<u>College Computer Courses</u>: Introduction to business computing; COBOL and C programming (2 courses each); database management systems (2 courses); business systems analysis; enterprise computing architectures (special elective course); and systems simulation.

<u>Professional Training Courses</u>: Advanced C programming (2 weeks); Oracle 7.3 (1 week); Oracle 7.3 stored procedures (1 week); Java programming (1 week); HTML programming (3 days); Introduction to Windows NT (3 days)

<u>Systems and</u>
<u>Technologies</u>

<u>Languages</u>: C (very experienced); Java (classroom work; worked on Java prototype application); PL/SQL (experienced)
<u>Platforms</u>: UNIX (very experienced); Microsoft Windows 95 (experienced); Microsoft Windows 98 (experienced); Microsoft Windows NT (classroom work)
<u>Technologies</u>: Three-tier client/server computing (experienced)

References available upon request.

DISCUSSION OF PRECEDING RÉSUMÉ

The word that most warms my heart when I see it on a résumé is "successful" (or a variation thereof, such as "successfully"). So note that in the description for Martin Elbert's current job the first sentence features that wonderful word. First and foremost in the minds of a hiring manager looking for someone with more than a year or two of experience is finding a person who has had a role in a successful implementation project. In this example, not only was the implementation successful, but there were also some fairly modern technologies involved (three-tier client/server computing).

If at all possible, you want to highlight a major success using the latest technologies in your résumé. If for some reason that's not possible—you keep getting bounced around from one project to another, or your company has an abysmal record of actually following through on IT projects (they keep canceling them and redeploying the teams), then try to put your best face on the words you choose. Emphasize the technologies, your own personal accomplishments (for example, your own tasks were successful, even if the project wasn't), and similar factors.

Note that I've also included lists of college courses (still important at the three- to four-year point, in my opinion); professional training (showing that your knowledge acquisition didn't stop on graduation day); and the various languages and technologies with which the person is familiar, together with an approximate experience level. In my opinion, you want to show off your breadth of knowledge, but you also need to be as up front as possible. Be careful not to overstate your experience (if you've only had classroom work with Java, you don't want to give the impression you are an experienced developer, for example).

I came across the web sites listed below while writing this book and have included this list for your ongoing research and learning. Be sure to periodically use an Internet search engine (Excite, Lycos, AltaVista, Yahoo, etc.) and search for some combination such as COLLEGE+COMPUTING+CAREERS to see what new sites are available to you.

These sites not only have valuable information within their own pages but also feature links to other sites and resources that should be of interest to you (they cover many of the topics discussed in this book) plus other subjects such as résumé preparation.

1. http://www.cs.vt.edu/refs/career-and-grad.html—the Virginia Tech Career and Grad School Resources site

2. http://www.occ.com/—Online Career Center

3. http://www.careermosaic.com/cm/cc/cc1.html—Career Mosaic College Connection

4. http://www.jobweb.org/catapult/catapult.htm—The Catapult on JOBWEB

INDEX